THE WHOLE BIBLE STORY

THE

Whole

BIBLE STORY

DR. WILLIAM H. MARTY

BETHANY HOUSE PUBLISHERS
Minneapolis, Minnesota

© 2011 by William H. Marty

Published by Bethany House Publishers
11400 Hampshire Avenue South
Bloomington, Minnesota 55438

Bethany House Publishers is a division of
Baker Publishing Group, Grand Rapids, Michigan.

Printed in the United States of America

Library of Congress Cataloging-in-Publication Data
William H. Marty.
    The whole Bible story : everything that happens in the Bible in plain English /
William H. Marty.
       p.   cm.
    Summary: "Bible College professor makes the stories of the Bible accessible by plac-
ing them in chronological order and simplifying the language"—Provided by publisher.
    ISBN 978-0-7642-0829-4 (pbk. : alk. paper) 1. Bible stories, English. I. Title.
    BS550.3.M34   2011
    220.9'505—dc22   2010048249

Cover design by Studio Gearbox
Cover scroll photograph by Steve Gardner, PixelWorks Studio

12   13   14   15   16   17   18   15   14   13   12   11   10

To my mother, a single mom, who sacrificed to give me what she never had—an education—and the students at MBI who challenged and motivated me to become a lifelong learner.

Acknowledgments

In a sense this book is not my own. The idea came from Andy McGuire at Bethany House. He also guided me in writing and organizing the content and started the process of transforming my academic content and style into a popular and contemporary story of the Bible. I would also like to give credit to Christopher Soderstrom, who used his editorial skills to put the manuscript into its final form. Having read the proofs, I have a new appreciation for editors. Without their revisions, this book would read like my lecture notes at Moody Bible Institute. Both men were positive and helpful encouragers when I am certain they could have been critical.

I owe a great debt, not so much for this book, but for my life as a follower of Christ and my career as a teacher to two of my former teachers. It was never my goal to go into ministry. After college, I was commissioned as an officer in the U.S. Army. After four years and a tour of duty in Vietnam, I resigned my commission and made a life-changing decision. I enrolled in Denver Theological Seminary. Because there wasn't an official diagnosis of post-traumatic stress syndrome, I didn't know why I was at risk emotionally. Two men, both of whom are now with the Lord, modeled for me what it meant to be a follower of Christ. Dr. Bruce Shelley, professor of Church History, and Dr. Vernon Grounds, president, and professor of Pastoral Ministry, not only taught what to believe but showed me how to live as an authentic Christian. Without their example and personal counsel, I would have never graduated from seminary and gone on to a career as a pastor and eventually a Bible teacher.

I am also grateful for my wife, who encouraged me in the challenging work of writing, and proposed using the book of Revelation as the Epilogue for the book. My wife is a wonderful gift from the Lord.

Contents

Introduction

A friend recently asked me for a Bible. Knowing that she didn't know anything about it, I gave her a study Bible.

She opened it and flipped through a few pages, then looked up with a bewildered expression and asked, "How do I read this? Where do I start? What's in it?"

I gave her a brief explanation and wrote down some of the biblical books she should start with, but I realized she needed more help than just this.

Simply reading the Bible from cover to cover is a daunting task. The Bible is long—sixty-six books from Genesis to Revelation—and it can be difficult to follow the storyline because the books are not recorded in chronological order.

Another challenge is content. The Bible is written in a variety of literary forms. In addition to historical narrative, there is poetry, law, prophecy, and parable. Epistles (letters) make up almost half of the New Testament.

Many of the Old Testament's prophetical books, plus Revelation, are what we call apocalyptic literature. This type of writing describes catastrophic events associated with the end of time in vivid and bizarre imagery. For someone first attempting to read the Bible, this all can be very confusing.

When you write a book, editors want you to be able to state its purpose in a sentence or two. Here's my attempt: *The purpose of this book is to tell the story of the Bible.*

It is not a paraphrase of the Bible's sixty-six books, and it is not intended to replace Bible reading. My hope is that it will motivate people to read the Bible.

This book skips important information. It is an effort to synthesize the storyline of the Old and New Testaments minus the laws, messages (sermons), prophecies, and parables (stories). It does not include Old Testament poetry (wisdom literature) and prophecy, and it does not include the New Testament Epistles.

It is not a direct translation of the Bible; instead, it tells the story in plain, simple English. With very little commentary, I'm trying to give "just the facts"—to tell the story as it is recorded.

One thing to keep in mind: Just because an event is recorded in the Bible does not mean God approves of it. The nature of historical narrative is to record what happened. The writers of Scripture assume the reader will look at events from God's perspective.

I need to warn you up front, also, that reading the Bible will change you. It's not like reading other books. The Bible compels you to become a participant in the story.

Simply put, the Bible is about God. It tells the true story of creation from his perspective. It is about God revealing himself to men and women who are in some respects like him, and who were made to have a relationship with him.

As you read you will discover that God has a plan for you and for all of creation. Though that plan has been corrupted by failure, God has not abandoned us. Those who enter into his story can experience what it means to enjoy life both now and forever.

Paul, who wrote most of the New Testament books, called the story of the Bible "good news." In the book of Romans he wrote, "I am not ashamed of the good news, because it is the power of God for saving everyone who believes the wonderful message of God's love that has been made known in Jesus Christ."

I hope this book not only helps and encourages you to read the Bible but also convinces you to join in God's story, which is also your story.

One

FROM CREATION
TO BABEL

Main Characters
God (the Lord)
Adam and Eve
Cain and Abel
Noah

Setting
Mesopotamia

CREATION

In the beginning God created the heavens and the earth. In its original state the earth was empty and dark. Like a bird watching over its young, the Spirit of God hovered over the watery surface of the earth.

God created light on day one. On day two, he placed the sky between the earth and the heavens. He made land and vegetation on the third day, and on the fourth day, he put the stars, the sun, and the moon in place. On day five, God filled the sky with birds and the oceans with creatures of the sea. God created animals on the sixth day, and finally, last but not least, he made humankind in his image. (This means they were like God in certain ways.) God enriched their lives by providing them food to eat and giving them responsibility for the rest of creation.

When God finished his work, he saw that everything he had made was perfect. There was absolutely no defect in his creation. He rested on the seventh day and set it apart as a day to rest and to remember that God is the creator of the universe.

The Lord God planted a garden in Eden and made Adam the caretaker. He made all kinds of trees grow in the garden, and in the middle of the garden he designated two trees as the tree of the knowledge of good and evil and the tree of life. The Lord gave man permission to eat from all the trees in the garden except the tree of the knowledge of good and evil. He warned Adam that if he disobeyed by eating from the tree of the knowledge of good and evil, he would immediately die spiritually and eventually die physically.

The Lord allowed Adam to name all the animals so he would realize none of them were made like him. But the Lord also knew Adam needed a wife. When Adam fell into a deep sleep, the Lord made a woman from Adam's rib. When Adam woke up, he was thrilled. The woman was perfect. Adam called her "woman" because she was made from his side. God united them in marriage, and though they were naked they did not feel embarrassed or think about exploiting each other.

THE FALL

Their relationship with the Lord and each other couldn't have been better until Satan came to Eve in the disguise of a snake and raised doubt in her mind about the integrity of God's prohibition. Satan lied and told Eve she would become like God and would be able to make moral decisions independent of God.

Satan's argument made sense. When Eve looked at the fruit, it looked good to eat, so she decided to eat it and then gave some to Adam. They immediately realized they had sinned. Both were overwhelmed with guilt and were shocked when they saw they were naked. Adam and Eve awkwardly tried to cover their nakedness by sewing fig leaves together.

When the Lord returned to the garden, Adam and Eve were so afraid they tried to hide. It didn't work. The Lord knew what had happened. When Adam and Eve didn't meet him, the Lord called out, "Where are you?" Like a criminal caught in the act, Adam tried to cover up his sin. He told the Lord he was afraid because he was naked; he was actually afraid because he knew the Lord would punish him for his disobedience.

When the Lord asked Adam if he had eaten the forbidden fruit, Adam tried to blame Eve. He said it was her fault. She had given him the fruit. The Lord then asked Eve what had happened, and she blamed Satan. She admitted Satan had deceived her.

Because Satan had taken the form of a snake to deceive Eve, the Lord cursed both the snake and Satan. The Lord said Satan would be humiliated and he would grovel in dust like a snake crawls on the ground. The Lord also predicted there would be a constant struggle between the followers of Satan and the descendants of the woman, but one of Eve's descendants would eventually crush the head of Satan.

As a consequence of her disobedience, the Lord said Eve would suffer pain in bearing children, and Adam and Eve's marriage relationship would suffer from a sinister conflict. Eve now would have a sinful desire to control and manipulate Adam; Adam would attempt to dominate and exploit Eve.

Because Adam had listened to his wife and had eaten the forbidden fruit, he would always struggle to eat. The soil of the earth would become his enemy; it would produce thorns and thistles. Adam would die and his body would return to the ground from which he was created.

But the Lord was also kindhearted to Adam and Eve. He covered their nakedness with the skin of an animal. Because of their sin, Adam and Eve forfeited the opportunity to eat from the tree of life, so the Lord expelled them from the garden and ordered angels to guard the tree of life.

THE SONS OF ADAM AND EVE

Adam slept with Eve, and she became pregnant and gave birth to a son. She was amazed; she was able to produce life just like the Lord had done. She named her son Cain and thanked the Lord for giving her a son. She then had another son, Abel.

When the two boys became adults, they chose different occupations. Abel became a herdsman and Cain a farmer. They both brought an offering to the Lord. Cain merely fulfilled an obligation by bringing some of his harvest, but Abel did his best to honor the Lord, bringing some of the best animals from his herd. God approved of Abel's offering, but not Cain's. This made Cain furious. He was red hot with anger.

The Lord tried to warn Cain. He told him his uncontrolled rage would lead to violence. Cain refused to listen. He tricked his brother by inviting him into one of his fields, and then he killed him.

The Lord knew what Cain had done but asked him a rhetorical question: "Where is your brother, Abel?" Cain defiantly lied and said he didn't know. He then expressed his contempt for the Lord with his own rhetorical question: "Am I my brother's keeper?"

The Lord told Cain there was an eyewitness to his crime. It was his brother's blood, crying out from the ground. Because of Cain's heinous murder of his own brother, the Lord banished him from the ground he had cultivated for his livelihood. Realizing he could not survive as a homeless wanderer, Cain was desperate. He complained that his punishment was more than he could endure. Someone would undoubtedly kill him if he was a homeless wanderer. The Lord understood and assured Cain of special protection. Cain was satisfied, but he refused to stay in the presence of the Lord. He went east and lived in the land of Nod (which means "land of wandering").

Cain married, and his wife had a son, Enoch. Instead of accepting his punishment, Cain started a city in the east and named it after Enoch. Enoch had several sons, including Lamech. Lamech married two wives, Adah and Zillah. Jabal, his son by Adah, became the first shepherd, and Tubal-Cain, his son by Zillah, was the first to make tools of metal.

Lamech killed a man who offended him. Knowing he might be held accountable, he boasted to his wives that if anyone tried to punish him, he would kill that person as well.

Eve had another son. She named him Seth, which means "in the place of" (because Cain had killed Abel). During the lifetime of Enosh, Seth's son, people began to worship the Lord through prayer and sacrifice.

NOAH

Adam lived for eight hundred years after he became the father of Seth. He was 930 when he died. The descendants from Adam to Noah lived for hundreds of years, but they all eventually died just as the Lord had said they would. There was one exception. Because Enoch was fully devoted to the Lord, God suspended the penalty of death and took him from the earth. One of Adam's descendants, Lamech, had a son at age 182 and named him Noah, which means "comfort," because he hoped his son would bring relief from the harsh struggle of living under the curse on the ground.

During the lifetime of Noah there was a population explosion. "The sons of God" lusted after beautiful women and married them. (There are three major views on the identity of "the sons of God." [1] They were fallen angels who took human bodies to cohabit with women; [2] they were godly descendants in the line of Seth, and "the daughters of men" were in the ungodly line of Cain; or [3] they were powerful tyrants who forced themselves on attractive women.) Their children were called Nephilim. (Some believe the Nephilim were mighty warriors, descendants of the union between "the sons of God" and "the daughters of men." Nephilim are mentioned later, in Numbers 13:33, but they could not be descendants of the Nephilim in this passage, since all humanity except for Noah and his extended family were destroyed in the flood. *Nephilim* is probably a general term referring to "physical giants" or "powerful warriors.") The Nephilim became famous superheroes and dominated the world. Until now, the Spirit of the Lord had spared humanity from judgment because of sin, but the Lord warned he would only withhold judgment for another 120 years.

A rampant explosion of wickedness throughout the earth both broke the heart of the Lord and made him angry. He was extremely disappointed in the people he had made but made the painful decision to destroy everything he had created.

In contrast to his contemporaries, Noah was a man of integrity and had a special relationship with God. His sons were Shem, Ham, and Japheth. The rest of humanity was totally corrupt. There was complete anarchy. Because of Noah and God's close relationship, God did not want to destroy Noah with the rest of humanity. God revealed his plan to Noah to destroy the world with a flood, and ordered him to build an ark out of gopher wood (probably cypress) and cover it entirely with pitch. He instructed Noah to build it so that it would not capsize during the flood. God said to build it with three decks but no windows, only an opening for ventilation eighteen inches from the top deck. Though there had never been a flood, Noah believed God and built the ark exactly as instructed.

After Noah finished building the ark, the Lord told him to take seven pairs of every clean animal, two pairs of every unclean animal, and seven pairs of every species of birds into the ark. (The distinction between clean and unclean animals is based on differences as defined in the Law of Moses.) The Lord then warned Noah the rain would begin in seven days and would continue for forty days and nights.

At age six hundred, Noah brought his wife, his sons and their wives, and all the animals on board. As soon as he finished loading, the rain began. In addition to the rain, gigantic tidal waves from the oceans swept across the earth, covering it for 150 days. Everything was destroyed; only Noah and those on the ark survived.

After the flood, God kept his promise to Noah and all the animals on the ark; he closed the huge underground caverns of water that had broken open, and he stopped the rain. He sent a powerful wind to accelerate the evaporation of water. (There are two views on the extent of the flood. Some believe it was universal, covering all the earth. Others believe it was local and destroyed life only in populated areas.)

After 150 days, the ark landed somewhere on the mountains of Ararat (southeast of the Black Sea bordering on today's Turkey, Armenia, and Iran). Noah and his family stayed in the ark for another two and a half months until the waters had receded enough for them to see the tops of other mountains.

To make certain it was safe to leave the ark, Noah released two birds. First he released a raven that flew until it found a place to land and did not return. Second, he released a dove that returned because it could not find a place to land. Noah waited seven more days, then released the dove again. When the dove returned with an olive leaf in its beak, Noah knew there was dry land. But to be absolutely certain, Noah waited another seven days and released the dove a third time. This time the dove did not come back.

Noah was now 601. It had been ten and a half months since the beginning of the flood, and Noah felt it was safe to remove the top covering of the ark. He could see dry land, but he waited another two months until the earth around him was completely dry.

Just as God had ordered Noah to board the ark, God ordered Noah to leave the ark and release all the animals to repopulate the earth. After he had set the animals free, Noah built an altar and sacrificed some of the approved animals and birds to thank the Lord for delivering him and his family from the flood. The Lord accepted Noah's sacrifices and was delighted with them. Though Adam's sin had permanently corrupted humankind, the Lord swore he would never totally destroy the world again. He promised there would always be a cycle of seasons to sustain life.

God blessed Noah and told him to repopulate the earth. Prior to the sin of Adam and Eve, the Lord had given humans dominion over animals but had not allowed them to eat meat. Now God gave humans permission to eat meat but said animals would fear people, perhaps because people would hunt them for food.

As a reminder of the high value of life, God did not permit the eating of blood—not because blood was unhealthy, but because blood was a symbol of life. God warned he would demand the life of anybody who killed (by implication, "murdered") someone.

To assure Noah and all humanity he would never again destroy life with a flood, God designated the rainbow as a special sign.

Unfortunately the flood did not eliminate the problem of sin. The tragedy of sin overtook Noah and his sons. Noah got drunk on wine he had made from the vineyard he himself had planted. In his stupor, Noah removed all his clothes. When his son Ham entered Noah's tent, instead of respecting his father by covering his nakedness, he did nothing and told his brothers. His brothers, Shem and Japheth, exercised extreme caution so they would not humiliate Noah by looking at his nakedness. They entered his tent backwards and carefully covered their father with a large blanket.

When Noah realized what Ham had done, he said Ham's flagrant act of disrespect would have consequences on future generations. Because his moral conduct exposed a serious character defect, Noah predicted Ham's son Canaan and his descendants would be oppressed by others. Noah also prophesied that God would bless the descendants of Japheth and Shem because they had shown respect for their father.

(Genesis 10 contains what is called "The Table of Nations." Though the list comes before the account of the tower of Babel in the book of Genesis, it shows the dispersion of the nations in the ancient Near East after God's judgment at Babel. It contains the names of individuals, tribes, nations, and even cities. All the people listed are in some way connected to Shem, Ham, and Japheth, the three sons of Noah.)

THE TOWER OF BABEL

The consequences of Adam and Eve's sin surfaced again in rebellion against God in Shinar (the ancient region of Babylonia or southern Mesopotamia; this area is today's country of Iraq). As the population began to increase after the flood, God commanded people to repopulate all of the earth. Instead of obeying, they settled on a plain in Shinar. Because stone was scarce in that area, they developed the technology to make bricks and constructed a city. Motivated by pride and the desire to establish some kind of powerful humanistic empire, the rebels erected a skyscraper type of temple-tower in the city center.

The rebels' blatant defiance of the Lord did not go unnoticed. There was no limit to what they might do if God did not stop them. At this time in civilization's development, everyone spoke the same language. The Lord, knowing exactly how to stop them, confused them with different languages and forced them to scatter all over the world. The tower was given the name Babel. (This is a play on words. In Hebrew, *Babel* means "confusion," but in Babylonian literature it refers to "the gate of god.")

🎵 Chapter Summary

God created the earth and the whole universe in six days. As the climatic act, he made Adam and Eve. When he had finished his work, God rested on the seventh day.

He placed Adam and Eve in Eden and provided everything they needed to live and enjoy life. He gave them instructions on how to live, and warned them not to eat from the tree of the knowledge of good and evil.

Satan deceived Eve; she and Adam disobeyed God.

God told Satan, Eve, and Adam what their punishments would be, and he assured Eve that one of her descendants would triumph over Satan. He covered their nakedness but banished them from the garden.

Eve gave birth to Cain and later to Abel. Abel did his best to respect God, but Cain was godless. Cain killed Abel because he was jealous of Abel's relationship with God.

As God had warned, Adam died. Because his sin affected the whole human race, as the population increased, the world became corrupt and violent. This broke the Lord's heart, but it made him so angry that he decided to destroy the world.

Noah was a good man. To protect Noah from the coming flood, God told him to build an ark for his family and for animals.

After the flood, God commanded Noah to repopulate the earth. He promised he would never destroy the world again with a flood, and gave the rainbow as his promise.

Instead of spreading out as God had ordered, people gathered to build a city and a tower. Because everyone spoke the same language, God put an end to their rebellion by confusing their tongues and scattering them across the earth.

The story of the Bible now narrows, from the history of humanity generally, to focus on Abraham and his descendants.

Two

ABRAHAM, ISAAC, JACOB, AND JACOB'S SONS

Main Characters
Abraham
Sarah
Ishmael
Isaac
Esau
Jacob
Joseph

Setting
Mesopotamia (Ur and Haran)
Land of Canaan
Egypt

ABRAHAM

Terah was a descendant of Shem, one of Noah's three sons. Terah also had three sons, one of whom was Abraham. While Terah and his family lived in Ur, the Lord appeared to Abraham. He told him, "Leave your country, your father's family, and go to a new land that I will show you. I will bless you, make you into a great nation, and bring a blessing to all people through you." (The promise to bless all people was ultimately fulfilled through Jesus Christ, a descendant of Abraham.)

After God had spoken to Abraham, Terah moved his family to

Haran. Abraham lived in Haran for several years, though the city was not in the land God had promised him. After the death of his father, Abraham moved to Canaan with his wife, Sarah, and his nephew Lot.

At this time, in the Promised Land, Abraham had to live like a nomad, moving from place to place because the Canaanites occupied the parts of the land that were fertile. God appeared to Abraham a second time and again promised his descendants would possess the land. Abraham worshiped the Lord by building a stone altar.

A severe famine then forced Abraham to move to Egypt. Because Sarah was extremely attractive, Abraham was afraid the Egyptians would kill him and abduct his wife. So Abraham lied; he told the Egyptians that Sarah was his sister.

The ruler of Egypt (Pharaoh—a title, not a name) was captivated by Sarah's beauty and attempted to take her as one of his wives. When the Lord inflicted terrible diseases on Pharaoh's household, he became suspicious and accused Abraham of lying. When Abraham admitted that Sarah was his wife, Pharaoh ordered him to leave Egypt.

Abraham returned to Canaan and decided to live in Bethel, where he had previously built an altar to the Lord. Abraham and Lot were grazing their sheep together, and both had become extremely wealthy.

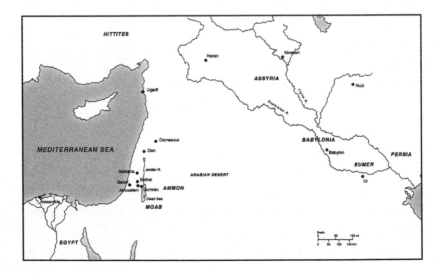

Their herdsmen quarreled over grazing rights, so the two men agreed to separate. Lot chose to live near Sodom, though the people in that area were exceedingly wicked.

After the departure of Lot, the Lord again assured Abraham that he would give him the land as far as the eye could see and predicted his descendants would be as numerous as the sand. Abraham built another altar to the Lord at Hebron.

When war broke out between kings in the region, one of the kings and his allies plundered the city of Sodom. They captured Lot and withdrew to the north. When Abraham found out his nephew had been captured, he organized 318 of his best warriors and pursued Lot's captors. He caught up with them north of Damascus and rescued Lot and all the other captives from Sodom.

After Abraham returned, the priest-king Melchizedek blessed him, recognizing God as creator and the one who had given Abraham victory. (*Melchizedek* means "king of righteousness.") Abraham expressed his appreciation to Melchizedek by giving him a tenth of the valuable goods he had captured.

When he gave back the captives to the king of Sodom, the king offered to reward Abraham, but Abraham refused because he did not want to become indebted to an ungodly king.

When Abraham decided to designate Eliezer, his most trusted servant, as his heir since he still didn't have a son, the Lord reassured Abraham that he would give him his own son. The Lord told Abraham to count the stars if he could, and then said, "Your descendants will be like the stars, too many to count."

Abraham reaffirmed his trust in God's promises by making an animal sacrifice, and the Lord himself passed between the animals in the visible form of a smoking firepot and flaming torch, assuring Abraham that God could be trusted. He promised that Abraham's descendants would possess the land from Egypt in the south to the Euphrates River in the north. The Lord would allow the Amorites (one of the nations living in Canaan) to occupy the land for four hundred years before removing them because of their sin.

Sarah became so impatient she refused to wait any longer for a son. She told Abraham to sleep with Hagar, her Egyptian servant. (In the ancient Near East, a husband could produce an heir by his wife's servant if his wife could not have children.) After Hagar became pregnant, she ridiculed Sarah, and Sarah despised Hagar. When Hagar attempted to run away because Sarah mistreated her, the angel of the Lord told her to return and submit to Sarah's authority, and promised Hagar her son would be great. When Hagar gave birth to her son, Abraham named him Ishmael. Abraham was eighty.

God appeared again to Abraham when the patriarch was ninety. He revealed himself as God Almighty and challenged Abraham to serve him faithfully. He expanded the original covenant, promising to make Abraham the father of many nations and assuring him it would be an everlasting covenant. He told Abraham to circumcise himself and every male child in his household. God made this ancient rite the distinguishing sign that Abraham and his descendants were God's covenant people.

God again promised to give Abraham and Sarah a son. The idea was so ridiculous that Abraham laughed to himself because he was one hundred and Sarah was ninety. To encourage the patriarch, the Lord told him to name his son Isaac (which means "he laughs") and promised he would be born in a year's time.

Later, three angels in the form of men visited Abraham's camp; when Sarah overheard one of them tell Abraham that within a year Sarah would have a son, she laughed because she thought her body was so old she could never become pregnant. The angel was the Lord himself, and he asked Abraham why Sarah had laughed. Sarah was so afraid that she denied she had scoffed at the Lord's promise.

As the three men were about to leave, the Lord decided to tell Abraham their intention to totally destroy the cities of Sodom and Gomorrah because they had become so evil. Abraham knew Lot and his family were still living in Sodom, so he pleaded with the Lord to spare at least ten people. The Lord graciously agreed.

Lot held some kind of official position in Sodom, so when two visitors arrived at the city gate, Lot invited them to stay at his house. The men of the city had become so perverse that when they spotted the visitors, they surrounded Lot's house and demanded he turn the visitors over to them for sex. Instead, Lot offered them his daughters.

The mob became violent, and the angels blinded them. Then they ordered Lot to get all his relatives out of the city immediately because they intended to destroy the whole area. Lot was hesitant to leave, so the angels forcibly removed him, his wife, and two daughters. Outside the city, the angels told Lot to flee and not look back. After Lot was safe, the Lord totally destroyed Sodom and Gomorrah with an eruption of fire and sulfur. Lot reached the village of Zoar, but in disobedience to the angels' command, his wife looked back and in consequence was turned into a pillar of salt.

Lot hid in a cave with his two daughters because he was afraid of the men in Zoar. His daughters thought all the men in the area had been killed, so they conspired to get their father drunk so they could have children. The oldest slept with her father first, and the next night the youngest. They conceived and the oldest gave birth to Moab, who became the father of the Moabites, and the youngest to Ammon, who became the father of the Ammonites.

When Abraham moved to the Negev, he lied again. He told Abimelech, a powerful ruler, that Sarah was his sister. (*Abimelech*, most likely a dynastic rather than a personal name, means, "My father the king.") Abimelech had Sarah brought to his palace, but fortunately, before he slept with her, the Lord warned him in a dream that Sarah was married.

Abraham had been wrong about Abimelech; he was an honorable man. When he realized Abraham had lied, Abimelech returned Sarah to him and even compensated the patriarch with a thousand pieces of silver for his mistake. Abraham prayed for Abimelech and his household, for the Lord had made all the women infertile because Abimelech had placed Sarah in his harem.

The Lord then surprised both Abraham and Sarah with the impossible. Sarah conceived in her old age and gave birth to a son. Abraham named him Isaac and circumcised him on the eighth day as God had commanded. Sarah was delighted and declared, "God has brought me laughter!"

When Ishmael ridiculed his stepbrother, Sarah demanded that Abraham banish Hagar and her son. The Lord assured Abraham that Sarah's demand was part of his plan to bless Isaac. Abraham provided food and water for Hagar and Ishmael and sent them into the wilderness of Beersheba. They almost died in the desert's heat, but God mercifully provided water and again promised to make Ishmael the father of a great nation. Ishmael grew up in the desert and married an Egyptian.

In an arid region, Abraham again found himself in a conflict over water rights. His shepherds fought over a well at Beersheba with the shepherds of Abimelech, a Philistine. Abimelech could see Abraham was a man blessed by God, so he made a peace treaty with him rather than risk God's judgment.

Then God shocked Abraham, testing his faith by telling him to offer Isaac, the son he greatly loved, as a sacrifice. Though an astounding command, Abraham obeyed. He climbed a mountain in the region of Moriah, built an altar, and prepared to sacrifice his son; instead, the Lord unexpectedly provided a ram as a substitute sacrifice. Abraham named the place "Jehovah provides." Because Abraham had been willing to sacrifice his own son, the Lord reaffirmed his promise to bless Abraham and make him a blessing to the nations.

Sarah died at age 127. Abraham purchased a field and a cave for her gravesite in the land God had promised to give to him.

Before Abraham died, he made arrangements for a wife for Isaac. Because he did not want Isaac to marry a Canaanite, he sent his most trusted servant to find a wife among his own people, who lived in the region of Haran. The servant stopped at a well; after asking the Lord for guidance, he met Rebekah. When he explained to Laban, her brother, the nature of his journey, Laban realized this was providential, and he explained to his sister the purpose of the man's visit. Rebekah agreed to go with Abraham's servant. When they arrived in Canaan, Isaac took Rebekah as his wife and fell in love with her.

After the death of Sarah, Abraham married Keturah and had several sons and grandsons. Abraham also had more sons by concubines. Though he provided for all his sons before he died at age 175, Abraham willed his inheritance to Isaac. Both Isaac and Ishmael buried their father in the cave at Machpelah, where Abraham had buried Sarah.

Ishmael fathered twelve sons, who became the heads of twelve tribes. They lived in an area from Havilah to Shur (in north-central Arabia). Ishmael died at age 137.

ISAAC

Rebekah gave birth to two sons. Contrary to ancient custom, God told her he planned to make the younger son greater than the older. Esau was born first; they named their second son Jacob because he was grasping Esau's heel when he was born. (The name *Jacob* is similar to the Hebrew word for "heel.")

Though twins, the two boys were radically different. Esau became an excellent hunter and loved the outdoors; however, he lived by his passions and had little regard for his privileged position as the firstborn son. Jacob was the stay-at-home type, but he was ambitious and manipulative. He also had a serious problem with integrity.

Isaac favored Esau, for he would bring savory wild game. Rebekah favored Jacob.

Jacob cunningly obtained Esau's inheritance. When Esau returned from hunting, he complained he was starving to death and asked for food. Jacob replied, "First, sell me your birthright." Esau was so famished that he traded his firstborn inheritance for a bowl of red stew. (His descendants eventually lived in an area distinguished by red cliffs.)

Like Abraham, Isaac was forced to move south because of a severe famine. He thought about moving to Egypt, but the Lord said, "Stay here, and I will bless you. Your descendants will be as numerous as the stars, and they will be a blessing to all nations of the earth." Isaac decided to stay in the south of the Promised Land.

Though Isaac was a man of faith, he was far from perfect. Because Rebekah was attractive, Isaac told the men of Gerar that she was his sister because he thought they might kill him and abduct her. When the Philistine king spotted Isaac embracing her, he knew she wasn't his sister. The king issued a warning that no one should touch Rebekah because she was Isaac's wife.

The Lord blessed Isaac. He became wealthy and powerful—so wealthy that the region's king asked him to leave. Though Isaac moved, his flocks were so large there was not enough water for them and those of the local shepherds. Isaac moved again, this time to Beersheba, where the Lord assured him he had nothing to fear. Isaac worshiped the Lord and made Beersheba his home. This was wise; the king made a nonviolent treaty with Isaac, and Isaac's servants found water while digging a well at Beersheba.

Esau continued to live as a godless rebel. Instead of finding a wife from his own people, he married Judith and Basemath, who were the daughters of foreigners.

Jacob again resorted to deception to obtain the patriarchal blessing that customarily would have been given to his older brother. When Isaac was old and had extremely poor eyesight, Rebekah helped Jacob disguise himself so Isaac would think he was Esau. The ruse worked, and Isaac blessed Jacob.

JACOB

Esau, who was furious, threatened to kill his brother; Rebekah warned Jacob to flee for his life. Before Jacob left, Isaac blessed his son and told him not to marry a Canaanite. Jacob went to Haran, where his uncle lived.

Jacob worked as a shepherd for Laban, who had two daughters, Leah and Rachel. Jacob fell in love with Rachel, the youngest. He asked Laban for permission to marry her, agreeing to work seven years as Laban's servant.

The man who had used deception to manipulate others met his match in Laban. On the wedding night, Laban gave Leah to Jacob to be his wife instead of Rachel. When Jacob realized he had been tricked, he complained; Laban replied that it was customary for the oldest daughter to marry first. To marry Rachel, Jacob was forced to commit to another seven years of work.

Jacob's wives competed with each other for his favor. Though Jacob loved Rachel most, Rachel was unable to conceive; the Lord, however, blessed Leah with four sons. In desperation, Rachel told Jacob to sleep with her servant to bear a son. Leah then allowed Jacob to sleep with her servant to give him another son. Finally, in answer to her prayers, the Lord gave Rachel a son, whom she named Joseph, which means, "May he add." (This expressed Rachel's hope that the Lord would give her even another son.) Rachel and Leah and their two servants gave Jacob a total of twelve sons and one daughter. (Jacob's twelve sons would become the leaders of the twelve tribes of Israel.)

After the birth of Joseph, Jacob began making plans to return to the land of Canaan. His uncle pleaded with him to stay; Jacob had made Laban extremely wealthy. He reluctantly agreed to let Jacob leave but was only willing to give him a small flock of sheep. Jacob, an extremely skillful shepherd, still was able to increase the size and quality of his flock.

When Jacob realized Laban's sons resented him because of his success, he decided to leave secretly. He informed his wives but told them not to tell their father. Laban discovered Jacob's departure and pursued. When he caught Jacob, the two men argued but finally agreed to a peaceful settlement. Jacob built a stone monument to mark the location, and offered a sacrifice to God.

Jacob had another problem to overcome before he could return home. He sent his servants ahead to find out if Esau was still angry enough to kill him. When the messengers reported that Esau was coming to meet him with four hundred armed men, Jacob asked the Lord for protection and sent ahead a gift of several hundred animals.

The day before he met Esau, Jacob sent his family across the Jabbok River and stayed by himself in the camp. During the night, Jacob encountered a man and wrestled with him until dawn. (The "man" was a visible, physical appearance of the Lord.) The man dislocated Jacob's hip, but Jacob grabbed his opponent and would not release him until he blessed him.

"What is your name?" the man asked.

"Jacob," was the reply.

"It isn't anymore!" the man told him. "It is Israel, one who fought with God." The man blessed Jacob, and Jacob called the place Peniel (which means "the face of God"), because he had survived a face to face encounter with the Lord. Jacob walked with a limp because of the severity of the blow to his hip.

Early in the morning, Jacob saw Esau and his men approaching. He went out ahead of his family, but instead of attacking, Esau ran to meet his brother. The two men embraced, and Jacob introduced his family to Esau. Esau offered to escort Jacob to his home in Seir, but Jacob declined. Instead he purchased land in Shechem, and as a witness of his faith, he built an altar to the Lord.

Though the Lord had promised the land of Canaan to Abraham and his descendants, it was not a safe place for Jacob. The relationship between his family and the people of Shechem was disastrous. Shechem, a Hivite, raped Leah's daughter, Dinah. Shechem told his father, King

Hamor, that he loved Dinah, so the king asked Jacob for permission for his son to marry Dinah.

Dinah's outraged brothers plotted revenge. They told the men of Shechem they could marry into their family only if they were circumcised. The men agreed, and all were circumcised. While they were incapacitated, Simeon and Levi, Dinah's brothers, rescued Dinah, killed all of Shechem's men, and then plundered the city. Jacob, shocked by what his sons had done, feared the other Canaanites would destroy them.

Because of the threat, Jacob ordered his extended household to completely trust in the Lord by destroying all their idols. They moved to Bethel, where Jacob had first built an altar. The Lord reaffirmed the Abrahamic promise to Jacob, and Jacob built another altar to him.

They intended to go to Ephrath (also called Bethlehem), but Rachel died giving birth to her second son, Benjamin, before they arrived in the city. Isaac died at age 180; Jacob and Esau buried him at Mamre (Hebron), where Abraham had lived.

Esau, who married three Canaanite women, moved south to Mount Seir because there was not enough land to support his livestock and Jacob's. The descendants of Esau were known as Edomites, and the area where his descendants settled was called Edom.

JOSEPH

Jacob made Canaan his permanent home. His twelve sons shepherded his large flocks, but there was trouble in his family. Though Joseph was not his oldest, Jacob favored him and gave him a beautiful robe, indicating that he intended to give Joseph most of the family inheritance. Joseph's brothers resented this and despised Joseph. The relationship deteriorated even further when Joseph had two dreams revealing that his brothers and even his parents would bow to honor him.

The brothers' hostility exploded in violence while they were grazing their flocks in an isolated location. Jacob sent Joseph to check on them, but when he found them they assaulted him and took his fancy robe. They planned to kill him, but Reuben pleaded that they not do so. Instead, they sold him to merchants who were on their way to Egypt. They smeared Joseph's robe with goat blood and told their father that Joseph had been killed by a wild animal, and they produced his bloody robe as evidence.

In Egypt, Potiphar, a military officer, bought Joseph to be his household slave. His wife tried repeatedly to seduce Joseph, but Joseph refused to sin because of his commitment to Potiphar and to God. In a last desperate attempt to seduce Joseph, she grabbed his cloak and said, "Let's have sex." Joseph ran from the house, leaving Potiphar's wife holding his cloak. Scorned, she accused him of rape and used his cloak as evidence.

Instead of executing Joseph, Potiphar had him put into prison. Though his brothers had betrayed Joseph, God had not abandoned him. The Lord continued to speak to Joseph through dreams.

Two other prisoners, one who had been Pharaoh's cupbearer and the other his baker, asked Joseph to interpret their dreams. Joseph told the cupbearer he would be restored to his former position; the baker would be executed. He asked the cupbearer to remember how he had helped him, but the man seemed to have forgotten about Joseph when he was reinstated.

Years later the Lord worked providentially to fulfill his purpose for Joseph. Pharaoh (the king) had dreams his advisors could not interpret. Then Pharaoh's cupbearer remembered Joseph's ability to interpret dreams. He informed Pharaoh, who ordered Joseph released and asked him to interpret the dreams that had baffled his other advisors.

Joseph gave the king good news and bad news. He told the ruler his dreams were prophetic about future economic conditions in Egypt. Joseph predicted seven years of prosperity followed by seven years of hardship. Pharaoh was impressed and made Joseph the second-highest ruler in Egypt.

As Joseph had predicted, Egypt enjoyed seven years of abundant harvest and then suffered seven years of devastating famine. During the prosperity, Joseph strategically stored grain for Pharaoh. When the famine struck, landowners were forced to sell their land to Pharaoh to survive. Pharaoh became extremely wealthy; Joseph, very powerful.

The famine was severe and widespread. It affected the land of Canaan, and Jacob's sons were forced to go to Egypt to buy grain. On their first visit, Joseph's brothers didn't recognize him, but he knew them and remembered his dreams that they would bow before him.

Instead of identifying himself, Joseph accused them of spying on Egypt and imprisoned them. After three days he released them, but said that to prove they were not spies they had to leave a hostage and bring their youngest brother back when they returned again. They left Simeon. Joseph ordered his servants to give them grain and hide their money in the grain sacks.

When they arrived in Canaan, they told Jacob an Egyptian ruler had imprisoned Simeon as a hostage and demanded they return to Egypt with their youngest brother, Benjamin. Jacob refused. He had lost two sons—Joseph and now Simeon—and he didn't want to lose his only other son by Rachel.

Because of the severity of the famine, Jacob (now called Israel) eventually was forced to send his sons back to Egypt, and he reluctantly agreed to let them take Benjamin after Judah promised he would protect him. On their second trip, Joseph's brothers expected trouble but were astonished at being treated like honored guests.

Joseph tested them one more time before identifying himself. (He wanted to find out if they would abandon Benjamin as they had abandoned him.) He ordered his servant to secretly place his silver cup in Benjamin's grain sack. After they began their journey back to Canaan, Joseph sent his servant after them. He accused them of stealing and said the thief would become Joseph's slave. They denied the charge and agreed that if any of them were found to have stolen the silver cup, he would become Joseph's slave.

They were shocked when the cup was found with Benjamin. When Judah pleaded for mercy, Joseph could no longer control his emotions. He wept and said to his brothers, "I am Joseph!"

They were astonished and terrified; Joseph, however, assured them they had nothing to fear. He realized that though their intentions had been evil, God had sent him to Egypt to save their lives by making him an advisor to Pharaoh and ruler over the land. Joseph told them to return to Canaan and bring their father and their families to Egypt.

When they returned and told their father that Joseph was alive and had become a powerful ruler, Israel didn't believe them. They were able to convince him by telling him what Joseph had said and showing him the provisions he had sent.

Israel agreed to make the journey to Egypt. While on his way, the Lord confirmed to the patriarch that this was all part of his plan to make Israel into a great nation.

Joseph asked Pharaoh for permission to settle his family in the land of Goshen and assured the king they were self-sufficient. After Israel, who was now 130, arrived in Egypt, Joseph introduced him to Pharaoh, and Israel blessed the king.

Under Joseph's administration, the people of Egypt were able to survive the famine, but ultimately had to give their land to Pharaoh in exchange for food. The people became Pharaoh's servants, and he assumed responsibility for their care.

Israel blessed Joseph's sons, Ephraim and Manasseh, but elevated Ephraim over Manasseh even though Manasseh was the oldest. Israel also predicted what would happen in the future for each of his sons, and he instructed them to bury him in the land promised to Abraham.

When Israel died, Joseph honored his father's request and buried him in Canaan. Now that Israel was dead, Joseph's brothers expected him to take revenge, but instead he made a remarkable statement of faith. He declared, "Don't be afraid. Am I in God's place? You intended evil, but God intended it for good, to accomplish the saving of many lives."

Before he himself died, Joseph blessed his two sons, Ephraim and Manasseh, and made his brothers promise to take his remains back to the land that God had promised to Abraham, Isaac, and Jacob.

♫ Chapter Summary

As the Lord had made a covenant with Noah to sustain the earth, he entered into a covenant relationship with Abraham that ultimately would bring a blessing to all people. The Lord promised Abraham a new homeland and descendants as numerous as the stars. Abraham believed God's amazing promise and left his home for the land of Canaan.

Abraham discovered that nothing is impossible with God; Sarah gave birth to Isaac when they were so old they had abandoned all hope of ever having children.

After Isaac's birth, the Lord tested Abraham's faith by telling him to offer his son as a sacrifice. Abraham obeyed. He built an altar, but the Lord provided an animal as a substitute.

Isaac and Rebekah had two sons. Jacob persuaded Esau to sell him the family inheritance, which was rightfully Esau's, as the oldest. When Isaac was nearing death, Jacob deceived him to obtain his father's blessing intended for the oldest son.

Jacob experienced a turning point in his life when he struggled with the Lord all night; his name was changed to Israel. He fathered twelve sons who would become the leaders of the twelve tribes.

Joseph, his favorite, became first a household slave, then an alleged rapist, and finally the chief economic advisor to the king of Egypt. Joseph guided the nation through extreme prosperity and severe famine; when he rediscovered his brothers, instead of seeking revenge, he provided for them and moved them all to Egypt.

Joseph realized that God had providentially used his brothers' attempt to destroy him for the preservation of his family. Before Joseph died, he asked his brothers to take his bones back to the land God had promised to Abraham, Isaac, and Jacob.

Three

MOSES AND THE EXODUS

Main Characters

Moses
Pharaoh, (the Egyptian king)
The Lord (God's covenant name, Yahweh)
The Sons of Israel (Israelites)

Setting

Egypt
Red Sea
Sinai Peninsula
Mount Sinai

MOSES

After the death of Joseph, the children of Israel prospered in Egypt. Their explosive growth in size and power alarmed the Egyptians. When a new Pharaoh, who didn't know what Joseph had done for Egypt, came to power, he feared the Israelites and enslaved their entire population, but their numbers continued to increase.

Pharaoh was so threatened that he ordered the midwives to kill all the Hebrew (Israelite) male children at birth. The midwives, however, refused to obey his murderous edict because they honored God more than Pharaoh.

Moses did not aspire to become the leader of Israel. He was thrust into the position by providential circumstances. When Moses was born, his mother recognized him as a special child and tried to hide him. When that was no longer possible, she placed him in a reed basket and set it afloat on the Nile River. The daughter of Pharaoh found the infant, adopted him, and chose Moses' mother as his nurse.

When he had grown up, Moses killed an Egyptian who was beating a Hebrew. Instead of recognizing Moses as their leader, his own people threatened to report him to Pharaoh. Moses fled to Midian (southern Sinai Peninsula) and didn't plan to return. He became a shepherd and married Zipporah, the daughter of Jethro.

One day when he was tending sheep, Moses saw a strange phenomenon: a bush that was on fire but didn't burn up. When he approached, the Lord spoke to Moses from the bush, "I am the God of your father Abraham, Isaac, and Jacob." The Lord had heard the cries of his people, and he wanted Moses to return to Egypt to rescue them.

Moses protested he was unworthy and inadequate for the task. The Lord repeated his command two more times, while Moses pleaded with him to send someone else. God told Moses his name, "I AM WHO I AM," pledged he would give him power to force Pharaoh to release his people, and promised that Moses' brother Aaron would help him. Moses reluctantly agreed.

THE PLAGUES AND THE EXODUS

After telling Jethro of his plans and meeting Aaron at the mountain of God (Mount Sinai), Moses returned to Egypt. It wasn't easy, but with Aaron's help he was able to convince the elders of Israel that the Lord had sent him to rescue them from Egypt.

Moses' next challenge was more difficult. He had to convince Pharaoh to free his labor force of slaves. Moses said, "The Lord, the God of Israel, says, 'Let my people go!' " Pharaoh scoffed and ridiculed God: "Who is your Lord? Why should I listen to him? I don't know him, and I will not let Israel go!"

Aaron and Moses insisted, but Pharaoh was obstinate. "The Israelites have been lazy," he charged, and he made their work harder. Moses now faced another crisis. The Israelite foremen complained that Moses was responsible for the harsher treatment. Moses in turn complained to the Lord.

Pharaoh's stubborn, cruel response provided the Lord with the opportunity to show the Egyptians and the Israelites he is "El Shaddai," the God Almighty. The Lord would force Pharaoh to release his people, and he would bring them into the Promised Land.

"How?" Moses said. "My own people won't listen to me." The Lord said he would make Moses so powerful that Pharaoh would think he was God and Aaron his spokesman.

Both Moses and Aaron confronted Pharaoh a second time. As a sign they had been sent by the Lord, Aaron threw down his shepherd's staff, and it turned into a serpent. Pharaoh was not impressed since two of his magicians were able to do the same, even though Aaron's staff swallowed the magicians' staffs.

It was obvious Pharaoh was so arrogant and stubborn that it would take a series of catastrophic disasters to force him to free the children of Israel. Moses unleashed ten destructive plagues on the land, the livestock, and even the Egyptians themselves. The plagues devastated Egypt, but the people of Israel were protected by the Lord.

Each time Moses announced a plague, he made it clear to Pharaoh he was God's spokesman by saying, "The Lord says, 'Let my people go!' " Pharaoh's magicians were able to imitate the first two plagues of blood and frogs, but after the third plague they declared, "This is the finger of God."

Though his own magicians realized Moses' power as supernatural, Pharaoh still would not release the Israelites. He attempted to bargain with Moses by allowing the people to worship God in Egypt and even promising to let them go but with restrictions.

After the eighth plague, the plague of locusts, Pharaoh's officials begged him to free the people before Egypt was completely destroyed, but Pharaoh was so hardhearted he threw Moses and Aaron out of his palace. He even confessed he had sinned against God, but he didn't change his mind about releasing the Israelites.

When the entire land of Egypt was shrouded in a thick darkness, Pharaoh summoned Moses and offered to let the Israelites worship the Lord, but he would not allow them to take livestock. Moses refused; Pharaoh exploded in anger and warned Moses that if he ever came into his presence again he would kill him.

The tenth plague was the most devastating: the death of the first-born sons. Instead of automatically protecting Israel from this plague, the Lord told Moses they would need to sacrifice a sheep or goat and place the blood over the doorframes of their homes and roast and eat the meat. When the Lord saw the blood, he would pass over those homes but strike the land of Egypt with the plague of death.

Along with the meat, they were to bake unleavened bread. Moses summoned the elders of Israel and gave them instructions for the sacrifice. The people did exactly as the Lord had commanded, and at midnight there was not a single death in the homes of the Israelites, but there was loud wailing throughout Egypt.

Moses and Aaron didn't need to go to Pharaoh; he sent for them and ordered, "Get out of the land of Egypt." Afraid they would all die, even the Egyptian people urged the Israelites to leave. The people of Israel took food, clothes, and large amounts of silver and gold, which the Egyptians had given them, and left Egypt after living there for 430 years.

In addition to eating the meat from the sacrificed animal, they baked bread without yeast to remind them they had left Egypt in a hurry. The Lord told Moses and Aaron to memorialize the sacrificing of an animal and the eating of bread without yeast by making it an annual celebration called Passover. Moses said to the people, "You are to remember this day forever. You must never forget the Lord kept his promise and brought you out of Egypt with the power of his mighty hand."

When the Israelites left Egypt, they did not take the direct, shortest route to Canaan; instead the Lord led them in a southerly direction with a cloud by day and a pillar of fire at night. While they were camped on the edge of the wilderness near the Red Sea ("Reed Sea" in the Hebrew text), Pharaoh realized he had made a foolish mistake by freeing his slaves. He ordered six hundred of his elite chariot commanders to go after the Israelites.

Panic set in when the Israelites saw the Egyptians rapidly approaching. They accused Moses of leading them out to die: "It would be better to be a slave in Egypt than a corpse in the wilderness." But Moses assured them the Lord would fight for them.

The angel of the Lord, who had been leading the people in the cloud, moved between the Israelites and the Egyptians. Moses raised his hand, opening a way through the waters of the sea, and the people walked through on dry ground. After they were all safely on the other side, Moses raised his hand again and the two walls of water collapsed, destroying Pharaoh's army, who had followed them into the sea.

When the Israelites saw how the Lord had destroyed the Egyptians, they trusted in the Lord and Moses and praised the Lord with a song of victory. Miriam, Aaron's sister, danced, played a tambourine, and led the women in a song:

> Sing to the Lord,
> for he has triumphed gloriously;
> He has hurled both horse and rider
> into the sea. (Exodus 15:21 NLT)

♔ Chapter Summary

(More than four hundred years passed from the time Joseph was taken to Egypt to the time of the exodus.)

Moving to Egypt was an advantage for the sons of Israel, who prospered. Their growth in numbers and power, however, alarmed a new Pharaoh, who didn't know how Joseph had saved Egypt. The king ruthlessly oppressed Israel, his tyranny climaxing in an order to kill all Hebrew boys at birth.

Though Moses was raised in Pharaoh's palace, Pharaoh's daughter chose his own mother to be his nurse, and because of her godly influence, Moses knew he was a Hebrew and not an Egyptian. But when he tried to help his people, one of them threatened to inform Pharaoh that Moses had killed an Egyptian.

While Moses was a shepherd, God appeared to him and identified himself as the Lord, who had heard the cries of his people. He commissioned Moses with divine power to rescue them from oppressive slavery.

Moses returned to Egypt and used all kinds of disasters as warnings to the king to release Israel, but each time Pharaoh imposed harsher demands. The Lord finally forced Pharaoh to release the Israelites when he passed through the land and killed all the firstborn males in homes not covered with the sacrificial blood.

Before the children of Israel left, they ate a Passover meal to commemorate the day the Lord delivered them from slavery; they dedicated their firstborn to the Lord.

He guided them to the sea before Pharaoh pursued with his chariots. Moses parted the waters so Israel could cross on dry ground. When the army attempted to follow, they drowned as the Lord withdrew his power and water came crashing down on them.

Four

WANDERING IN
THE WILDERNESS

Main Characters
Moses
Joshua
Caleb
Aaron
The people of Israel

Setting
Sinai wilderness
Mount Sinai
**Kadesh Barnea (an oasis on the southern border of the Promised
    Land)**
Plains of Moab (area east of the Jordan River)

THE LORD'S PROVISION

Moses and the people of Israel now faced a different threat: how to
survive in an arid desert without food and water. A month after leaving
Egypt, they began to run out of supplies, and the water they found was
brackish. They complained to Moses and Aaron; Moses responded by
reminding them the Lord had not brought them to the desert to die.
He would provide.

He gave them quail in the evening and a perishable bread–like sub-
stance in the morning, but they could only collect enough for one day.
They had never before seen anything like the bread, so they called it
manna (which means, "What is it?"). To avoid violating the restriction

from working on the Sabbath (the seventh day), on the sixth day the people could collect enough bread for two days.

To remember this gracious provision, the Lord told Moses to preserve a small amount of manna so future generations could see what the Lord gave them in the wilderness. This manna was later placed in the ark of the covenant, and the miraculous provision continued for the entire forty years until Israel entered the Promised Land.

The water problem was solved when the people camped at Rephidim (exact location unknown). When they couldn't find a natural supply, they again complained. Moses cried out to the Lord for help because he thought the people were so angry they might stone him. The Lord told him to assemble the elders and stand on a large rock and strike it with his staff. Moses hit the rock, and water poured out of it. (He named the place *Massah*, which means "test," and *Meribah*, which means "arguing," because the people tested the Lord and argued with Moses.)

Here Israel faced an unexpected threat when they were attacked by Amalekites. Moses told Joshua (whose name means "savior") to pick some men for battle.

Moses climbed a nearby hill and raised his staff above his head. As long as he held it high in the air, the Israelites defeated the Amalekites, but when his arms tired and he lowered it, the Amalekites advanced against Joshua and his men. To enable Joshua's complete victory, Aaron and Hur stood on each side of Moses and helped him hold up his arms. Then the Lord told Moses to name the place Yahweh-nissi, which means "the Lord is my banner."

Jethro, Moses' father-in-law, heard about the exodus from Egypt and came to see Moses. He too praised the Lord for delivering Israel from the powerful hand of Pharaoh, and he ate a sacrificial meal with the elders.

He also gave Moses wise counsel. Moses had assumed responsibility for resolving conflict, and on some days he was listening to complaints from sunrise to sunset. Jethro said, "Moses, you can't continue to do this. You will wear yourself out! Teach the people how God wants them to live, organize them into groups, and appoint capable leaders over the groups to solve the minor problems and bring only the difficult cases to you."

MOUNT SINAI

Exactly two months after they left Egypt, the people arrived at Mount Sinai. After they had set up camp, Moses climbed the mountain to meet with God, who spoke to him from a thick cloud on the mountaintop. He assured Moses if Israel honored him as their "great king" by obeying the covenant, then they would be his treasured people, "a kingdom of priests and a holy nation."

When Moses told the elders about his meeting with God, they enthusiastically agreed to do everything the Lord had commanded. Moses climbed the mountain again and told the Lord the elders agreed to obey and trust him. After speaking with God, Moses returned to the people and told them to prepare to meet with God in three days.

Before meeting with the Lord, the people had to purify themselves by bathing and washing their clothes, and by abstaining from sexual relations. They could come close to the mountain but could not cross the boundary that Moses had set up around its base. Moses warned, "Any person or animal that crosses the boundary or even touches it must be put to death."

When Moses met again with the Lord, he gave Moses the Ten Commandments. Because the Lord had rescued Israel out of Egypt, he demanded total loyalty. He said, "You must not worship any god but me, bow down to any kind of idol, or denigrate the name of God." As a reminder that God had created everything in six days, the seventh day (Sabbath) was a holy day of rest. His people were to honor their father and mother. They must not commit murder or adultery, steal, make false accusations against another person, or covet anything that belongs to another person, especially his wife.

When the people heard thunder and saw lightning, they trembled. Afraid they would die, they begged Moses to approach God and speak for them. Moses assured them they had nothing to fear. God's awesome display of power was to keep them from sinning.

With the people standing at a distance, Moses approached God, whose form was shrouded in a dark cloud. He gave Moses detailed instructions about sacrifices, prayers, and offerings. The civil laws included issues of slavery, murder, theft, lending, and lying. Because Israel would become primarily an agricultural nation, the Lord even told them how to plant and harvest their crops.

Moses repeated all the instructions to the people, and with one voice they said, "We will do everything the Lord has commanded." To ratify the covenant, Moses built an altar and erected twelve pillars, one for each of the twelve tribes. After the sacrifice of several bulls, Moses splattered half the blood on the altar and the rest on the people. He read from the book of the covenant, and again the people agreed to fully obey the Lord.

After Moses and Israel's leaders had eaten a covenant meal, the Lord summoned Moses back to the mountain. Though the Lord's glory descended in the form of a blazing fire partially shrouded by a mysterious cloud, Moses had to wait six days before the Lord met with him. On the seventh day, the Lord descended in a pillar of fire and summoned Moses to meet with him in the cloud that covered the mountain.

Moses stayed forty more days to receive instructions for the building of the tabernacle (the tent of meeting), a temporary place for worship while Israel was in the wilderness. They were to use animal skins, wood, gold, silver, and bronze.

In addition to the outer structure, the Lord gave precise instructions for furnishings. God told Moses to make the ark of the covenant (a box to hold the two stone tablets) and said he would speak to him from between the two golden angels on the top of it. There also was an altar for making sacrifices, a table for holding ceremonial bread, a golden lampstand (menorah), the altar of incense, and a basin for ceremonial washing.

Aaron and his sons were chosen to serve as priests to lead in worship and provide access to the Lord. They were to wear "garments of holiness" to distinguish them so that even their clothes brought dignity to their position and beauty to the worship.

The primary distinguishing piece of clothing for Aaron was an elaborate vest-like garment embroidered with gold and colored thread, which contained two stones used for determining God's will. For their ordination, Aaron and his sons were anointed with oil and the blood of sacrificial animals. Their responsibilities included making daily sacrifices in the morning and evening on behalf of the people.

For the maintenance of the tabernacle, each person over twenty was required to pay a half shekel (a silver coin weighing about six grams). For the actual construction and furnishings, the Lord said he would choose skilled individuals and fill them with his Spirit. After reminding Moses again of the importance of observing every seventh day as a day of rest, the Lord gave Moses two stone tablets with the Ten Commandments carved with his finger.

THE GOLDEN IDOL

Unfortunately, during Moses' extended absence, the people lapsed into idolatry. They collected their gold jewelry and persuaded Aaron to make an idol resembling a young bull. The next day the people brought sacrifices to the idol and celebrated the worship of their new god.

Knowing the people had rebelled against him, the Lord told Moses he would destroy them and make another nation for Moses to lead into the Promised Land. Moses pleaded with the Lord for mercy, asking him to remember the covenant he had made with Abraham and his descendants. The Lord honored Moses' request and withheld judgment.

Moses descended the mountain carrying the two stone tablets. Joshua met him before he reached camp and said the noise was the sound of warfare. When Moses saw the golden calf and the people dancing, he exploded in anger and broke the two tablets into pieces. He burned the golden calf, ground it into powder, mixed it with water, and made the people drink the idol they had worshiped.

When Moses asked Aaron why he had made it, he tried to blame the people. He said the people wanted an idol so he asked for their gold, and when he threw the gold in the fire, miraculously an idol came out. Moses, outraged, stood at the entrance to the camp and said, "Whoever is on the Lord's side, come stand with me." He then ordered the Levites to execute all the idolaters. There were no exceptions, even if it was their brother, friend, or neighbor; all idolaters were to be killed. They executed about three thousand.

Moses realized the people had committed a grievous offense against the Lord, so he returned to the mountain and asked God to punish him for their sins. God forgave Moses, but he placed a deadly plague on those who had made the golden calf.

Though Israel had broken its covenant promises, God remained faithful to his promise to make the descendants of Abraham into a great nation. He told Moses, "Go to the land I swore I would give to Abraham, Isaac, and Jacob." However, because the people were stubborn and rebellious, God said he himself would no longer lead them; instead, he would send an angel to guide them and fight for them. Plus, because the people had worn flashy jewelry and clothes while worshiping the golden calf, Moses said they were prohibited from ever dressing like that again.

MOSES AND THE GLORY OF THE LORD

Moses continued to act as a mediator between God and the people. Those who wanted to make a request of the Lord would meet with Moses at the entrance to the tent of meeting, and Moses would convey their request. The people would watch Moses enter the tent from a distance, and they would bow down in front of their tents.

One day when Moses met with the Lord, he made a bold request. (Moses was concerned the Lord would not lead his people into the Promised Land. He knew God's name and was privileged to meet with the Lord, but he wanted to know the Lord more intimately—his character and the motives for his actions.)

The Lord assured Moses he could trust him to keep his promises to Israel, but Moses still was not satisfied. He asked, "Show me your glory." The Lord told Moses he could glimpse his glory but not see his face, because no one could look directly at God's glory and live. Moses was concealed in the crevice of a rock and saw a reflection of God's glory after he had passed by.

The Lord told Moses to return to the mountain with two new stone tablets to replace the ones he had broken. After he had chiseled out two new tablets, Moses climbed early in the morning, and the Lord descended in the form of a cloud, calling out to Moses, "I am Yahweh, the LORD! I am a God of compassion and mercy. My love is unfailing, and I forgive the people's rebellion and sin." Moses fell facedown on the ground, worshiped the Lord, and asked him to renew the covenant with his chosen people.

The Lord promised again to confirm Moses as leader and to lead the people into the land, but he reemphasized the importance of obedience. Because the land's inhabitants worshiped idols, the Lord stressed that Israel must not make treaties with them. Making a treaty with people who worshiped idols could influence them to worship other gods.

As a further precaution, the young men were prohibited from marrying the young women of the foreign peoples because they would seduce the men to bow down to idols. To keep themselves fully devoted to the Lord, the Israelites were expected to observe annual festivals and offer special sacrifices to the Lord.

At the end of the forty days and forty nights, the Lord wrote the Ten Commandments on the new tablets. When Moses returned, his face was so radiant with God's glory that the people were afraid to come near him. Moses covered his face while speaking with the people but uncovered his face when speaking with the Lord, so every time he met with the Lord, Moses' face had a fresh radiance.

THE TABERNACLE

Moses assembled the people and repeated the command to observe the Sabbath as a day of rest and worship. To begin construction on the tabernacle, he asked them to bring their gifts to the Lord voluntarily. When the people returned to their tents, the Lord stirred their hearts to bring items of gold, linen, leather, oil, and other materials needed to construct the tabernacle exactly as he had commanded.

The people were so eager to help that even after the work began they continued bringing materials. Finally, Moses had to tell them to stop because they had more than enough for the project. For the tabernacle's actual construction, Moses put Bezalel and Oholiab, two skilled craftsmen, in charge of the work.

In addition to the structure, the craftsmen made the furniture and clothes for Aaron and the priests. After the work was finished, Moses inspected it and commended the workers because they had made everything exactly as the Lord had directed.

On the first day of their New Year (in March or April), they set up the tabernacle, which consisted of three separate areas: the Holy of Holies, the Holy Place, and the outer courtyard. The innermost area, the Holy of Holies, was enclosed with a large curtain. The sacred lamps and the altar of incense were put in the Holy Place, which was isolated by another large curtain. The largest area was the outer courtyard, also enclosed by curtains. A basin for ceremonial washing and an altar for sacrifices were set up in the tabernacle's one and only entrance. After all the furniture was put in its designated place, it was sprinkled with oil to dedicate it to the Lord.

Moses assembled Aaron and his sons at the entrance, placed their priestly robes on them, and anointed them with oil to serve as priests from generation to generation. The climatic event was the placing of the

Ten Commandments in the ark of the covenant. The priests attached poles to the ark and carried it into the Holy of Holies; Moses closed the curtain shielding the ark from view as the Lord had commanded. Moses lit the lamps and burned incense on the altar in the Holy Place, and he filled the basin for ceremonial washing with water in the outer courtyard.

At the exact moment Moses finished, a cloud covered the tabernacle and the glory of the Lord filled the Holy of Holies. For the remainder of Israel's journey to the Promised Land, whenever the cloud moved, the people would follow it; otherwise, they would stay in the place where the cloud stopped. At night, a bright fire burned inside the cloud so that even when it was dark the people could see the Lord's presence.

🎵 Chapter Summary

After the exodus, Israel needed God's help to survive in the desert. He provided food and water for them. He also protected them. When they were attacked, Moses, Joshua, Aaron, and Hur, along with some of Israel's best fighting men, gained victory.

Jethro came to visit and gave wise counsel. Because Moses was overwhelmed with his responsibilities, Jethro advised him to appoint assistants to help with minor decisions.

At Mount Sinai, God gave Moses instructions for organizing Israel into a unique nation, one that worshiped the Lord. He inscribed the Ten Commandments on stone tablets and gave additional guidelines for worship and case law.

Moses ratified the covenant when he read it to the people and they agreed to obey it.

As commanded, Moses appointed Aaron as high priest and his sons as priests. The Lord identified gifted individuals for building the tabernacle (where the people would meet with God) and its sacred furniture.

When the people lapsed into idolatry, Moses had to plead for mercy; God was prepared to destroy Israel and choose a new nation. The Lord relented, but with a deadly plague he punished those who worshiped the golden calf.

Moses wanted to know the Lord more intimately, so he was allowed to glimpse the Lord's glory but not look directly at his face.

Tabernacle construction started when the Lord stirred the people's hearts to give materials they had brought from Egypt. Two skilled craftsmen supervised the making of the structure, the furniture, and the priests' clothes.

After the tabernacle was finished and dedicated, the Lord filled the Holy of Holies with his glory—visible as a cloud during the day and a glowing fire inside the cloud at night. For the remainder of their journey to the Promised Land, Israel followed the cloud when it moved and stopped when it stopped.

Five

The Wilderness and the Death of Moses

Main Characters

Moses
Joshua and Caleb
The people of Israel
Balak
Balaam

Setting

Mount Sinai
The wilderness
Kadesh-Barnea
Plains of Moab

Preparations for the Journey— From Mount Sinai to Kadesh

The story of the Israelites' journey from Mount Sinai to the plains of Moab is a dramatic account of human failure and God's faithfulness. The Israelites repeatedly tested God's patience, and though he judged those who rebelled, and an entire generation perished in the harsh desert of Sinai, the Lord prepared a new generation to inherit the Promised Land.

To determine their military strength, Moses counted all the men who were twenty and older and capable of going to war. All were counted except Aaron, his sons, and the tribe of Levi—they were put in charge of moving and setting up the tabernacle. The number of men of military age was staggering: 603,550.

Each tribe was assigned an order in the march and a location for setting up camp in relation to the tabernacle. The area near the front of the tabernacle was reserved for Moses, Aaron, his sons, and the Levites. If anyone else came too close, they were to be put to death.

In preparing for the journey, no detail was too small. To ensure that no one sinned out of ignorance or was unjustly accused of sinning, Moses explained the laws for ritual and moral purity. If someone was not a Levite, they could impose stricter spiritual self-restraints by taking a temporary (Nazirite) vow. The Nazirite vow involved voluntary restraint from (a) drinking anything made from grapes; (b) cutting the hair; and (c) touching anything dead. At the end of the vow, sacrifices were brought to the Lord.

Before leaving Mount Sinai, Israel celebrated its second Passover. For those unable to celebrate on the regularly scheduled day, Moses said it was possible to make up the Passover a month later.

Moses needed some way to communicate with the people while marching. The Lord told him to make two silver trumpets to be used for signaling the tribes and to warn of a threat from their enemies.

Israel was now ready for the journey. It was a momentous event when the cloud lifted up from the tabernacle and began to move. Moses asked his brother-in-law to serve as their guide; he was a Midianite and knew the desert far better than Moses.

With the ark of the covenant at the head of the column, the Israelites walked for three days after leaving Mount Sinai. Each time they began to move, Moses would shout, "Arise, O Lord, and let your enemies be scattered before you." When they stopped, Moses would shout, "Return, O Lord, to your people."

ON THE WAY TO KADESH—A SPIRIT OF COMPLAINING

The journey began as a wonderful experience. But once they left Sinai, the people faced the hardships of an inhospitable desert and immediately began to complain. This was the first of many occasions when they would do so on the way to the Promised Land. When they complained, God punished them, but he never totally abandoned them.

The first time, God destroyed the complainers with a raging fire. They begged Moses for help, and when he prayed, the fire stopped. The place was named Taberah ("place of the burning fire").

Even after the terrifying judgment of fire, the people continued to complain. Some Egyptians, who'd left Egypt with the Israelites, craved spicy food and complained about the bland diet of manna. When the Israelites also complained, Moses became so frustrated he wanted to die.

The Lord intervened and told Moses to select seventy men to assist him and relieve some of the stress of leadership. To provide them with the wisdom they needed for making decisions, the Lord gave them his Spirit. As punishment, God flooded the camp with quail and inflicted a terrible plague on the rebels.

When the Israelites arrived at Hazeroth (location unknown), Miriam and Aaron criticized Moses for marrying a non-Israelite; they also claimed they were as qualified as Moses to lead the nation. The Lord inflicted Miriam with leprosy.

When Aaron saw what had happened, he cried out to Moses for forgiveness. Moses prayed for Miriam, and the Lord healed her.

AT KADESH—REBELLION

Kadesh-Barnea, an oasis, was a strategic location on the southern border of the Promised Land. Moses sent out twelve men, one from each of the tribes, to make a reconnaissance. The spies went through the arid region of the Negev and traveled as far north as Rehob (north of Damascus—total distance of over two hundred miles).

On their return, they brought a large cluster of grapes and reported that the land was exceptionally fertile, but there was also a serious problem: The land was inhabited by powerful people who lived in fortified cities.

Though Joshua and Caleb urged the people to trust God and enter the land, the Israelites refused. The report of the spies spread through the camp like wildfire. Soon the entire nation was ready to reject Moses, choose a new leader, and return to Egypt. They even threatened to stone Joshua and Caleb.

For their lack of faith and disobedience, the Lord threatened to destroy the whole nation. As he had done previously, Moses interceded. God pardoned the people, but he judged the faithless generation to wander in the desolate desert of Sinai for forty years.

When the people realized they had made a serious mistake, they decided to enter the land without the help of the Lord or the ark of the covenant. They made it as far as the hill country in the south, but they were repulsed by the Amalekites and Canaanites, who chased them almost all the way back to Kadesh.

ON THE WAY TO MOAB—SPIRITUAL DEFEAT AND MILITARY VICTORY

After the failure at Kadesh, thousands died in the wilderness and never made it to the Promised Land. Some died from natural causes, but most by divine judgment. When Korah incited a rebellion against Moses, the ground split open; Korah and the other rebels fell into a fiery pit.

The Lord killed thousands of others with a deadly plague. To stop the plague, Moses told Aaron to grab an incense burner and wave it before the Lord between the dead and the living. The plague stopped, but not before 14,700 died.

After Korah's revolt, the Lord instructed Moses to set up a test to settle the matter of Aaron's leadership. He told the tribal leaders to bring their staffs to the tabernacle. He placed their staffs along with Aaron's in front of the ark of the covenant. The next day Aaron's staff had blossomed and produced almonds. Moses placed Aaron's staff in front of the ark as a permanent warning to any potential rebels. The people were so frightened they thought they were doomed.

Because so many people died in the desert, there was a special means of purifying those who became ceremonially unclean from disposing of a dead body. The Lord instructed Moses to prepare water of purification from the ashes of a red heifer. In addition to bathing and washing their clothes, they were sprinkled with water mixed with cedar, hyssop, a scarlet thread, and the ashes of a red heifer.

While the Israelites were camped at Kadesh, their water supply dried up. The people criticized Moses and Aaron; the Lord told Moses to summon the people and speak to a rock to bring water out of it. Instead of speaking to the rock, Moses struck it twice. Because Moses and Aaron did not follow exactly the Lord's instructions, they were not allowed to enter the Promised Land. The place was called Meribah (place of "arguing").

As they neared the Promised Land, the Israelites encountered resistance from the people who occupied territory adjacent to Canaan. The king of Edom mobilized a large blocking force and refused to let Israel pass through his country. He warned, "Keep out of our land. You are not welcome here!"

When Israel reached Mount Hor (exact location unknown), Aaron died, and his office was passed on to Eleazar, his son.

While the Israelites were camped at Mount Hor, the Canaanite king who ruled over the region attacked and took prisoners. Israel vowed to completely destroy all the towns in the area if the Lord would help rescue the prisoners. He answered their prayer, and they totally annihilated their enemies. The place was called Hormah ("destruction") because the Israelites destroyed all the Canaanites and their towns.

Though they won an important military victory, the people were still inflicted with a spirit of ungratefulness. When forced to take the longer route around Edom, the people criticized God and Moses: "Why have you led us into this wilderness to die? Not only that, but there is nothing to drink or eat except this horrible manna."

This time the Lord sent poisonous snakes into their camp. To keep those who were bitten from dying, Moses erected a bronze snake in the center of the camp. When someone was bitten, if they looked at the bronze snake, they did not die.

As Israel moved north out of the vast Sinai Desert, they occupied the territory of two Amorite kings. After these two victories, Israel camped on the plains of Moab (east of the Jordan River and northeast of the Dead Sea).

BALAAM—A PROPHET FOR HIRE

Balak, the king of Moab, became alarmed when it was reported that large numbers of foreigners had entered his country. He sought help from a pagan prophet named Balaam, who lived in Pethor near the Euphrates River, northeast of Moab. (Balaam was some kind of diviner who sold his services.)

When Balak's messengers first arrived, Balaam refused to go with them; instead he invited them to spend the night while he sought a word from the Lord. God warned him, "Do not go with them to curse my people, for they are blessed."

When they reported to Balak that Balaam refused his offer, the king didn't give up. He sent several princes, who promised Balaam that Balak would give him whatever he wanted if he would curse Israel. This time the Lord allowed Balaam to go but made it clear he could only speak exactly what the Lord commanded.

The next morning Balaam saddled his donkey and left for Moab. God, however, was angry with Balaam and sent an angel to block the road.

Balaam's donkey could see the angel blocking the path, but Balaam couldn't. He beat his donkey, assuming the animal was uncooperative. This happened twice, and the third time the donkey saw the angel of the Lord, the animal lay down.

In a fit of rage Balaam furiously beat the donkey, but instead of getting up, his donkey spoke to him, "What have I done to deserve a beating?"

Balaam complained that the donkey had made him look foolish.

The donkey spoke again and asked, "You have ridden me all your life. Have I ever done anything like this?"

Balaam was forced to say, "No!"

At this point the Lord opened Balaam's eyes so he could see the angel standing in the path with a drawn sword. The angel reprimanded Balaam for his lack of spiritual perception and his foolish disobedience.

Balaam offered to go home; the angel said he could go to Moab, but again made it clear that Balaam could say only what the Lord commanded.

When Balaam met Balak, he explained what had happened and informed the king he didn't have personal power to do anything, and he could only speak the Lord's message.

Balaam built seven altars and prepared seven bulls and seven rams for sacrifice. Both Balaam and Balak sacrificed two animals, but then Balaam announced that Israel was a unique people who had been chosen by God.

Balak, confused, demanded an explanation. "Why have you done this?" he asked. "I paid you to curse my enemies. Instead you have blessed them."

He took Balaam to another location, thinking the location might make a difference. Location didn't matter. Though he built seven more altars, the Lord only permitted Balaam to bless Israel. Totally frustrated, Balak scolded Balaam: "If you won't curse them, at least don't bless them."

Balak wanted to try a third time, so he took Balaam to Mount Peor (location unknown). Balaam built seven altars for sacrifice, but instead of resorting to divination, he sought a message from God. The Spirit of the Lord moved the prophet to announce his third message. This time Balaam not only blessed Israel but prophesied they would crush all of their enemies.

Balak ranted and raved: "I called you to curse my enemies; instead you have blessed them. I promised to reward you, but you will not get anything from me. Get out of here, and go back home."

Balaam said he would leave, but first he told Balak what would happen in the future. He predicted the defeat of Israel's enemies and the emergence of a powerful king in the distant future: "A star will rise from Jacob, and a scepter from Israel." (Christians believe this prophecy refers to the Lord Jesus Christ.)

Before returning to Pethor, Balaam told Balak how he could defeat Israel. He advised him to have the women of Moab seduce the men of Israel into sexual immorality and idolatry, and then God himself would judge them.

The plot worked. The women of Moab enticed the men of Israel with sex to worship the gods of Moab.

The Lord's anger blazed against Israel. He ordered Moses to publicly execute the ringleaders, and he punished other offenders with a deadly plague.

When one Israelite blatantly took a Midianite woman into his tent, Phinehas, a priest, grabbed a spear and thrust it through them as they were having intercourse. His zeal turned away the Lord's fierce anger and stopped the plague. God honored Phinehas by granting him and his descendents permanent priestly status.

A SECOND CENSUS

After the plague, Moses took a second census, counting Israel's military strength by tribe. Some tribes had increased in size; others were smaller. Overall, the population was less than when they left Mount Sinai (601,730).

Based on the census, Moses assigned the land by lot, according to the size of each tribe. He did not count the Levites because they did not receive a land allotment.

The result of the census was shocking. It revealed that, except for Joshua and Caleb, the entire generation that had come out of Egypt had died in the wilderness.

Afterward, Moses made final preparations for the invasion of Canaan.

Because families would actually possess their own land once they were in Canaan, it was necessary for Moses to resolve the question about inheritance of family property. To keep the land in the family, Moses ruled that if a man died and didn't have a son, the property should be given to his daughter or to any other relative.

When Moses disobeyed the Lord by striking the rock instead of speaking to it, he lost the privilege of entering the Promised Land. He would be permitted to see it, but not enter. So Israel needed a new leader. The Lord put his Spirit on Joshua and instructed Moses to commission him. In a public ceremony, Moses' decision was confirmed by Eleazar, the high priest.

Once the people settled in the land, they needed a schedule for daily, weekly, and monthly offerings and annual religious festivals, so Moses set up a religious calendar for the feasts of Passover, Harvest, Trumpets, and Tabernacles. He also warned about making hasty, thoughtless vows and not keeping them.

Because the women of Midian had cooperated with the Moabites to seduce Israel, the Lord ordered Moses to destroy the Midianites. For the assault, Moses put together a force of twelve thousand men—one thousand from each of the twelve tribes.

The Israelites attacked Midian and killed all the men, including five kings and Balaam, who had advised Balak on how to seduce Israel into immorality and idolatry. The soldiers burned all the towns in Midian but did not destroy the women and children.

When Moses found out they had not killed the women and children, he was outraged, and he ordered the soldiers to kill all those who had participated in the seduction. Only young girls who were virgins were to be spared.

The soldiers who participated in the attack and the captive virgins were required to purify themselves, including their clothes and the plunder not destroyed by fire, and remain outside the camp for seven days. Half of the plunder was given to the soldiers; the other half to the rest of the people. Because not a single Israelite was killed in the attack, the officers brought thank-you offerings of gold to the Lord.

Before Israel crossed the Jordan to occupy land west of the river, the tribes of Reuben and Gad made a surprising request. They had significantly more livestock than the rest of the tribes and asked if they could settle in the lush grazing land to the north and east of the Jordan River. (This land had been captured from the Amorites and the king of Bashan.)

Moses was shocked. He asked, "Do you intend to stay here in safety while your brothers risk their lives to occupy the land?" If they didn't occupy the land, they'd be guilty of the same kind of disobedience as the generation that perished in the wilderness, and they would threaten the unity of the new nation.

The Reubenites and Gadites said Moses misunderstood. They only wanted to build fortified towns for their families to live in safety. They assured Moses, "We will fight with our brothers until they have safely occupied all of the land."

Their pledge convinced Moses, and he gave them and half the tribe of Manasseh permission to settle east of the Jordan.

When Israel arrived on the plains of Moab (opposite Canaan, east of the Jordan River), the Lord commanded Moses to drive out all the Canaanites and destroy all their pagan idols. There were to be no exceptions, because any people permitted to remain in the land would be a military threat and entice Israel to worship their gods.

In anticipation of the occupation, Moses identified the boundaries of all the land that God had promised to Israel, and then he assigned Eleazar and Joshua the responsibility of dividing the land among the remaining nine and a half tribes.

The tribe of Levi did not receive any land; instead they were assigned forty-eight cities within the boundaries of each of the tribes. These cities were also places of protection for anyone who accidentally killed another person. Family members could not take revenge on those who fled to the cities of refuge until it could be determined if the death was accidental or intentional. If the death was accidental, the person had to live in the city of refuge until the death of the high priest. If it was determined that the death was murder, based on the testimony of witnesses, then the offender was to be executed to keep the land from becoming polluted by the blood of the victim.

MOSES' FINAL MESSAGES TO ISRAEL

Moses was Israel's first and greatest leader, but knowing that the end of his life was near, he gave a final series of speeches to the infant nation on the plains of Moab. After reviewing God's faithfulness during the forty years of wandering in the Sinai Desert, Moses emphasized that God chose Israel because of his great love, not because they were better than any other people.

God loved Israel, and he wanted his people to love him with "all their heart, mind, and soul." As a "holy nation," God would bless them, but more than that he wanted Israel to become his witness to the world. This required total obedience to the Lord's commands and complete separation from the sin and idolatry of other nations.

Because of the other peoples' indescribable and incurable evil, Israel was still to destroy or drive out the seven nations that occupied the land.

If Israel did this, God would give them victory, protect them from their enemies, and make them a great nation as he had promised.

But Moses also warned that failure to fulfill their covenant obligations would bring disaster. God would drive them out of the land and scatter them over the earth. However, even then, if Israel would repent and return to the Lord, he would forgive them and restore them to the Promised Land.

Moses said Israel had a choice "between life and death, between blessings and curses." They could choose by faithfully loving and fully obeying the Lord their God.

MOSES' DEATH

After his final messages, Moses alone climbed Mount Nebo (a high peak in the Abarim mountain range, south of the plains of Moab). From this vantage point, Moses was able to see the land God had promised to Abraham, Isaac, and Jacob.

After seeing the land, Moses died and was buried in Beth Peor. The people mourned for thirty days. Joshua assumed leadership of Israel, and he was immediately recognized as a man with a spirit of wisdom.

In his obituary, Moses was recognized as Israel's greatest prophet. No one ever had such an intimate relationship with the Lord that God spoke to him "face to face," as he did with Moses. And no one ever performed miraculous signs and wonders like Moses did when he delivered Israel from Egypt.

𝕎 Chapter Summary

After a census, the Israelites left Mount Sinai when the cloud lifted from the tabernacle and began to move. Then the people faced desert hardships and they started to complain. Each time God punished them, yet he never totally destroyed his people.

At Kadesh-Barnea, Moses sent out twelve men to scout the land.

They reported that it was an ideal place to live, but they were terrified by the people living in it.

Though Joshua and Caleb urged the people to trust God, they refused, and God condemned them to wander in the Sinai Desert for forty years. Many thousands never entered the Promised Land.

Instead of speaking to a rock to provide water for the people, Moses struck it twice. For his defiance, he and Aaron were not allowed to enter Canaan.

When the Israelites started to move toward Moab, they faced resistance but were victorious with God's help.

Balak, king of Moab, hired Balaam to curse Israel, but Balaam could only bless Israel because they were God's chosen people. Moab's women, however, seduced the Israelites to worship their gods, and God punished his people with a deadly plague.

A second census was taken before entering the land of Canaan.

Moses saw the Promised Land from Mount Nebo. The Lord himself buried Moses in Moab.

Six

THE PROMISED LAND

Main Characters
Joshua
The Twelve Tribes
Rahab
Achan

Setting
Land of Canaan

After forty years of wilderness wandering, Israel was ready to possess the Promised Land. Moses was dead. Joshua was the new leader.

Leading God's people in the conquest would be difficult and dangerous. Joshua needed to know the Lord would help him as he had promised Moses.

The keys to success were simple. Three times the Lord told Joshua to be courageous and obey all the instructions given to Moses. "Meditate on the law, day and night; do everything it says, and you will succeed in everything you do." If Israel trusted in the Lord and was obedient to his word, God assured them of victory over all their enemies.

To get ready, Joshua summoned the officers and told them to make preparations for the invasion in three days. All the tribes accepted Joshua as their leader and promised to obey his orders as they had obeyed Moses.

Joshua sent two spies to infiltrate Jericho, a strategic city in the center of Canaan. Once inside, the spies went to the house of Rahab, a prostitute. She unexpectedly helped them by giving them vital information and hiding them when the king found out two strangers had come into the city. She helped them because the reports she had heard about the exodus convinced her that the Lord was God.

When guards went to the house of Rahab, she lied and said the men had left. In exchange for her help, she asked the spies to spare her and her family when the Israelites destroyed the city. They told her to display a piece of scarlet rope on one of the windows of her house so the soldiers would know she was the one who had helped them. After the spies escaped, they reported to Joshua that the inhabitants of the land were terrified.

The eastern boundary of Canaan was protected by a formidable natural barrier—the Jordan River. Plus, Jericho was protected by high stone walls. The Israelites did not have equipment for a river crossing or for breaking through the walls of a fortified city.

The problem of crossing the Jordan was solved when Joshua told the army to follow the ark of the covenant at a safe distance. The Lord told Joshua to send the priests into the river's center with the ark of the covenant, and he would block the flow of the water so the Israelites could cross on dry ground. Though it was overflowing its banks because of the spring runoff, when the priests reached the middle, the water was held back until all the people had crossed.

To commemorate the miracle, the people set up two memorials. They took twelve stones from the center of the Jordan and erected a monument at Gilgal, where they spent their first night in the land. They made a second stone monument in the middle of the river. (This apparently would be visible when the water was low.)

When the kings in southern Canaan heard about the crossing, they were terrified. The Israelites had a significant psychological advantage.

THE CONQUEST

Now that they were in the Promised Land, Joshua instructed the people to circumcise all men who had been born during the forty years of wilderness wandering. And while still camped at Gilgal, they celebrated their first Passover in Canaan. The next day the manna stopped, since Israel could now eat from the produce of the land.

Joshua still faced the problem of the fortified city of Jericho. It was resolved when the Commander of the Lord's Army appeared and gave him instructions for the city's capture. Because it was dedicated to God for destruction, he wanted the Israelites to march around Jericho for six days behind the ark of the covenant. On the seventh day, they were to walk around seven times, and on the seventh time they were to blow trumpets and shout, and the Lord would collapse the walls.

When the army attacked, they did exactly as the Lord had commanded for six days, and on the seventh day, the walls collapsed as God had promised. The Israelites captured the city without suffering a single casualty, and they completely destroyed the city and all its inhabitants except for Rahab and her family. Joshua also placed a curse on Jericho, warning that if anyone tried to rebuild it, his firstborn and youngest sons would die.

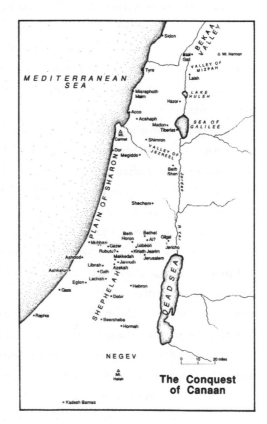

The Conquest of Canaan

Unknown to Joshua and the people, a man named Achan had violated God's order to destroy everything, and he secretly took some of the spoils. When the Israelites attacked Ai, which was a significantly smaller and more vulnerable town, they were unexpectedly repulsed, and thirty-six soldiers were killed.

The people were humiliated and frightened. They feared the defeat would embolden the Canaanites to attack and destroy them. Joshua cried out, "Sovereign Lord, why did you bring us across the river so the Canaanites could kill us?" The Lord immediately revealed that Israel had disobeyed. Someone had stolen items devoted to the Lord for destruction. The Lord would not tolerate disobedience. They would never defeat their enemies unless they purified themselves and punished the offender.

The next morning Joshua assembled all the tribes, conducted an investigation, and discovered that Achan had stolen a robe, silver coins, and a bar of gold. Achan and his family were stoned and their bodies burned. The bodies were buried under a pile of stones and the place was called Valley of Achor (which means "trouble").

This time when the Israelites attacked Ai, they assembled a larger force and used an ambush. Joshua hid a small force west of the town and made a frontal attack with the main army. When Ai's men came out, Joshua pretended to retreat. When they had lured all the men, the soldiers waiting in ambush charged into the defenseless city and set it on fire, then attacked the men of Ai from behind. Joshua and the rest of the army then turned on the men of Ai, who were trapped and totally destroyed. The Israelites burned Ai and executed its king.

After the victory, Joshua built an altar of uncut stones on Mount Ebal and offered sacrifices to the Lord. On the stones he copied the instructions Moses had given, and he read the curses and blessings in the book of the law to every single person in Israel.

When the kings west of the Jordan heard about the defeat of Jericho and Ai, they consolidated their forces to fight against Israel. The people of Gibeon, however, decided on a different strategy: They sent messengers to Joshua to make a peace treaty.

However, to make the treaty they had to convince the Israelites they were from another country. The messengers wore old, dusty clothing and even brought dry and moldy bread to make it appear they had traveled a long distance.

Joshua was suspicious, yet the ruse worked. When he asked where they had come from, they said, "We are from another country and have heard how the Lord your God delivered you from Egypt; we are your servants; please make a treaty with us."

The Israelites did not consult with the Lord. They made a peace treaty with the Gibeonites and sealed it with an irrevocable oath.

Three days later, the Israelites discovered they had been tricked. Because they had made a vow in the Lord's name, they honored the treaty but forced the Gibeonites to become their servants.

The Canaanite king of Jerusalem heard how the Israelites had totally destroyed Ai and Jericho and that Gibeon had made a peace treaty with the invaders, so he mobilized a coalition of four other kings to retaliate against the Gibeonites. When threatened, they appealed to Joshua for help. He honored the treaty, quickly mobilizing to protect Gibeon.

Israel's army marched all night and made a surprise attack at sunrise. The armies of the coalition panicked and were completely routed. As they retreated, the Lord rained down hailstones, killing more of them than the Israelites had killed. Joshua prayed, asking God to lengthen the day so they could pursue and annihilate the enemy force. After the victory, Joshua and the army returned to Gilgal.

When Joshua found out the five kings had escaped and were hiding in a cave, he ordered them to be impaled on poles and said their bodies were to be buried in that cave.

Joshua then moved quickly to complete the conquest of southern Canaan. With the help of the Lord, the Israelites either captured or burned all the major cities in the south.

Victory in the north was as swift and decisive as the southern campaign. The king of Hazor organized the northern kings to repel the invaders, but Joshua made a surprise attack and destroyed the coalition army, even though they had the advantage of chariots. Joshua burned the fortress at Hazor, which had been the capital of the northern kingdoms.

As the Lord had commanded Moses, Joshua destroyed the Canaanites. But the Israelites kept some of the spoils of victory and livestock for themselves and did not burn all the cities.

Though a few areas had not been conquered, the conquest was extensive enough that Joshua could distribute the land to the twelve tribes exactly as Moses had ordered. All the tribes except three received land west of the Jordan River. Manasseh, Reuben, and Gad settled east of the Jordan, as had been agreed.

Both Caleb and Joshua were given individual allocations of land because of their unwavering faith in God. Caleb's endurance was amazing. At age eighty-five he said, "I am as strong now as when we started on this journey, forty-five years ago."

Joshua established cities of refuge and assigned the tribe of Levi to live in towns within the boundaries of the other tribes. The conquest was an amazing accomplishment: "Not one single promise of God was unfulfilled. Everything God promised came true."

With the occupation complete, Joshua released Reuben, Gad, and the half tribe of Manasseh to return to their land east of the Jordan. On the way home, they built a large altar west of the Jordan. The other tribes assumed it was for another god and that those tribes had abandoned the Lord. They were outraged but mistaken. The three tribes had built the altar so that future generations would know they had a right to worship the Lord east of the Jordan River: "It is a witness to all of Israel that we worship the Lord God."

REDEDICATION TO THE LORD

As he neared the end of his life, Joshua assembled the group of men to lead Israel in the future. He reviewed how the Lord had helped them defeat their enemies, and he urged them to obey the law of Moses and to love and serve the Lord. He warned of disastrous consequences for worshiping the gods of the Canaanites; if they did, God's anger would burn against them, and he would drive them out of the land.

Joshua also summoned all the people to Shechem for renewal of the covenant. He reminded them of their special relationship with the Lord. God had promised Abraham and his descendants a home, he had rescued them from slavery, and he had given them victory over the inhabitants of the land.

Joshua said Israel had to decide who they would follow. Joshua had made his decision: "As for me and my family, we will serve the Lord." The people accepted Joshua's challenge, saying, "We will never forsake the Lord and serve other gods."

He told them to get rid of their idols, and they said a second time, "We will worship the Lord and obey him." With their verbal commitment, Joshua made a covenant with the people and set up a large stone under a tree as a memorial to their agreement. After the ceremony, Joshua dismissed the people to return to the land of their inheritance.

Three important individuals were buried in the land now possessed by Israel. Joshua died at age 110 and was buried in the territory of Ephraim. The remains of Joseph were buried in Shechem. Aaron's son, Eleazar the high priest, died and was also buried in the territory of Ephraim.

⚯ Chapter Summary

Moses was dead. Israel was ready to conquer the Promised Land. Joshua needed help; the Lord inspired him with courage, assuring him of total victory and promising he would possess every square inch of land where he set his foot if he would completely obey God.

Joshua secretly sent spies to Jericho. Rahab hid the spies and asked them to spare her. On returning to Joshua, the spies reported that everyone in the land was terrified.

Though the Jordan River was high, the Lord stopped the flow of water and the Israelites crossed it on dry ground. The miracle further terrified the Canaanites and confirmed that the Lord had chosen Joshua to lead in the conquest of the Promised Land.

Israel celebrated the Passover, and the manna stopped.

Because they trusted the Lord, Israel successfully destroyed the fortified city of Jericho and all its inhabitants; only Rahab and her family were spared. Because of Achan's disobedience, Israel was defeated when they attacked the small town of Ai, but after they judged Achan, they attacked a second time and captured it.

The Gibeonites tricked Israel into making a peace treaty. The deception worked because Israel did not seek the Lord's counsel.

When southern Canaanite kings formed a coalition, Israel's army routed them. The Israelites destroyed all the major cities in the south, leaving no survivors.

The campaign in the north was also decisive. The Canaanites were put under a divine curse and destroyed, as God had commanded Moses.

Though they had not conquered all the land, God told Joshua to divide it among the tribes and said he would help them drive out the remaining Canaanites. The people of Israel now had a home where they could live in peace.

Before he died, Joshua charged Israel to love and obey the Lord. If they abandoned God, he would drive them out just like the Canaanites. As his final act, Joshua led all of Israel in a renewal of their covenant relationship.

Seven

THE TIME OF THE JUDGES

Main Characters
The Israelites
Canaanites and other inhabitants Joshua had not driven
    out of the land
Othniel
Deborah
Gideon
Jephthah
Samson
Ruth

Setting
Land of Canaan (territories of the Twelve Tribes)
Land of Moab
Bethlehem (in Israel)

ISRAEL'S FAILURE AND GOD'S FAITHFULNESS

Joshua's generation and the following generation, who had witnessed
God's miraculous power in delivering them from Egypt and possessing
the Promised Land, continued to worship the Lord. The subsequent
generation, though, did evil. They worshiped images of Baal and Asherah
and other gods of the people they had not driven out of the land.

Their apostasy made the Lord so angry he actually helped their
enemies defeat them: "Every time Israel fought against an aggressor,
the Lord fought against his own people to defeat them just as he had
sworn he would do." The situation was dreadful.

Even so, God had compassion for Israel and raised up judges

(charismatic leaders) to rescue them from their oppressors. God would help them while the judge was alive, but as soon as the judge died, the people were so stubborn and evil they would lapse back into the sin of worshiping other gods.

This made God furious. Because they broke the covenant the Lord had made with their ancestors, God did not help them drive out the nations Joshua had not conquered.

Israel's failure was also an opportunity. The Lord said, "I will use these pagan nations to test Israel and find out if they will follow me." The presence of idolaters in the land forced God's people to choose between him and the gods of the Canaanites.

To survive in the hostile environment of the ancient world, Israel also needed to develop skills for war. Fighting against the Canaanites helped Israel gain valuable military experience. Unfortunately, as God had warned, his people intermarried with the people left in the land, and this led to the worship of their gods.

EARLY LEADERS

This entire period of history was characterized by the recurring theme of blatant apostasy, cruel oppression, and merciful deliverance. From the people's perspective, what they needed was a king. Though they repeatedly asked, God did not give them one. Instead he raised up military leaders (judges) to rescue them from oppressors.

Despite God's mercy, though, the people quickly abandoned him. God would allow their enemies to enslave them, and when they'd cry out again for help, God would answer by raising up another judge. This downward spiral of spiritual and military failure, followed by deliverance, was repeated over and over again.

Because the Israelites worshiped Baal and Asherah, God helped the king of Aram enslave them. When they pleaded for help, the Lord sent Othniel, an ideal judge. The Spirit of the Lord strengthened Othniel, and he defeated Aram. After they were set free, Israel enjoyed peace for forty years.

When Israel sinned again, three nations east of the Jordan River invaded and captured the hill country of Ephraim and Benjamin. God responded to Israel's pleas for rescue by sending Ehud, a left-handed judge.

Ehud brought a double-edged dagger with him when he went to pay tribute to Eglon, king of Moab. After paying, Ehud told the king he had a secret message. The king agreed to meet Ehud privately in an upstairs room.

When they were alone, Ehud stabbed Eglon, but he couldn't pull the dagger out: "It was so deeply imbedded in Eglon's stomach the handle disappeared in the fat."

Ehud escaped and sounded the call to arms; the tribe of Benjamin mobilized for war. Ehud told the people to follow him because "the Lord has granted victory." The Israelites defeated the Moabites and enjoyed peace for eighty years.

Though little is known about the judge named Shamgar, he killed six hundred Philistines with a metal spike from an ox cart.

When Ehud died, Israel sinned again, so the Lord handed them over to Jabin, a Canaanite king. Sisera, general of Jabin's army, commanded a force of nine hundred iron chariots. Through overwhelming military advantage, the Canaanites brutally oppressed Israel for twenty years. This time God used a woman to deliver them.

Deborah was ministering as a prophetess and also judging Israel. She summoned Barak, promising the Lord would give him victory. Barak was unwilling to lead the army unless Deborah went with him. She agreed but told Barak he would not receive any honor for the victory.

Barak put together an army of ten thousand from his tribe of Naphtali and the tribe of Zebulun. When Barak attacked Sisera, the Lord helped Israel by flooding the Kishon River. Because their chariots were immobilized by the mud, the Canaanites panicked. Barak routed Sisera's army, and no one escaped except Sisera.

Sisera fled to the tent of Jael, a woman who pretended to offer him hospitality. After drinking warm milk, Sisera fell asleep in what he thought was safety. She grabbed a tent peg and a hammer and drove the peg though Sisera's temple.

GIDEON

Israel enjoyed forty years of peace until attacked by marauding bands of Midianites. The Midianites would wait until the Israelites planted crops, then they made surprise raids, stole livestock, and trampled fertile fields with their camels. These seasonal attacks continued until Israel was devastated and cried out to the Lord.

God had compassion on his people and sent the angel of the Lord to Gideon, who was threshing wheat in an abandoned winepress. The angel called to Gideon, "Mighty warrior, the Lord is with you."

Gideon, dumbfounded, asked, "If so, why have we been oppressed by our enemies? Why haven't we seen miracles, and where is the Lord who brought us out of Egypt?"

The angel assured Gideon he would help him. Still, Gideon protested, "How can I rescue Israel? I'm a wimp from the smallest clan in the weakest tribe."

Promised a second time the Lord would help him destroy the Midianites, Gideon asked for proof that the Lord was on his side and told the angel to wait until he returned with an offering. Gideon rushed home to bring meat and bread.

The angel of the Lord touched Gideon's offering with his staff, and it erupted into flames; then, as suddenly as the Lord had appeared, he was gone. Gideon was terrified when he realized he had been speaking to the sovereign Lord.

The Lord assured Gideon he would not die. Gideon built an altar and named it "Yahweh-Shalom," which means "the Lord is peace."

That night the Lord instructed Gideon to make a second sacrifice and use the wood from the community's altar as fuel.

Gideon offered the sacrifice with ten of his servants. The next morning when the people of the town discovered he had destroyed the altar to Baal, they planned to execute him, but Gideon's father defended his son. He mocked them, saying, "If Baal is truly God, let him defend himself." This courageous and defiant act earned Gideon the title *Jerubbaal*, which means "Let Baal defend himself."

When nomadic armies occupied the valley of Jezreel (in northern Israel, west of the Sea of Galilee), Gideon sounded a call to arms. Though thousands responded, he still had doubts. He asked God to prove he would help defeat the coalition.

Gideon placed lamb's wool on the threshing floor at night and asked the Lord to make it wet with dew and the ground around it dry. The next morning when Gideon squeezed the fleece, it was saturated with water and the ground was dry. That was still not enough. Gideon asked for God to do the opposite the next night. God complied.

When Gideon recruited an army of 32,000 soldiers, the Lord said he had too many: "If you defeat the Midianites with such a large force, the Israelites will boast they saved themselves." He ordered Gideon to send everyone home who was afraid; 22,000 departed. Then he reduced the army one more time, leaving Gideon with just three hundred men.

Gideon and a servant sneaked into the enemy camp at night. They heard soldiers talking about a dream that they would be defeated. This was enough for Gideon. He and his army attacked, blowing trumpets and shouting, "A sword for the Lord and for Gideon!"

The Midianites were so confused that they turned on each other in the darkness. Warriors from three other Israelite tribes pursued and killed both Midianite commanders.

Though his men were exhausted, Gideon joined in pursuit of the other survivors. He caught the remnants of the army and captured the two Midianite kings. On his return from the battle, Gideon punished the elders of Succoth and executed the men of Peniel because both cities had refused to give his men food while pursuing the Midianites.

When Gideon ordered his oldest son to kill the Midianite kings, he refused, so Gideon killed them himself and took their royal necklaces.

Gideon's victory was so inspiring that the Israelites wanted to make him king. Gideon refused but asked each of the elders to give him an earring from the plunder. Gideon used the gold to make a sacred idol, which he set up as an altar in his hometown. The people worshiped the idol; even Gideon and his family were enticed to worship it.

After the defeat of the Midianites, Israel lived in peace for forty years. Gideon had seventy sons by multiple wives. After his death, the Israelites worshiped Baal and forgot about Gideon's remarkable victory and all the good he had done.

One of Gideon's sons, Abimelech (which means, "my father is king"), conspired with the leaders of Shechem to make him king. Then he hired hit men to kill all of Gideon's other sons. Only Jotham, Gideon's youngest, escaped; he denounced Abimelech and pronounced a curse on him.

Abimelech ruled for three years, but then Shechem rebelled. When Gaal, a stranger, offered to overthrow Abimelech, the people of Shechem placed their troops under Gaal's command. The city commissioner tipped off Abimelech about the plot; he set an ambush for Gaal and his men, and most of the conspirators were killed. Abimelech massacred the people of Shechem, including one thousand men and women who had taken refuge in the Tower of Shechem.

Flush with victory, Abimelech attacked the nearby city of Thebez, but his skull was crushed when a woman dropped a large millstone on his head. He was mortally wounded, and the next day he ordered one of his soldiers to kill him so he would not be humiliated at dying by the hand of a woman. Jotham's curse was fulfilled, and the men of Shechem were punished for their evil deeds.

After the death of Abimelech, Israel spiraled further into spiritual and religious chaos. Tola and Jair served as judges, but there was no peace under their leadership.

Israel again worshiped pagan gods, yet this time their apostasy was different: They totally abandoned the Lord. The Lord's anger burned against his people, and for fifteen years they were oppressed by the Philistines and Ammonites.

Finally, in desperation they cried out for help. The Lord, however, said, "Cry out to your new gods. Let them rescue you!" Israel confessed they had sinned and pleaded fervently for help. When Ammonites invaded the territory of Gilead, they said they would follow the first person courageous enough to lead them in battle.

Jephthah was a great warrior, but he was illegitimate—Gilead's son by a prostitute. Gilead's other sons by his wife despised Jephthah and forced him out of their family.

He had left home and become the leader of a gang of outlaws, so the elders of Gilead appealed to him to lead them in fighting the Ammonites. Jephthah refused because of the way he had been shunned, but then he negotiated for a better offer. He said he would help if they made him "ruler," not just a military commander. The elders agreed.

When Jephthah tried to negotiate peace with the Ammonite king, the king ignored his message. The Lord inspired him with courage to attack the Ammonites, but Jephthah made a famously impulsive vow: "Whatever comes out of my house when I return in victory, I will sacrifice to the Lord."

Jephthah crushed the Ammonites, yet when he returned victoriously, his daughter came out of his house, singing and rejoicing. Jephthah was beside himself. He cried out, "You've caused me disaster! I promised the Lord a sacrifice, and I must keep my vow."

His daughter said, "Father, keep your vow, because the Lord has given you victory over the Ammonites."

After she spent two months with her friends, Jephthah did as he had promised. It became a custom for the young women in Israel to commemorate Jephthah's daughter's courageous act of trust in the Lord.

The victory over the Ammonites did not bring peace. When the tribe of Ephraim ridiculed the men of Gilead, Jephthah attacked and killed forty-two thousand.

Three judges ruled Israel after Jephthah, but none of them were able to bring peace either. Israel remained trapped in their downward spiral of sin and oppression.

SAMSON

After the Philistines had oppressed Israel for forty years, the angel of the Lord appeared to Manoah's wife. The couple was childless, but he told her she was going to conceive and have a son. He instructed her to dedicate him as a Nazirite, which meant he was not to drink wine, cut his hair, or touch anything ceremonially unclean. Also, the Lord promised him power to deliver Israel from the Philistines.

Manoah couldn't believe it—the promise was too wonderful to be true. He asked for confirmation, and the angel of the Lord appeared a second time, repeating the instructions about being a Nazirite. Manoah prepared a sacrifice to offer to the Lord; when he placed it on an altar, flames shot into the air and the angel ascended in the fire. Manoah and his wife were so awestruck they fell on their faces. They realized they had seen God.

When Manoah's wife gave birth to a son, she named him Samson. The Lord empowered Samson and filled him with his Spirit. However, though the Lord wanted Samson to honor and serve as a man of God, Samson was indifferent to God's will and used his strength to satisfy his selfish desires and ruthlessly exploit the Philistines.

When visiting the city of Timnah, Samson spotted an attractive

Philistine girl and asked his parents to let him marry her. He badgered them until they reluctantly agreed.

On his way to Timnah, Samson was attacked by a lion, but the Spirit of the Lord empowered him and he tore it apart with his bare hands. Later, when he returned to marry the girl, he saw a swarm of bees in the lion's carcass and scooped honey out of it. He didn't tell his parents he had violated his Nazirite vow by touching a dead animal.

In Timnah, Samson hosted a party and tried to humiliate the Philistines by betting them thirty expensive sets of clothes that they couldn't solve a riddle. He said, "Out of the one who eats came something to eat; out of the strong one came something sweet."

The Philistines forced Samson's girlfriend to get the answer by threatening to kill her family. They won the bet, but, in a sense, they lost, because Samson killed thirty Philistines and took their clothes to pay the bet. Then the girl's father gave her to Samson's best man.

Though married, the girl continued to live in her father's house. When Samson wanted to have sex with her, her father wouldn't let him—he told Samson to marry her younger sister. Samson was so mad that he destroyed the Philistines' grain harvest. He caught three hundred foxes, tied their tails together in pairs, and put a torch in the tails of each pair. He lit the torches and set the foxes loose in the fields.

The Philistines retaliated by murdering Samson's wife and her father. Samson was furious and slaughtered the murderers, ripping them limb from limb. This only escalated the violence; the Philistines attacked Judah. Instead of seizing the opportunity to overthrow their oppressors, Samson let the men of Judah tie him up with ropes, and when he was turned over to the Philistines, he easily broke the ropes and killed a thousand Philistines with the jawbone of a donkey.

Samson went to the city of Gaza and had sex with a prostitute. When the men of the city heard Samson was there, they plotted to ambush him at dawn. Instead of spending the entire night with the prostitute,

Samson got up at midnight, ripped off the city gates, and carried them to the top of a hill near Hebron (a distance of about forty miles).

A short time later, Samson fell in love with a Philistine woman named Delilah. The Philistines realized this was an opportunity to defeat Samson, so they bribed Delilah to find the secret of his strength. After four attempts, Samson revealed the truth: "My hair has never been cut."

While Samson slept in the lap of Delilah, she cut his hair. When Samson woke up he didn't realize the strength of the Lord had left him. The Philistines captured him, gouged out his eyes, and forced him to grind grain like an animal.

The Philistines held a festival to celebrate Samson's capture and praised their god Dagon for their victory. When they were drunk, they brought Samson into their temple to ridicule him. Because he was blind, Samson asked a servant to place his hands on the pillars supporting the temple.

Samson asked the Lord to restore his strength; pushing mightily, he prayed, "Let me die with the Philistines!" The temple collapsed, killing several thousand Philistines and Samson. His brothers retrieved his body and buried him in the family gravesite.

After the death of Samson, Israel didn't have a king to provide national leadership. The tribes disintegrated into spiritual and social chaos. Micah, who was from Ephraim, stole silver coins from his mother. When his mother cursed the thief, Micah confessed he had stolen the coins himself. Instead of disciplining her son, she commended him for admitting he had stolen and made an idol from some of the coins. Micah used the idol to set up an altar in his home and hired a Levite to serve as his personal priest.

Scouts from the tribe of Dan, still looking for places to settle, discovered that the residents of Laish had a good life and were living in peace. The scouts also found out about Micah's shrine, so en route to Laish, six hundred armed men went by Micah's home, confiscated the sacred objects, and forced Micah's priest to serve their entire tribe.

They made a surprise attack, burned Laish to the ground, rebuilt it, and named it Dan. For their religious shrine, they appointed a descendant of Moses as their priest and worshiped Micah's idol.

A Levite decided to take a concubine (secondary wife) from the town of Bethlehem, but after he brought her home she despised him and returned to Bethlehem.

After four months the Levite decided to go and persuade the woman to come home again with him. He convinced her father to give him his daughter.

On the way home, they spent the night in Gibeah, in the tribal area of Benjamin. They were sitting in the town square when an older man offered to let them stay at his house. While they were eating the evening meal, a group of violent young men demanded the older man give them his visitor so they could have sex with him. The man refused, offering instead his daughters.

They became threatening, so the Levite gave them his concubine. After they raped her all night, she stumbled back to the house and collapsed at the front door. When the Levite found her in the morning, she was dead. He took her body home, cut it into twelve pieces, and sent a piece to each tribe of Israel.

Everyone was appalled. The leaders of the tribes, along with four hundred thousand warriors, assembled at Mizpah. When the Levite testified to what had happened, they unanimously agreed the offenders should be executed.

But the tribe of Benjamin refused to hand the offenders over for punishment; this amounted to a declaration of war. The Benjaminites were highly skilled warriors and, though outnumbered three to one, they defeated the other tribes twice, inflicting heavy casualities.

After their second defeat, the other tribes were ready to give up, yet the Lord encouraged them to attack a third time. They made a frontal attack, luring Benjamin's warriors into an ambush. It worked, and the Benjaminites fled; Israel pursued the survivors and killed all but six hundred men. They systematically slaughtered people and animals in all the towns of the tribe of Benjamin.

The Israelites had sworn they would never permit their daughters to marry anyone from Benjamin, but now they felt sorry for almost annihilating the tribe. They decided to fix the matter by punishing the town of Jabesh Gilead for not joining them in the war.

They attacked and killed everyone except for four hundred virgins. They gave these to the remaining Benjaminites for wives. When two hundred of the surviving warriors still did not have wives, the Israelites allowed the warriors to kidnap their virgin daughters when they went to Shiloh for the annual grape festival.

Because there was no king, everyone did what seemed right in his own eyes.

RUTH

Not everyone was trapped in Israel's destructive cycle of sin and oppression. An outsider named Ruth became the great-grandmother of David and an ancestor of Jesus Christ.

A famine forced Elimelech and his family to move from Bethlehem to Moab (a country southeast of the Dead Sea). His two sons married Moabite women, but then Elimelech and his sons died unexpectedly.

Elimelech's wife, Naomi, decided to return to Israel, but gave her Moabite daughters-in-law permission to stay. Ruth, though, loved Naomi and made a surprising commitment to her and to God. "Wherever you go, I will go. Your people will be my people, and your God will be my God."

In Bethlehem the two women struggled to survive until Ruth went out to glean in the fields of Boaz. Boaz noticed the attractive young woman and told his workers to respect her and make sure she was able to gather enough grain for food.

When Naomi asked Ruth who owned the fields where she was gathering grain, she discovered they belonged to Boaz, who was a close relative. Naomi told Ruth to meet Boaz at his threshing floor, where he slept to guard his grain, and tell him she was available to marry him.

Boaz could not believe Ruth wanted to marry him. She was much younger and was not obligated to marry within her mother-in-law's family. Boaz assured Ruth he would do everything necessary to provide for the two women.

Though he wanted to marry Ruth, Boaz knew a closer relative had the first right of marriage. Boaz explained the situation, but the man declined; he did not want to endanger his inheritance. Boaz didn't waste any time. The elders were witnesses that Naomi's closest relative had declined his option to marry Ruth, so Boaz took Ruth as his wife.

They named their son Obed. Obed had a son named Jesse, and Jesse had a son named David. In an amazing unfolding of events, Ruth, an unknown woman from the land of Moab, became the great-grandmother of Israel's greatest king.

🪕 Chapter Summary

The third generation after Joshua became trapped in a vicious cycle of sin, oppression, and deliverance. The tribes repeatedly attempted to go it alone with total disregard for God's will. This led to disaster after disaster.

God used the enemy nations Joshua had not driven out of the land to enslave his people. Harsh oppression forced them to cry out to God, who answered by raising up charismatic military leaders (judges) to defeat their oppressors.

After a period of peace, Israel would lapse into sin, usually worse than before, and God again would allow their enemies to oppress them. This cycle was repeated over and over for two centuries. Israel lacked national spiritual and military leadership. The tribes needed a king.

A wonderful love story about a woman from Moab explains how the void of a national leader was filled. After Ruth married Boaz, she gave birth to a son who would become the grandfather of King David.

Eight

THE KINGDOM UNITES

Main Characters
Eli
Samuel
Saul
David
Jonathan

Setting
Israel

SAMUEL

A Levite named Elkanah had two wives; Peninnah had given him two sons, but Hannah was unable to have children. When she went to Shiloh to offer an annual sacrifice, Hannah poured out her heart to the Lord and promised to dedicate her son to him as a priest if he would enable her to have a child. The Lord heard her prayer, and she gave birth to Samuel, which means "asked the Lord." Samuel was a gift from God.

She kept her promise and dedicated Samuel to serve in the tabernacle at Shiloh under the high priest, Eli. There Samuel grew both physically and spiritually.

In contrast to Samuel, who served the Lord with honor, Eli's sons were godless and self-indulgent. They extorted sacrifices from worshipers and seduced young women. Eli knew his sons were wicked but made only feeble attempts to discipline them. God held Eli responsible for the sins of his sons and sent a godly man to announce judgment.

God had never spoken to Eli or his sons, so the first time the Lord spoke to Samuel, even Eli didn't realize it was the Lord. Instead of communicating with only one tribe, Samuel carried the Lord's message to all Israel—from Dan in the far north to Beersheba in the south. The Lord was beginning to unify the tribes into a single nation through the ministry of Samuel as both judge and prophet.

The judgment on Eli and his sons was fulfilled when the Israelites took the ark of the covenant into battle against the Philistines, thinking it would give them victory. Instead, thirty thousand Israelites were killed, including Eli's sons. When a survivor reported to Eli about the demoralizing defeat, Eli was so shocked he fell over backward and broke his neck.

The Philistines thought they had captured Israel's sacred idol, but they soon realized they were dealing with a "god" far more powerful than their man-made idols. When they placed the ark in their temple, their idol of Dagon fell over, breaking off his head and his hands. They decided to move the ark to another town, but every time they moved it, people were infected with a deadly plague. The God of the ark was obviously more powerful than the Philistine gods, so their priests advised returning the ark to Israel. (The Israelites then kept the ark in Kiriath Jearim and put Levites in charge of it.)

Samuel restored the nation's spiritual dynamic by gathering all Israel at Mizpah. He challenged them to get rid of their idols and recommit themselves to the Lord. The people fasted and prayed, pleading with the Lord to save them from the Philistines.

When the Philistines attacked, the Lord used a storm to throw them into confusion, and they suffered a devastating defeat. Samuel set up a large stone as a memorial and called it Ebenezer, "the stone of help." The Philistines never threatened Israel again during the lifetime of Samuel.

SAUL

Though Samuel was a man of God, his two sons were godless. When Samuel grew older, he appointed his sons as judges, but the people protested. The elders demanded a king like other nations.

Their request was a personal insult to Samuel. He felt rejected and asked the Lord what he should do. Samuel was to give the people what they wanted: "It is me they are rejecting, not you," said the Lord; "they don't want me as their king."

Samuel warned the people that a king like the nations had would come at a high cost. He would tax them and force them to serve in the army.

His warning fell on deaf ears. The Lord said to Samuel, "Give them a king," so he agreed and sent the people home.

Saul, son of Kish, came from a wealthy family and was physically impressive, but he had never even thought about becoming king. When Samuel first saw Saul, he and his servant were searching for lost donkeys. Samuel invited them to stay at his house overnight, but before they left the next day, Samuel poured a flask of oil over Saul's head and said, "The Lord has told me to anoint you as ruler over his people."

He then told Saul the donkeys had been found and he would meet a band of prophets on his way home. When Saul met the prophets, the Spirit of the Lord came upon him, and he prophesied like a prophet. Saul told no one—not even his father—what Samuel had said.

Having anointed Saul in a secret ceremony, Samuel was now ready to publicly proclaim him. When he summoned the tribes to identify Saul as Israel's first king, though, they couldn't find him—he was hiding behind the baggage. When they found him, the people enthusiastically shouted, "Long live the king!" Most people were excited that they now had a king like other nations, but a few diehards refused to accept him.

It wasn't long before Saul had the opportunity to prove he was qualified as a military leader. The Ammonites surrounded Jabesh Gilead, and when its people offered to surrender, the king of Ammon said he would spare them only on the condition they gouge out the right eye of everyone in the city.

Jabesh Gilead sent an urgent plea to Saul. He responded quickly and decisively, summoning troops from all of Israel and, in a surprise attack, routing the Ammonites. After this, some wanted to execute those who had refused to accept Saul as their king, but he would have none of it. Instead he insisted that everyone thank the Lord for Israel's great victory.

In his final address to the nation at Gilgal, Samuel reaffirmed Saul as king and reminded the people that God still expected them to honor him as Lord. He said they had sinned in demanding a king, but God would protect them if they didn't abandon him to worship idols. Though his rule as judge was finished, Samuel promised to pray for Israel.

Unfortunately, Saul turned out to be a disaster as Israel's first king. He was foolish and disobedient, quickly losing the divine right to rule God's covenant people as he made one bad decision after another.

In his first major engagement with the Philistines, his army was incapacitated by fear while they waited for Samuel to make a sacrifice to the Lord. Instead of waiting, Saul panicked and made the sacrifice himself though he was not a priest.

Before he was done, Samuel arrived and asked, "What have you done?"

Saul tried to explain that the army was deserting and the Philistines were preparing to attack, so he felt compelled to make the sacrifice asking for the Lord's help.

"How foolish!" Samuel shouted, announcing judgment on Saul. "Had you obeyed the Lord, he would have established your kingdom forever, but your kingdom will not last. The Lord has rejected you and will seek a man after his own heart." Most of the three thousand troops Saul had called up went home; only six hundred remained.

(In addition to their superior numbers, the Philistines also had an advantage in that they had the technology to make iron weapons.

The Israelites even had to purchase their farm implements from the Philistines.)

Saul's son Jonathan proved himself to be a more courageous and capable soldier when he and his armor bearer attacked a Philistine outpost. When they killed about twenty, the Philistine army thought they were under attack from a larger force and fled. When Saul's men saw them fleeing in confusion, they attacked. Later, they reminded Saul that it was because of Jonathan's courage they had defeated the Philistines.

Saul did win victories over several of Israel's enemies, but he never totally defeated the Philistines. Because he was constantly at war with them, Saul drafted the strongest and bravest young Israelite men for his army.

Another devastating mistake came in a campaign against the Amalekites. Samuel had instructed Saul to destroy them for opposing Israel when they came out of Egypt. Saul defeated the Amalekites, but instead of destroying all of the plunder, his men kept valuable animals and items and only destroyed what was worthless.

When the Lord revealed to Samuel that Saul had disobeyed, Samuel confronted Saul. Saul lied and said he had kept the animals to sacrifice to the Lord. Samuel replied, "Obedience is better than sacrifice. Because you have disobeyed the Lord, he has rejected you as king."

Saul sought forgiveness, but Samuel said the Lord of Glory would not change his mind. "He will give the kingdom to someone whose heart is fully devoted to the Lord," said Samuel. Not only would Saul's dynasty end, but now he would not even be allowed to finish his rule.

SAUL AND DAVID

The Lord told Samuel to go to Bethlehem and anoint one of Jesse's sons as Israel's eventual king. The Lord said, "Don't look at someone with an impressive physical appearance; look for someone with a heart for me." When Samuel informed Jesse the Lord had chosen one of his sons as king, Jesse had seven of his sons appear before the prophet, but Samuel was not led to anoint any of them.

Jesse's youngest son, David, was out watching the sheep. Jesse sent for him, and when he came home, the Lord said to Samuel, "This is the one; anoint him." On that day, the Spirit of the Lord came powerfully upon David.

After Samuel anointed David, the Spirit of the Lord left Saul, who was then tormented by an evil spirit. For relief, Saul looked for someone to play calming music. He recruited David, an outstanding young man and an excellent musician. David would play his harp to calm Saul when he was emotionally upset. Saul was so impressed with David that he made David his armor bearer.

The Israelite and Philistine armies were holding positions on opposite sides of a valley. One Philistine, Goliath, was over nine feet tall and wore armor that weighed over a hundred pounds; the shaft of his spear weighed fifteen pounds. Each day he would taunt the Israelites: "I defy you. Send your champion to fight me." But no one had the courage to fight Goliath. The taunting went on day and night for forty days.

Jesse sent David with supplies for his three oldest brothers, who were serving with Saul's army. When David arrived on the battlefield, he heard Goliath taunt Saul's soldiers and watched them cringe in fear. They said that the man who killed Goliath would be rewarded with the marriage of one of Saul's daughters and be exempt from taxes.

After David talked with many soldiers, Saul heard that someone was asking about Goliath and sent for David. David told Saul, "I'll go fight him." The idea was ridiculous in Saul's opinion, but when David told how he had killed a lion and a bear while protecting his father's sheep, Saul agreed and gave David his armor.

The armor was so large and bulky that David left it behind and instead picked up five stones from a stream and his shepherd's staff. When Goliath saw that David was only a boy, he sneered at him and cursed him.

David wasn't intimidated. He ran toward the giant and shouted, "I have come against you in the name of the Lord, the God of the armies of heaven and Israel!" David hurled one stone with his sling, hitting Goliath in the forehead and stunning him; he fell facedown. David raced forward and killed Goliath with the giant's own sword and then cut off his head. When they saw that their champion had been killed, the Philistine army fled with the Israelites in hot pursuit. The dead and wounded littered the road for miles.

David's victory led to a lifelong friendship between David and Saul's son Jonathan. When the two men met they instantly bonded. But not everyone was thrilled about the stunning defeat of Goliath. When the army returned home, women gathered from all over Israel to honor the victorious soldiers. They danced and sang, "Saul has killed his thousands, and David his ten thousands." Saul became insanely jealous because David was receiving twice the honor for the victory. He made David commander of a thousand men, but David was so successful in battle that Saul became even more fearful of his popularity.

Instead of giving David his daughter as he had promised, Saul said David had to win more battles against the Philistines, and then he could marry Saul's oldest daughter. Saul hoped David would be killed while fighting. David eventually married Saul's oldest daughter, but he fell in love with Saul's other daughter, Michal.

Saul was obsessed with getting rid of David and saw this as another opportunity for David to be killed. Saul told David he could marry Michal if he killed a hundred more Philistines, but instead of losing his own life, David and his men killed two hundred Philistines, and Saul gave Michal to David as his wife. David continued to prove himself a capable leader in battle after battle with the Philistines, yet his victories only made Saul more convinced David was a threat to his kingship.

Saul's deceitfulness and murderous intentions forced David to become a fugitive from the man he had sworn to serve. Saul tried to get his servants and Jonathan to kill David, but Jonathan and David were close friends; Jonathan warned David instead. Jonathan tried to reason with his father, and though Saul vowed he would not kill David, he immediately broke his promise and hurled a spear at him.

This was enough. David was convinced that his life was in danger. Michal deceived her father and helped David escape to Ramah. When Saul sent soldiers, the Spirit of the Lord prevented them from capturing David. When Saul himself went, the Spirit took control of him, and Saul stripped off all his clothes and lay naked all night and prophesied. People wondered if Saul had become a prophet rather than the king.

David and Jonathan met secretly, and David asked whether there was any hope of reconciliation with Saul. They set up a secret sign to inform David so his life would not be at risk, and made an enduring pact of friendship. At the monthly festival, Jonathan asked his father if David could return home to Bethlehem. Saul flew into a rage, cursed Jonathan, and even hurled a spear at him. Jonathan knew it was useless to reason with his father. He shot a series of arrows to signal David of his father's insane determination to kill him. The two friends met for one last time, and then David became a fugitive.

David hoped to find safety with Ahimelech, the high priest, in the town of Nob, but Ahimelech was afraid of Saul and suspicious of David. When David asked for a weapon, the only one Ahimelech had was the sword of Goliath. David took it and left because Doeg, Saul's chief herdsman, was there and spotted David and his men.

David made a risky decision: He fled to Gath, a Philistine city and the former home of Goliath. But he had a problem, because the Philistines recognized him as the one who had killed Goliath. Fearing for his life, David acted insane, scratching on doors and drooling down his beard. The king of Gath was insulted that his men would let a crazy madman into his city and then expect him to show hospitality.

David then went south to the cave of Adullam where his brothers, relatives, and other fugitives joined him. David now had about four hundred men with him. They went farther south to Moab, and David asked the Moabite king if his father and mother could stay while David hid out in his stronghold in the desert.

The prophet Gad advised David to return to Judah, but when Saul found out about that plan, he was certain David was conspiring to become king. When Doeg told Saul that Ahimelech had provided David's men with food and the sword of Goliath, Saul summoned Ahimelech and ordered his men to kill the high priest.

They refused, so Doeg killed him and eighty-five other priests. They killed all the priests in Nob and their entire families; only Abiathar, Ahimelech's son, escaped, and he joined David, who promised to protect him. Though he was a fugitive from Saul, David gained popular support by defending Israelite towns when the Philistines raided them.

Saul was relentless in his pursuit of David and almost captured him on several occasions, but each time the Lord helped David escape. When Saul found out David was at Keilah, the Lord warned David, and he and his men fled into the wilderness. Saul's men searched day after day, but the desolate, dry, vast Judean desert provided protection for David.

Jonathan, however, was able to find David, and he renewed his pledge of friendship and support for his close friend. He assured David that his father would never capture him and that David would someday become king of Israel. Jonathan returned home and never saw David again.

Though David knew he was destined to become king, he refused to kill Saul because the Lord had anointed him. When Saul and three thousand elite troops went to En Gedi (a rocky, rugged area west of the Dead Sea), Saul went into a cave to relieve himself, not knowing David and his men were hiding deeper in the cave.

David cut off a piece of Saul's robe without his knowing it. David's men wanted to kill Saul, but David wouldn't let them: "The Lord forbid that I should attack the king, the Lord's anointed one." After Saul left the cave, David waited until he was at a safe distance and then called, "Why do you listen to people who say I want to kill you? Look, I have a piece of your robe in my hand. I could have killed you today if I wanted. The Lord will judge between you and me."

Saul had to admit that David was a better man and that he deserved to be king. Knowing David would become king, Saul asked him to spare his family and not kill all of his descendants when he took the throne.

After Samuel's death, David moved farther south into the desert wilderness. When he and his men needed supplies, he sent them to Nabal (whose name means "fool"), a wealthy sheep rancher.

Nabal was crude and mean-spirited. He mocked David's men and called them a band of outlaws. When David heard what Nabal had said, David took four hundred armed men to kill Nabal the fool.

Nabal's servants told his wife that David was coming. Abigail acted quickly, putting together enough food for a feast and going with her servants to take it to David. When she met him, Abigail showed respect and convinced him it would be wrong to murder her husband.

David was impressed and said, "Return home in peace. I promise I will not kill your husband." When Abigail arrived home, Nabal was partying and drunk. The next morning when Abigail told Nabal about meeting David, he suffered a paralyzing stroke and died ten days later. When David heard Nabal was dead, he asked Abigail to marry him. She agreed and became David's wife.

David also married Ahinoam. Saul had given his wife Michal to a man named Palti.

David had a second chance to kill Saul when he found out Saul again was searching for him with three thousand elite troops. He and Abishai crept into Saul's camp at night and penetrated the inner circle of guards. As before, Abishai wanted to kill Saul, but David wouldn't let him. David took Saul's spear and a jug of water near Saul's head, and then sneaked out of the camp.

From a nearby hill David taunted Saul's general, Abner: "If you are such a mighty warrior, why haven't you protected your king?" David showed him the spear and the jug. By this time, David's voice had awakened Saul. David told him again that he could have killed him but refused. Saul acknowledged that he himself was a sinful man and that David was honorable and heroic. This was the last time Saul and David met.

David knew Saul would not stop hunting for him, though, so he made the risky choice to hide out among the Philistines. When Saul heard David was with the Philistines he stopped searching. The Philistine king Achish allowed David to live in the city of Ziklag. During the year and a half David was there, he raided Canaanite towns but lied to Achish, telling him he had raided towns in Judah. Achish believed David and thought, "How his own people must hate him!" Achish was so convinced David was his ally that when the Philistines prepared for another war with Israel, Achish made David his personal bodyguard.

Witchcraft was strictly forbidden in Israel, but when Saul saw the size of the Philistine army, he was terrified. Because Samuel had died, Saul couldn't consult with him, so he asked his advisors to find a medium. So she wouldn't recognize him, Saul disguised himself and asked the witch of Endor to call up the spirit of a man who had died.

She refused at first and accused him of trying to get her killed, since Saul had forbidden mediums from contacting the dead. But she asked who he wanted her to call from the dead. When he said Samuel, she screamed, "You have deceived me; you are Saul!"

Saul reassured her that she would not be harmed, and Samuel did appear, but he told Saul what he already knew: The Lord had abandoned him and would not help him in the battle. Samuel predicted Saul and his sons would be killed, the army of Israel defeated. Saul fell down, paralyzed with fear and weak from hunger because he had not eaten for a full day. Saul's men finally convinced him to eat so he could regain his strength. The witch prepared a meal, and after eating, Saul and his men left under the cover of darkness.

When the Philistine army assembled for battle, David and his men were with Achish in the rear of the formation. But when the officers found out Israelites were in their ranks, they were outraged. They didn't trust David because they remembered how he had killed Goliath. Though Achish assured them he had complete confidence in David's loyalty, they were adamant that David not go into battle with them. Achish advised David and his men to leave secretly.

When David and his men returned to Ziklag, they discovered that the Amalekites had destroyed the city and taken all the women and children captive. David sought the counsel of the priest Abiathar, who assured David that the Lord would help him recover all the captives and everything stolen.

David pressed so hard in pursuit of the Amalekites that two hundred men became exhausted and had to be left behind. The pursuers found an Egyptian slave who had been abandoned by the Amalekites because he was sick; he guided them to the raiders.

David and his men caught the Amalekites by surprise and totally wiped out the raiding party. They recovered everything, including the women and children. Some of David's men did not want to divide the plunder with the two hundred men who had been unable to pursue, but David insisted everyone receive a share of the spoils. He also sent gifts to the towns that had provided support for David and his men.

Saul's rule as Israel's first king came to an end when the Israelites suffered a devastating defeat. Three of Saul's sons, including Jonathan, were killed, and Saul was mortally wounded by an archer. He ordered his armor bearer to kill him so the Philistines could not capture and torture him, but the armor bearer refused; Saul then killed himself with his own sword.

The next day the Philistines found Saul's body and cut off his head. They placed his armor in the temple of one of their gods and nailed Saul's body to a wall in Beth Shan. When the men of Jabesh Gilead heard how the Philistines had desecrated Saul and his sons, they recovered their bodies and buried them under a tree.

Saul had ruled as Israel's king for forty years. Now Israel was in the same situation it was at the end of the era of the judges. God's people didn't have a king.

⚱ Chapter Summary

Samuel, a transitional figure in Israel's history, was the last judge and the first official prophet. He was born in answer to prayer and dedicated to serve as a priest.

When the Philistines captured the ark of the covenant, Samuel gained prominence as a charismatic leader by defeating them and returning the ark to Israel. When he grew old, the people pressured him to give them a king. The Lord said to grant their request.

Saul was anointed as Israel's first king. He vacillated between wanting to do right and flagrantly disobeying the Lord's commands. He quickly lost his anointing as Israel's king by defying God.

The Lord guided Samuel to the house of Jesse, and there he anointed David as Israel's king-elect. David had been an unknown like Saul, but he gained national recognition when he killed the Philistine champion, Goliath.

David's popularity made Saul paranoid. He chose David as his personal musician, but he was certain David was plotting to kill him and seize the throne. David and Jonathan became close friends even though Jonathan knew that David, and not he, would become Israel's next king.

Saul's delusion became so severe that David was forced to flee for his life. He had several opportunities to kill Saul, but he refused because Saul was the Lord's anointed.

Before his final battle, Saul acted foolishly again, seeking counsel from a witch to learn the outcome. In some kind of séance, instead of promising victory, Samuel returned from the dead, rebuked Saul, and predicted Israel's defeat and Saul's death.

Nine

DAVID AND SOLOMON

Main Characters
David
Bathsheba
Nathan
Absalom
Solomon

Setting
Israel

THE RULE OF DAVID

After David returned from victory over the Amalekites, a straggler from the battle with the Philistines reported Saul's defeat and death. Thinking David would reward him, the man claimed that he himself had killed Saul to put him out of his misery. He was wrong; David ordered him executed because he had dared to use his sword on the Lord's anointed king.

David did not become king immediately after Saul's death. He and his followers moved to Hebron, within the tribal area of Judah. He tried to unite all the tribes, but Abner, commander of Saul's army, conspired to make Ishbosheth, Saul's son, king.

Abner proclaimed Ishbosheth king over a coalition of tribes in the north and set up a capital at Mahanaim (east of the Jordan River), but the tribe of Judah supported David. This led to civil war between Judah and the coalition of tribes in the north.

The conflict started when Joab, commander of David's forces, and

Abner met at the pool of Gibeon. What started as peaceful negotiations became twelve-on-twelve combat between handpicked young warriors. This quickly deteriorated into a full-scale deadly battle during which Abner killed Joab's brother Asahael.

When it became apparent that David would win the war, Abner secretly offered to support him and convinced the elders of Israel to do likewise. However, Joab murdered Abner in revenge for the killing of Asahael. Knowing people would suspect him, David swore he had not ordered the execution of Abner and publicly mourned his death.

When Ishbosheth heard Abner had been killed, he decided to surrender. But then two of his own soldiers murdered him and brought his head to David. Instead of rewarding them, David ordered them executed for killing an innocent man.

After this, the elders of all the tribes of Israel anointed David as king. At age thirty, David began his rule that lasted forty years.

He captured Jerusalem, a Jebusite fortress, made it the political capital for all Israel, and called it the City of David. David strengthened his power through marriage to multiple wives and concubines. He also defeated the Philistines in two major battles.

To honor God as their ultimate ruler, David brought the ark of the covenant to Jerusalem. While they were moving it on a cart, the ox stumbled, and the Lord killed Uzzah for touching the ark to keep it from falling. The death of Uzzah so terrified David that he left the ark in a house for three months before attempting to move it again.

Because God blessed that house, David decided to move the ark again. This time, men carried it with poles. As they moved it to Jerusalem, David and the people made sacrifices and sang and danced before the Lord. When they arrived, David blessed the people and gave them gifts. It was a glorious occasion.

Everyone celebrated except Michal, Saul's daughter and David's wife (he had taken her back). She was filled with contempt and criticized

David for celebrating publicly with common people. She and David never had any children.

Because he was living in a palace and the ark was only in a tent, David summoned the prophet Nathan and told him he wanted to build a temple for the ark. Nathan was certain the Lord would honor David's plans, but instead the Lord promised he would establish David's dynasty forever, saying, "Your house and kingdom always will endure." One of his descendants, not David, would build a house for the Lord.

When Nathan told David what the Lord had revealed, David thanked God for his goodness and promised to honor him. He prayed, "How great you are, Sovereign Lord! There has never been a God like you. You have made Israel your people forever."

David was a superb military strategist and political organizer. He expanded his kingdom through military victories by capturing Gath, the largest Philistine town, and conquering Moab to the east, Aram to the north, and Edom to the south. His royal staff included military officers, a historian, priests, a secretary, and bodyguards.

David did not forget his promise to Saul. When he found out the sole survivor of Saul's dynasty was Mephibosheth, Jonathan's son who was handicapped, he assured him he had nothing to fear and promised to care for him for the remainder of his life.

David's greatest military success was against armies east of the Jordan River. King Nahash of Ammon had been a loyal supporter, so when Nahash died, David sent representatives to his funeral. But Nahash's son humiliated them by cutting off their beards. David considered this a declaration of war and ordered Joab to mobilize the army.

Though trapped between Ammonite and Aramean forces, Joab defeated both opposing armies. After their defeat, the Arameans realized that under David the Israelites had become powerful, so they assembled a larger army to attack. David mobilized the entire army, and the Israelites killed seven hundred charioteers and forty thousand foot soldiers. The Arameans surrendered and never again went to war against Israel.

Over time, David's success turned into a serious moral failing. Instead of going with the army on a military campaign, David decided to stay in Jerusalem. One evening he saw Bathsheba, a beautiful married woman, bathing on her rooftop balcony. Instead of resisting, he invited her to the palace.

They had sex, and later she sent David a shocking message: "I am pregnant." David attempted to hide the affair by summoning her husband, Uriah, who had been with the army. David hoped Uriah would spend a night with his wife in Jerusalem, but Uriah refused out of respect for his fellow soldiers who were separated from their wives.

David resorted to a drastic and deadly cover-up. In the siege to capture Rabbah, David had Joab send Uriah, along with other soldiers, near enough to the city wall that the archers could shoot them with arrows. Uriah and others were killed.

When Uriah's death was reported, Bathsheba mourned for her husband and then became David's wife. David didn't think anyone knew what he had done, but the Lord knew and sent Nathan the prophet to confront him.

Nathan told David a parable about a rich man and a poor man. Instead of killing one of his own lambs, the rich man took the poor man's only lamb to feed his guests. David was furious and said, "The rich man must repay the poor man with four lambs." Nathan said to David, "You are the rich man," and he announced that because of David's sin, his own family would be devastated by violence and his wives publicly violated.

David deserved to die for abusing his royal power, but he confessed his sin and the Lord forgave him. However, Nathan said that the child born of the adulterous relationship would die. When David's son became ill, David grieved and begged God for mercy and even fasted, but after seven days the boy died. David immediately resumed his normal activities, and his advisors were amazed at how quickly he ceased mourning. He replied, "When the child was alive, I fasted and prayed, hoping the

Lord would let him live. But after his death, he cannot return to me. I will go to him when I die."

God was gracious to David and Bathsheba. She eventually gave birth to their son Solomon (whose name means "peace"). Nathan told them to give the child a second name, Jedidiah, which means "beloved of the Lord."

David's son Absalom had a beautiful sister named Tamar. Amnon, Tamar's half brother, became insanely obsessed with her but couldn't have sex with her because she was his sister.

Amnon pretended he was sick and asked David if his sister could take care of him. When they were alone, Amnon tried to seduce Tamar; when she resisted, he raped her. Amnon's lust then turned to disgust, and he had her thrown out of his room.

Tamar was disgraced and wept. When Absalom found out what had happened, he arranged for Tamar to live in his house. David was angry but didn't punish Amnon. Absalom, however, hated Amnon for what he had done.

Absalom waited two years and then invited all of David's sons to a royal banquet. Absalom then ordered his men to kill Amnon when he was drunk. It was initially reported to David that all his sons had been murdered, but in fact the rest of them safely returned to Jerusalem.

Absalom feared David would have him executed for what he had done, so he fled to Geshur (northeast of Israel) and stayed with his grandfather for three years. Eventually David abandoned any desire for revenge, and instead wanted reconciliation. However, he refused to take the initiative, so Joab devised a plan to convince David he should contact Absalom. Joab asked a woman to help, but by telling a story about a father and an estranged son, she reminded David that God finds ways to be reconciled with those who offend him. She reasoned that it was in the best interests of the people for David to restore his son.

David allowed Absalom to return to his own house in Jerusalem, but Absalom was never to enter into the presence of the king. After two years Absalom forced Joab to intercede with David on his behalf, and David agreed to a formal meeting in the palace.

About eleven years after Absalom had killed Amnon, he initiated a strategy of undermining David's credibility as king. Absalom was extremely handsome and proud of his massive head of hair. He paraded around Jerusalem in a chariot with bodyguards, as if he were the king, and he told people with grievances what he would do if he, rather than David, ruled.

Absalom gained enough support to plot a conspiracy. He secretly arranged for the twelve tribes to recognize him as king when he was crowned in Hebron. Then, after going to Jerusalem, as public evidence that he had usurped all of David's royal authority, Absalom had sex with David's concubines on the palace roof.

When David discovered the coup, he and his household, except the concubines, fled Jerusalem. Zadok, the high priest, and the Levites attempted to take the ark of the covenant with them; David, thinking the rebellion would be short, ordered them to take it back into the city.

After escaping, David sent one of his loyal supporters, Hushai, back to Jerusalem as a secret agent to keep him informed of Absalom's plans. Hushai went immediately and declared his willingness to serve as Absalom's adviser.

Hushai suggested that Absalom mobilize the entire army to totally annihilate David and his men. The Lord somehow influenced Absalom and his men to accept Hushai's plan because the Lord was determined to destroy Absalom.

David received fresh supplies and organized his troops in preparation to engagae Absalom's forces. He wanted to lead them into battle, but they convinced him it was too risky. "You are more valuable than ten thousand," they said. "Stay here in safety, and if we need help we will send for you." David agreed but gave Joab and his officers strict orders not to kill Absalom.

The battle raged all day in the rugged forest of Ephraim. Absalom became separated from his men, and then his long hair got tangled in the thick branches of a tree. One of David's men found him and told Joab, who disregarded David's orders and stabbed Absalom in the heart with three daggers. Joab and his armor bearers threw the body into a pit and covered it with stones.

Absalom's army fled. The rebellion was over.

Messengers were sent to inform David of the victory. When David asked about Absalom, one of the men replied, "May all of your enemies suffer the same fate as Absalom." David went into a room alone and burst into tears, crying out, "O my son Absalom, I wish I would have died instead of you, O Absalom, my son, my son."

When Joab heard David was mourning, he told him his actions were discrediting and demoralizing to his soldiers, who had won a great victory. They had saved the life of David and his entire family. David recovered and assumed leadership of his army.

David's return to Jerusalem was controversial. The northern tribes debated whether they should accept him as king; the tribe of Judah met him at the Jordan to escort him. Others pledged their loyalty, and David rewarded them. Some from Israel complained that David had shown preference to the tribe of Judah, and this contention was not resolved; it became an ongoing point of contention between Judah and the other tribes.

Throughout his reign, David's mightiest warriors fought against the Philistines, defeating them with courage and strength. Some of these Philistines were giants, descendants and relatives of Goliath. Many great warriors and mighty men fought on David's side and gained much renown.

For an unstated reason, though, the Lord became extremely angry with Israel, and he permitted Satan to provoke David to take a census. Afterward, David felt guilty and asked the Lord for forgiveness. The prophet Gad presented David with three options as punishment: three years of famine; three months of military defeats; or three days of plague.

Reasoning it would be better to place Israel's fate in the Lord's hands, David accepted the third option.

After seventy thousand died, the Lord relented of the judgment. David confessed his guilt: "I am the one who has sinned," he said. "The people are as innocent as sheep."

Gad told David he should build an altar to the Lord for stopping the plague. David tried to buy Araunah's threshing floor; Araunah offered to give him the property and even the animals. David refused, saying his sacrifice would be meaningless if it didn't cost him anything. After building the altar, David offered animal sacrifices and peace offerings to the Lord, declaring that the location would be the future site of the temple.

THE RULE OF SOLOMON

The transition of the kingdom from David to Solomon was marked by intrigue and violence.

As David neared the end of his life, his son Adonijah boasted, "I will make myself king." He attempted to get support from Joab and Abiathar the priest.

Zadok, Nathan, and Benaiah, David's personal bodyguard, refused to support Adonijah. When Adonijah held a massive banquet for his supporters, it became clear he was maneuvering to become king. Bathsheba and Nathan warned David of his son's intentions and urged him to announce his choice for the next ruler.

David summoned Bathsheba and assured her he would keep his promise that Solomon would be king. He ordered Zadok, Nathan, and Benaiah to publicly anoint Solomon in a ceremony. The royal bodyguard escorted Solomon to the Gihon Spring where Zadok anointed him and the people shouted, "Long live king Solomon!"

When Adonijah's supporters heard the shouting and celebrating, they fled the banquet in fear for their lives; they knew the attempted coup had failed. Adonijah went into the tabernacle and grabbed the horns of the altar for protection. When it was reported to Solomon that Adonijah was pleading for his life, Solomon promised he would not kill him if he pledged to support Solomon as king. Adonijah was brought to the king and bowed before him. Solomon released him and sent him home as promised.

In his final counsel to Solomon, David gave spiritual and practical advice. He told Solomon that if he courageously and faithfully obeyed the decrees of Moses, the Lord would bless his descendants for generation after generation. He warned Solomon that his military commanders were dangerous and couldn't be trusted.

David died and was buried in the City of David (Jerusalem), and his son Solomon became Israel's third king.

Solomon took action to eliminate rivals for the throne; Benaiah became his hit man. Adonijah made a second unsuccessful and foolish attempt to become king, asking Bathsheba if she would appeal to Solomon for permission for him to marry one of David's concubines. Solomon recognized this as a clandestine claim to the throne and ordered Adonijah's death. Solomon gave amnesty to Abiathar the priest but ordered Benaiah to execute Joab. Shemei, another supporter of Adonijah, violated Solomon's orders not to leave Jerusalem, so Solomon had Benaiah kill him too.

Then Solomon made a political alliance with the king of Egypt by marriage to his daughter. He brought her to live in Jerusalem.

Like his father, Solomon loved the Lord and on one occasion gave a thousand burnt offerings. That night the Lord appeared to Solomon in a dream and asked, "What do you want? I will give you whatever you ask." Solomon realized he could not govern Israel without God's help, so he asked for wisdom. The Lord was pleased with Solomon's request and said, "I will give you a wise and understanding heart, and I will also give you what you did not ask for—riches and fame."

Solomon had an opportunity to demonstrate his wisdom when two prostitutes came to him with a complaint. Both said they had given birth to a son, but one child had died, and both claimed the living child was their son.

After hearing their story, Solomon said, "Bring a sword; cut the living child in two, and give each woman half." One woman cried out, "No, my lord, give the child to the other woman, but please do not kill him!" The other said, "Good enough, cut the child in half and give each of us half." Solomon knew the real mother was the one willing to give the child to the other woman so he would live, and he ordered the child be given to her. The people recognized God had given Solomon special wisdom for ruling with justice.

Israel enjoyed peace and prosperity under Solomon's skillful, energetic leadership. He organized Israel into twelve administrative districts and required that each support his court for one month of the year. He expanded the borders of Israel to the north and south. He composed thousands of proverbs and songs and was so eloquent on a variety of subjects that ambassadors came from other countries to hear the wisdom of Solomon.

When Hiram, king of Tyre, sent ambassadors to congratulate him, Solomon asked him to provide cedars from Lebanon and workers for a massive building project—the temple of the Lord. Hiram agreed and made a contract with Solomon. Solomon conscripted thirty thousand workers from Israel and sent them in shifts of ten thousand to work for one month at a time in Lebanon. He also had seventy thousand common laborers, eighty thousand quarry workers, and 3,600 foremen.

After the exterior structure was erected, the interior rooms were paneled with cedar and olive wood and overlaid with gold. Solomon asked a master craftsman named Huram to make the bronze and gold furnishings; he took the gifts of silver and gold that David had collected and placed them in the temple along with other valuable objects. The temple became Israel's national treasury.

After seven years the temple was completed, and Solomon assembled all Israel for a historic dedication ceremony. When the people and the elders had arrived, the priests took the ark of the covenant into the inner Holy Place, and the glory of the Lord descended on the temple in the form of a thick cloud.

Solomon began the dedication service with a prayer of praise: "Praise the Lord, the God of Israel, who has kept his promise. I have built this temple to honor his name, the Lord, the God of Israel. There is no God like you." Standing before all the people, he lifted his hands toward heaven and said, "The highest heavens cannot contain you—how much less this temple that I have built. But hear our prayer, and watch over this place and your people, Israel." The celebration lasted fourteen days, and the people returned home thankful and praising God for how good he had been to them.

The Lord appeared to Solomon a second time and said, "I have heard your prayer, and I will watch over this place you have built to honor my name." But the Lord also warned Israel about the consequences of disobeying his commands and worshiping other gods: "If you abandon me, I will expel you from this land and reject this temple and make you a mockery of the nations."

Solomon's pursuits did not end with the temple's completion. He built towns and fortified cities on Israel's borders, where he stationed horses and chariots for defense. He forced Canaanites still living in the land to work as laborers, and he recruited Israelites for military and government positions.

He built a new palace for Pharaoh's daughter. He was the spiritual leader of the nation. Three times a year he presented sacrifices and offerings to the Lord. He built a fleet of ships and a seaport, and he established extensive trade with other nations. On one voyage, his ships returned to Israel with sixteen tons of gold.

The Queen of Sheba (southwestern Arabia) heard about Solomon's wisdom and wealth but didn't believe it, so she came to Israel to find out for herself. She brought spices and large quantities of gold and jewels. After meeting with Solomon, hearing his wisdom, and seeing his building projects, she exclaimed, "Everything I have heard is true!" She recognized it was God who had made Solomon great, and she said, "Praise the Lord, who has placed you on the throne of Israel." She gave him nine thousand pounds of gold along with other valuable gifts, and Solomon likewise honored her with generous gifts before she returned home.

The wealth and splendor of Solomon's kingdom made him famous. Each year he received about twenty-five tons of gold in addition to other merchandise, including ivory and exotic animals. People came from other countries to consult with him and hear his wisdom. He imported horses and chariots, and then sold them to other nations.

However, Solomon made several devastating mistakes that led to the division of the kingdom. In addition to Pharaoh's daughter, he married women from Moab, Ammon, Edom, Sidon, and the Hittites. The Lord had clearly warned his people that "you must not marry women from other nations because they will turn your heart to their gods."

Solomon had seven hundred wives and three hundred concubines. In his old age, his wives influenced him to worship their gods. He even built shrines and altars for them to worship their gods, one on the Mount of Olives.

The Lord was extremely angry. He had appeared to Solomon twice, yet Solomon had not obeyed God's commands. He said, "I will surely tear the kingdom away from you and give it to one of your servants." The Lord also said he would not take the kingdom away during Solomon's lifetime but from his son's, and he would let Solomon's son rule over one tribe because of the Lord's love for David and for Jerusalem, his chosen city.

The Lord used other nations to punish Solomon for his sin. Hadad from Edom and Rezin from Aram (Damascus) hated Israel and became bitter enemies of Solomon. The Lord also sent the prophet Ahijah to anoint Jeroboam as rival king of the northern tribes.

Solomon had placed Jeroboam in charge of repairing the city walls of

Jerusalem. One day when Jeroboam was leaving, he was met by Ahijah. The prophet took Jeroboam's cloak, tore it into twelve pieces, and gave him ten of the pieces. Ahijah then prophesied that God indeed would tear the kingdom from Solomon for worshiping other gods; again, he would allow Solomon's son to rule one tribe (Judah). When Solomon found out about the prophecy, he tried to kill Jeroboam, but Jeroboam fled to Egypt until Solomon died.

Solomon ruled for forty years and was buried in Jerusalem. His son Rehoboam became king.

𝕌 Chapter Summary

After Saul's death, civil war broke out between Judah, which supported David, and the other tribes. When it ended, Israel recognized David as king.

David captured Jerusalem, making it his political and religious capital. He defeated Israel's enemies, completing the conquest of the Promised Land.

David wanted to build the Lord a temple, but Nathan said that because David had been continuously involved in violent warfare, his son would build it instead. God, however, made a covenant with David, promising that one of his descendants would rule on the throne forever.

David slept with Bathsheba, the wife of another man, and then murdered her husband to cover up his sin. God knew it; Nathan confronted David and announced the dreadful consequences, which included continuous strife and fighting within his own household.

Absalom plotted David's overthrow and led a rebellion; David was forced to flee. Absalom's forces were defeated, and Joab, disregarding David's orders, killed Absalom.

At the end of David's life, his sons were hovering like vultures around the throne; David designated his son Solomon as his successor.

Solomon honored God, who then blessed him with wisdom.

Solomon also became famous for his wealth, and his crowning achievement was the construction of a magnificent temple honoring the Lord.

Though his rule was a testimony to the Lord's keeping of his covenant promises, Solomon played the fool and violated God's commands against marriage to foreign wives. His wives and concubines divided his heart; he built temples for their gods and abandoned wholehearted devotion to the Lord.

For his apostasy, the Lord announced that after his death, Solomon's kingdom would be divided.

Ten

A KINGDOM DIVIDED: NORTHERN KINGDOM

Main Characters
Kings of Israel
Jeroboam I (first king of Israel)
Ahab and Jezebel
Elijah and Elisha
Jonah

Setting
Israel (Northern Kingdom)
Judah (Southern Kingdom)
Aram (Syria)
Assyria

THE DIVISION OF THE KINGDOM

After Solomon's death, his son made a political decision that fulfilled the Lord's announcement about the division of Israel into two kingdoms. The kingdom in the north was called Israel; the kingdom in the south, Judah.

Rehoboam went to Shechem (in the northern tribes' territory) to become king of all Israel, but he faced a threat from a rival. When Jeroboam I, who had sought asylum after Solomon's attempt to kill him, heard Solomon had died, he returned from Egypt.

The northern tribes appealed to Rehoboam for relief from the harsh labor and heavy taxes imposed on them by Solomon. He discussed this with both his older and younger advisors. The older advisors said he could gain support by granting their request, but his younger advisors recommended a show of force by increasing demands.

Rehoboam followed the latter advice and arrogantly declared, "My father beat you with whips, but I will beat you with scorpions" (whips with pieces of metal embedded). This choice fulfilled the prophecy about the kingdom's division. The northern tribes rebelled and said, "Down with the dynasty of David! Rule over your own house."

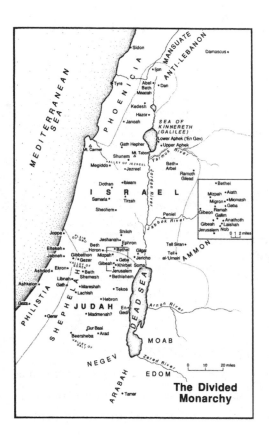

The Divided Monarchy

Rehoboam made the situation even worse by sending the officer in charge of labor to force compliance. The people stoned him to death and made Jeroboam their king.

When Rehoboam returned to Jerusalem, he mobilized the army to force the northern tribes to recognize him as their king, but Shemaiah the prophet warned him against starting a war with the north.

Jeroboam made Shechem his political capital but was concerned about the lack of a worship center in the north. He was afraid if people continued to worship in Jerusalem, they would eventually give their allegiance to Rehoboam. He made it easy for people in the north by encouraging them to worship two golden-calf idols at Bethel and Dan, and by appointing priests from the common people instead of the Levites. To give legitimacy to the shrines in the north, Jeroboam offered a sacrifice on the altar at Bethel and instituted a special religious festival for all of Israel.

The Lord commanded a prophet from the southern kingdom to go to Bethel and denounce Jeroboam's apostate worship. When Jeroboam pointed to him and ordered him seized, Jeroboam's hand and arm were instantly paralyzed and the altar split apart as the man had predicted. Jeroboam pleaded with the man for mercy, and his hand was restored.

The man of God had refused to eat with the king but accepted an invitation to eat with an old prophet living in Bethel—even though the Lord had commanded him to leave the north immediately. While the man was eating, the old prophet received a divine revelation condemning the man for disobeying God's command.

After the evening meal, the man left on his donkey and was killed by a lion. The old prophet retrieved his body and buried it in his own grave, instructing his sons to bury his body there too because his message of judgment against the shrines in the northern kingdom would certainly come true.

Even after these dramatic events of warning and judgment, Jeroboam persisted in appointing apostate priests, which doomed his dynasty to destruction.

When his son became ill, Jeroboam instructed his wife to disguise herself, go to the prophet at Shiloh, and ask if his son would recover. The disguise was useless. The prophet knew she was Jeroboam's wife.

He said, "I have bad news for you. Tell Jeroboam the Lord appointed him to rule over his people, but Jeroboam has made me furious by encouraging the people to worship golden calves. The Lord will destroy his dynasty, and his family will die and be devoured by dogs and vultures."

The prophet told the king's wife to go home, and when she entered the city her son would die. He predicted that the Lord would raise up a king who would destroy the family of Jeroboam, and Israel would be expelled from the land the Lord had given them.

After Jeroboam ruled for twenty-two years, he died and his son Nadab became king.

THE HISTORY OF ISRAEL—KINGS AND PROPHETS OF THE NORTHERN KINGDOM

The history of northern Israel is a tale of divine judgment on religious apostasy, political treachery, and brutal murder. None of the kings repented and abandoned the sin of Jeroboam (idolatry). Some, like Ahab, even promoted the worship of Canaanite gods.

Jeroboam's dynasty did not last long, as Ahijah had predicted. Nadab continued in the ways of his father and ruled for only two years. He was assassinated by Baasha while engaged in the siege of a city. Baasha seized the throne and immediately killed all of Jeroboam's descendants.

Though he was not a descendant of Jeroboam, Baasha followed his example and practiced idolatry. He fought constantly with Asa, king of Judah, and made Tirzah the capital of Israel. His idolatry stirred up the anger of the Lord, who sent Jehu to warn Baasha that he and his family would suffer the same fate as the family of Jeroboam.

After twenty-four years, Baasha's son Elah became king but ruled only two years before he was assassinated by Zimri. Zimri murdered all of Baasha's family and even his friends. Baasha and Elah had provoked God to anger by worshiping worthless idols.

Zimri's rule lasted seven days. When the army learned Zimri had assassinated the royal family, they rebelled and made Omri, their general, king of Israel. Omri attacked Tirzah, and when Zimri realized the city was lost, he went into the inner fortress of the palace and burned it down on himself.

Only half of Israel supported Omri. The rest wanted to make Tibni king, but his supporters were defeated and he was killed by Omri. Omri ruled for six years in Tirzah and then relocated the capital to Samaria, where he ruled for six more years. He was powerful, but he continued in the sin of Jeroboam.

Elijah

When Omri's son Ahab became king, he plunged Israel even further into apostasy and provoked the Lord to greater anger than any of the other kings of Israel. He had married Jezebel, daughter of the king of Sidon and a devoted worshiper of Baal, and then he built a temple and altar for Baal worship in the capital city of Samaria.

To challenge Baal worship, God raised up Elijah the prophet. Elijah confronted Ahab on numerous occasions with miraculous signs to prove that the Lord, not Baal, was the only true and living God.

Elijah's ministry began with an announcement of a drought. He told Ahab, "As surely as the Lord lives, the God of Israel, it will not rain until I give the word." During the drought, the Lord cared for Elijah by a brook. The brook provided Elijah with water, and God sent ravens to bring him food each morning and evening. When even the brook dried up, God told Elijah to leave Israel and go to the village of Zarephath near Sidon. (Zarephath was in Phoenicia, a Gentile area.)

There Elijah went to the home of a widow. He asked her for water and bread, but she had only a handful of flour and a cup of cooking oil, which she planned to use to prepare a last meal for herself and her son. Elijah assured her that if she trusted him and fed him first, the Lord would provide for her until it began to rain again. So she did as Elijah had said, and as Elijah had promised, the Lord miraculously provided flour and oil.

When her son became ill and died, the woman thought Elijah was punishing her for her sins, but Elijah stretched himself out over the boy three times and prayed, "O Lord, please restore this child's life." Life returned to the boy, and Elijah took him to the widow. "Look!" he said, "your son is alive!"

The woman said, "Now I am certain you are a man of God, a prophet of the Lord."

In the third year of the drought, the Lord told Elijah to announce to Ahab that it would end. Obadiah, a prophet of the Lord, arranged for the meeting.

Ahab blamed Elijah for the drought and called him a troublemaker. Elijah replied, "You and your family are the troublemakers; you have not obeyed the commands of the Lord." Elijah challenged the prophets of Baal and Asherah to a contest at Mount Carmel (near the Mediterranean Sea in the north, the location of a major Baal worship shrine).

Elijah told the prophets of Baal to sacrifice an animal on an altar of wood, then call on the name of their god, while he would call on the Lord: "The god who consumes the sacrifice with fire is the true God!" All the people agreed this was a fair test.

Elijah allowed the prophets to make their sacrifice first; when nothing happened he began to ridicule them. "Shout louder," he said. "Perhaps Baal is daydreaming or relieving himself. Or maybe he's on a trip or asleep and needs to be awakened."

The prophets of Baal shouted louder and louder and even cut themselves with knives until they were dripping with blood. They danced and whirled around in a frenzy all day until the time of the evening sacrifice, but nothing happened. Baal was impotent!

At the time of the evening sacrifice, Elijah called the people to come closer as he prepared the altar. He rebuilt it with twelve stones, one for each tribe of Israel, then dug a trench around the altar, piled on wood, and cut the bull into pieces.

He filled the trench with water, soaked the altar and sacrifice with gallons of water, and then offered a simple prayer. "O Lord, God of Abraham, Isaac, and Jacob: prove this day that you are God in Israel and I am your servant. O Lord, answer me, so these people will know that you are the Lord God and have brought them back to yourself!" Fire from the Lord immediately consumed the sacrifice, the entire altar, and even the water in the trench. The people fell on their faces and cried out, "The Lord—he is God!"

Elijah ordered the people to seize all the prophets of Baal. They took them to the Kishon Valley and killed them.

Elijah returned to Mount Carmel and prayed for rain. He told his servant seven times to look for rain, and the seventh time he saw a small cloud; the sky turned black and unleashed a heavy rainstorm. Ahab rode in a chariot for Jezreel to escape the torrential downpour, but the Lord enabled Elijah to outrun Ahab.

When Ahab told Jezebel what Elijah had done, she swore by the gods she would kill Elijah, just as she had killed all the other true prophets in Israel. Elijah was so afraid that he fled south toward Mount Sinai (a distance of approximately two hundred miles). He felt defeated and prayed, "I can't take anymore, Lord. Take my life."

Instead, God sent an angel who encouraged Elijah and gave him food and water for his journey. After forty days he arrived at Mount Sinai and hid in a cave.

The Lord appeared and asked, "What are you doing here?" Elijah complained that he had zealously served the Lord, but it was futile— the people had not kept their promises to serve the Lord faithfully and had killed all the prophets. "I am the only one left, and they are trying to kill me," he said.

The Lord told Elijah to stand outside the cave, and he would speak. The Lord sent a tornado-like wind, an earthquake, and a fire, but he did not appear in any of them; instead the Lord spoke to Elijah in a gentle, calming voice.

He told Elijah to retrace his route, go through the land of Israel, and travel all the way to Damascus (northeast of Israel) to anoint three individuals: Hazael to be king of Aram (modern-day Syria), Jehu to be king of Israel, and Elisha to replace himself as prophet in Israel. The Lord said he would use these three to execute judgment on Israel.

God also assured Elijah that there were seven thousand prophets in

Israel who had not abandoned the Lord to worship Baal. Elijah obeyed and anointed Elisha as his successor by symbolically throwing his cloak over the shoulder of the young man.

Ben-Hadad of Aram put together a coalition of thirty-two kings to attack Israel. He sent three delegations to offer terms of surrender. The first delegation demanded gold, silver, and hostages. Ahab agreed, but Ben-Hadad wasn't satisfied. The second delegation wanted Ahab to grant Ben-Hadad's officials access to Ahab's palace. Ahab refused, so Ben-Hadad sent a third delegation with a terrifying message: "May the gods strike me if there remains enough dust from Samaria for a fistful for each of my soldiers."

The attempt to intimidate did not work. Ahab was defiant, so Ben-Hadad ordered his forces to prepare to attack.

Unexpectedly, a prophet came to Ahab and assured him of victory. Though outnumbered, he told Ahab to attack the enemy's army first. Ahab attacked at noon when Ben-Hadad and his troops were drunk from celebrating their victory even before they had mounted their chariots. The Israelites routed the Arameans; Ben-Hadad and a few of his officers escaped. Before he left, the prophet warned Ahab to prepare for a second attack next spring. (Military campaigns were usually in the spring and early summer.)

The following spring, Ben-Hadad's officers told him they were defeated because the Israelite gods ruled the hills. They urged him to engage the Israelites on the plains where they would have the advantage with their chariots. This time a man of God assured Ahab of victory not only for the sake of Israel but as proof that the Lord is the only true God.

When the two armies met on the field of battle, the Arameans again suffered staggering losses. Ben-Hadad was forced to beg for mercy from Ahab. Ahab let him live, but Ben-Hadad surrendered territory to Ahab and signed a treaty with him.

Allowing Ben-Hadad to live was a mistake; God sent one of his prophets to announce judgment on Ahab. The prophet communicated the message symbolically by disguising himself as a wounded soldier. He told Ahab he had been ordered to guard a prisoner but the prisoner had escaped. Ahab said it was his own fault and that he deserved to die.

The prophet then said to Ahab, "The Lord says: Because you allowed the man the Lord ordered destroyed to live, you will die in his place and the people of Israel will die instead of his people."

Instead of repenting, Ahab became angry and went home.

Ahab's defiant attitude led to another offense when he tried to buy Naboth's vineyard. He made a generous offer, but Naboth refused it.

Ahab, sullen and brooding, refused to eat.

Jezebel asked, "What's the matter?"

Ahab complained that Naboth wouldn't sell him his vineyard.

Jezebel said, "You are the king. Don't worry, I'll get you his vineyard!"

She forged Ahab's name on letters and sent them to the elders of Jezreel. The letters instructed them to call an assembly and get two reprobates to accuse Naboth of cursing God and the king. They did as Jezebel had instructed, and the elders stoned Naboth to death.

When Ahab went to claim the vineyard, Elijah was there. The prophet announced judgment on Ahab: "Because you have killed Naboth and attempted to steal his property, dogs will lick your blood in the very place where they have licked the blood of Naboth."

Elijah also predicted that because they worshiped Baal, dogs would eat Jezebel's body, and that all the members of Ahab's family would be eaten by dogs and vultures.

After Elijah's announcement, Ahab repented. He mourned and even wore burlap, so the Lord withheld judgment on his family until after Ahab's death.

Following three years of peace, Ahab decided to go to war against Aram. While Jehoshaphat, king of Judah, was visiting, Ahab convinced him to join him in a campaign to recapture the strategic city of Ramoth Gilead. Jehoshaphat agreed but wanted prophetic confirmation before going into battle, so Ahab summoned four hundred prophets of Israel. Though they all assured Ahab of victory, Jehoshaphat was suspicious. He asked, "Is there another prophet? We should ask him."

Ahab said there was Micaiah, but he hated him because Micaiah always prophesied disaster. Jehoshaphat was insistent, so Ahab ordered one of his officers to bring Micaiah.

Ahab and Jehoshaphat dressed in their royal robes and sat on thrones near the gate of Samaria. Though the four hundred prophets continued to predict victory, Micaiah said, "As surely as the Lord lives, I will only say what the Lord tells me to say."

At first Micaiah sarcastically promised Ahab victory, but Ahab knew it wasn't true; he demanded that Micaiah speak the truth in the name of the Lord. So Micaiah told Ahab that the Lord had sent a lying spirit to his prophets in order to entice Ahab to go to battle, where he would be killed. Ahab angrily ordered Micaiah imprisoned until he returned.

Ahab disguised himself before going into battle, hoping no one would recognize him; one of the Aramean archers, however, fired an arrow that pierced his armor.

Ahab ordered his chariot driver to take him from the field of battle. He remained propped there all day but bled to death as evening approached. When they realized Ahab was dead, his troops fled.

Ahab was buried in Samaria, and the dogs licked his blood when his chariot was washed at a pool where prostitutes bathed.

Ahab's son Ahaziah became king but ruled only two years. He worshiped Baal like his father and mother and practiced idolatry like Jeroboam.

Ahaziah's life ended with a tragic accident. When he fell through the latticework in one of the upper rooms in his palace, he sent messengers to the temple of Baalzebub to find out if he would recover. Elijah intercepted them and said, "Ask Ahaziah: 'Is there no God in Israel?

Why are you going to Baalzebub for help? You will never recover and get out of bed; you will die.' "

Ahaziah sent fifty soldiers to seize Elijah, but he destroyed them with fire from heaven. Ahaziah sent fifty more soldiers, and the same thing happened. When Ahaziah sent a third unit, their officer approached Elijah on his knees and asked for mercy. The angel of the Lord told Elijah to go with the third officer.

Elijah repeated his message of judgment and told Ahaziah, "Because you sought help from Baalzebub rather than God, you will never recover. You will die in bed." Ahaziah died as Elijah had predicted.

Ahaziah's brother Joram became king because Ahaziah did not have a son. Joram, who ruled for twelve years, was evil like his brother, but he did destroy some of the sacred pillars Ahab had built to worship Baal.

Elisha

While Elijah and Elisha were traveling together, Elijah ordered Elisha three times to stay behind, but Elisha refused. When they came to the Jordan, Elijah struck it with his cloak, and the water separated so that the two men were able to cross the river on dry ground.

Elijah asked Elisha to tell him what he wanted before the Lord took him to heaven.

Elisha replied, "Please give me a double portion of your prophetic spirit."

Elijah said that it would be difficult, but if Elisha saw him when he was taken into heaven, he would know the Lord had granted his request.

Suddenly a chariot of fire appeared and carried Elijah to heaven in a whirlwind. Elisha picked up Elijah's cloak, struck the waters of the Jordan, and crossed on dry ground. When the other prophets saw what had happened, they shouted, "The Spirit of the Lord that energized Elijah now rests on Elisha!"

Like Elijah, Elisha became God's prophetic spokesman to the kings of Israel, and his miracles confirmed he was a true prophet. His first miracle was an answer to a request from the leaders of Jericho, who complained the town's water supply had become polluted. Elisha asked for a new bowl with salt in it and purified their water supply by throwing salt into the town spring.

When Elisha left Jericho for Bethel, a group of young boys ridiculed him, chanting, "Go away, you bald-headed man." Elisha announced divine judgment on them, and two bears came out of the woods, mauling forty-two of them.

King Mesha of Moab refused to pay tribute to King Joram of Israel, so Joram assembled his army for war. He asked King Jehoshaphat of Judah to join forces with him, and the king of Edom also joined them. But after the armies had marched south for seven days, they ran out of water. Jehoshaphat recommended they seek help from a prophet.

When they asked Elisha, he sarcastically told Joram to get help from the pagan prophets his father and mother worshiped, but out of respect for Jehoshaphat, Elisha promised that the valley they were camped in would have water and they would defeat Moab. The next day the valley was filled with pools of water that looked like blood to the Moabite army, so they attacked, thinking the three kings had turned on each other.

They were caught by surprise by the Israelite army and retreated to Moab. Israel destroyed several cities and attempted to capture Kir-hareseth, but Moab's king sacrificed his oldest son on the city wall, causing the Israelites to withdraw and return home.

Unlike those who served pagan gods, Elisha used the Lord's power to help people. The widow of a prophet who served Elisha asked for help when a creditor threatened to take her two sons as slaves. All she had was a small flask of oil.

Elisha told her to get as many empty jars as she could find and fill them. The supply of oil did not run out until she had filled all the jars.

Elisha told her to sell the oil and pay her debt. She had enough money left over for her and her two sons to live on.

Whenever Elisha visited the town of Shunem, he stayed at the home of a wealthy woman. When Elisha found out the woman didn't have any children, he promised her a son; however, when she finally had her son, he died unexpectedly as a young boy.

The woman didn't tell anyone her son had died because she was confident Elisha could raise him from the dead. Elisha's servant tried to restore the boy's life but couldn't. Elisha brought the child back to life by praying and lying down on the boy's body.

Elisha's power was also revealed in miracles related to food. When one of the prophets unknowingly put poisonous herbs in a pot of stew, Elisha threw in flour that neutralized the poison. Elisha also multiplied twenty loaves so there was enough to feed a hundred people, with bread left over.

Elisha's ministry was not limited to the people of Israel. Naaman, a distinguished commander of the Aramean army, had leprosy, but he was informed about this prophet in Israel who could heal him.

The king of Aram offered to help by providing Naaman with a letter of introduction to the king of Israel along with gifts of silver, gold, and expensive clothes. When the king of Israel heard what Naaman wanted, he tore his clothes in despair. He thought it was a ploy to start a war.

When Elisha heard how the king had responded, he sent the following message: "Why are you complaining? Send Naaman to me. I will heal him, and he will know there is a prophet of the Lord in Israel."

Naaman went to Elisha with his military escort of chariots and waited at the door of his house. Elisha didn't come out; instead he sent his servant to tell Naaman to go wash seven times in the Jordan River. Naaman was insulted and left in a rage. He said, "Aren't the rivers of Damascus better than any rivers of Israel?"

His officers calmed him down and persuaded him to at least try. He had nothing to lose, they reasoned. When Naaman dipped himself seven times in the Jordan, he was cured of his leprosy. They went back to Elisha's house with the gifts and Naaman said, "Now I know there is no God in all the world except in Israel."

Elisha refused the gifts and told Naaman, "Go in peace." But Gehazi, Elisha's servant, secretly followed Naaman and told him that Elisha had changed his mind and wanted the gifts. Naaman gave him twice as much as he had originally offered. When Gehazi returned home, Elisha confronted him, knowing what he had done. Elisha said, "Because of this, you and your family will suffer from leprosy forever." As soon as Gehazi left the room he was covered with leprosy.

There was no limit to Elisha's miracles. When the prophets were cutting logs for a new building and the ax head flew off its handle and into the Jordan, Elisha threw a stick into the water and the head floated to the surface so Elisha could grab it.

When the king of Aram would make plans to attack cities in Israel, Elisha knew their plans in advance and would warn the king, who would tell the cities to prepare. This happened so many times that the king of Aram became suspicious. One of his officers told them it was Elisha—and that he even knew what the king was saying in his own bedroom.

The king found out Elisha was at Dothan and surrounded the city under the cover of darkness. Elisha's servant woke up the next morning and was terrified to see the Aramean troops. Elisha told him to look again. This time he saw that the hills were filled with chariots of fire.

When the Arameans advanced, Elisha asked the Lord to blind them. Then Elisha led them to Samaria and asked the Lord to open their eyes. The king of Israel wanted to kill them, but Elisha told him to give them food and set them free.

The king of Aram surrounded Samaria and attempted to starve its people to death. The people became so desperate for food they resorted to cannibalism. A woman complained to the king saying: "This woman proposed that we eat my son today and her son tomorrow. We cooked and ate my son, but the next day she hid her son so we couldn't eat him."

The king was furious; he blamed Elisha and planned to behead him. He sent a messenger to summon Elisha, but Elisha wouldn't open the door. He sent a second messenger. Elisha predicted that the next day food would be so abundant, they could buy bags of flour with a single coin.

The king's chief military advisor said, "Impossible, it will never happen!" Elisha said because of his skeptical attitude he would not live to enjoy the abundant provision.

The next day four lepers decided it was better to surrender to the Arameans than starve to death. They sneaked out of the city at sunset and headed for the camp, but when they arrived they were shocked: The Lord had frightened the Arameans with the sounds of an approaching army, and they had fled, leaving behind all their supplies.

The lepers gorged themselves on food and wine but then felt guilty: "If we don't tell the people in the city, something terrible will happen to us." When it was reported to the king that the Arameans had abandoned their camp, he thought it was a trap and sent out scouts to see if it was true. Then the king ordered his advisor to control the people, but instead they stampeded out of the city and trampled him to death, as Elisha had predicted.

Though Elisha was stern when confronting his opponents, he was a man of compassion to those who needed help. He warned the woman whose son he had brought back to life about a famine and told her to leave Israel. She returned after seven years but had lost her house and land.

She decided to appeal to King Joram. Though Joram hated Elisha, he had asked Gehazi, Elisha's servant, to tell him about the prophet's amazing ministry. Gehazi was telling the story about Elisha raising the widow's son right when she walked in to ask for help. When she confirmed that it was accurate, King Joram returned her property plus the income lost during her absence.

Elisha's reputation as a prophet of the Lord was known beyond the land of Israel. When Ben-Hadad, the king of Aram, became gravely ill and heard Elisha was in Damascus, he sent his advisor Hazael to ask the prophet if he would recover. Elisha told Hazael to tell the king he would recover, even though he knew Ben-Hadad would die. Elisha looked straight into the eyes of Hazael and predicted he would become the next king of Aram, but then Elisha began to cry. Hazael asked, "Why are you so sad?" Elisha said, "Because I know when you become king you will attack Israel and brutally slaughter men, women, and children."

Hazael returned and told Ben-Hadad that he would recover, but the next day he murdered Ben-Hadad by smothering him with a blanket soaked in water; then he seized the throne.

Elijah had announced judgment on Ahab's dynasty, so Elisha sent one of the prophets to anoint Jehu as king. The prophet went to Ramoth Gilead, where Jehu was camped with the army. He told Jehu he had a message from Elisha and asked to meet with him privately. He poured oil over Jehu's head and announced, "The Lord, the God of Israel, anoints you as king. You are to destroy the family of Ahab because they murdered the prophets."

When Jehu returned to his officers, they wanted to know what the prophet had said. The word got out, and the soldiers shouted, "Jehu is king!"

While fighting against Aram, Joram was wounded and returned to Jezreel to recover. When Jehu heard Joram was there, he ordered his men to surround the city and not let anyone leave.

As Jehu approached, Joram sent out a messenger to ask if Jehu's intentions were peaceful. The messenger didn't return, so he sent a second messenger. When he also didn't return, Joram and Ahaziah, king of Judah, rode out in their chariots to meet Jehu. Joram demanded to know if Jehu had come in peace, but it was too late. Joram tried to escape; Jehu killed him with an arrow. Instead of burying Joram, Jehu ordered his body left exposed on the land that had belonged to Naboth before Ahab confiscated it.

Jehu was a violent assassin. When he rode into Jezreel, Jezebel shouted "Murderer!" from a second-story window. Jehu ordered her thrown down, and he trampled her with his horses. Later he ordered his men to bury her because she was the daughter of a king, but when they looked for her body they found only a skull and a few bones.

Elijah's prophecy of judgment had been fulfilled. Jezebel had been eaten by dogs.

Jehu also ordered the ruthless slaughter of Ahab's family, who lived in Samaria. Jehu sent a letter to the city's elders and the guardians of Ahab's sons. He wrote, "Select the best leader as your king and prepare to fight for Ahab's dynasty." This in-your-face challenge so terrified the elders and guardians that they said they would do whatever Jehu wanted. He sent a second letter telling them to bring the heads of Ahab's sons to him at Jezreel. They killed all of Ahab's sons and brought their heads to Jehu in baskets. He ordered their heads displayed overnight in two piles on either side of the city gate.

Jehu's purge of Ahab's dynasty was not limited to the former king's immediate family. The next morning Jehu spoke to the people and accepted full responsibility for the death of Joram and Ahab's sons; then he killed the rest of Ahab's relatives, friends, and officials in Jezreel. He even killed relatives of King Ahaziah, who were simply going to visit the sons of Ahab. He killed all the members of Ahab's family in Samaria.

He killed all the priests of Baal by deceiving them. He called for a town meeting and said, "Ahab's worship of Baal was nothing compared to how I will worship him." He told the people to summon all the prophets and worshipers of Baal for a great celebration.

The invitation went out to all Israel. He ordered special robes for the worshipers. After they were all in Baal's temple, he gave this order to eighty men: "Go in and kill all of them. Don't let a single person escape!" After his soldiers killed them all with their swords and wrecked the temple, Jehu made it into a public toilet for the city of Samaria.

Jehu completely wiped out every trace of Baal worship in Israel, but he did not destroy the golden calves set up by Jeroboam that caused Israel to sin.

Before the end of Jehu's rule, the Lord reduced the size of Israel's territory. Hazael of Aram captured land east of the Jordan and in the north. After he had ruled for twenty-eight years, Jehu died and was buried in Samaria. His son Jehoahaz became king.

Jehoahaz did not worship Baal, but he continued Jeroboam's idolatrous practices. This made the Lord furious with Israel, and they were defeated time and time again by Aram. Because Jehoahaz asked for the Lord's help, the Lord sent someone to rescue them, and they lived briefly in peace. By the end of Jehoahaz's seventeen-year rule, he had only fifty charioteers, ten chariots, and ten thousand soldiers.

Jehoash, Jehoahaz's son, ruled over Israel for sixteen years. He did not abandon the sins of Jeroboam but continued to practice idolatry. He did, however, visit Elisha on his deathbed. While weeping for Elisha, the king saw an army of chariots. Elisha told him to get a bow and shoot an arrow out the east window.

"The arrow," said Elisha, "is the arrow of victory over Aram." He told Jehoash to strike the ground with a handful of arrows. The king struck the ground three times. This made Elisha angry. He said Jehoash should have struck the ground five or six times for a complete victory over the Arameans. Now he would be victorious only three times.

Elisha's miraculous ministry continued even after his death. When a burial party of Israelites saw a band of Moabite raiders, they quickly threw the corpse they were carrying into Elisha's grave and fled. As soon as the man's body touched Elisha's bones, he sprang back to life.

As Elisha had predicted, on three occasions, Jehoash defeated Aram and recovered Israelite towns. Jehoash also went to war against Judah.

He captured Amaziah, marched to Jerusalem, destroyed part of the city wall, and looted the temple and the royal palace.

When Jehoash died, his son Jeroboam II became king. Israel prospered militarily and economically under his rule, but he continued the practice of idolatry.

Even so, because of the Lord's faithfulness to his covenant promises, he helped Jeroboam II recover territory in the east and extended Israel's boundary beyond Damascus in the north.

Jonah

During Jeroboam II's rule, God sent the prophet Jonah, who was from Israel, to warn Nineveh (the capital of Assyria) of God's judgment for their military savagery and demonically inspired idolatry and immorality. The Lord said, "Go to Nineveh and announce my judgment on that great city because they are extremely wicked."

Instead, Jonah fled to the port city of Joppa and boarded a ship sailing for Tarshish (a city hundreds of miles in the opposite direction). On board, Jonah fell asleep only to be awakened by frantic sailors amid a terrifying storm.

In desperation, the sailors "cast lots" to find out who had offended the gods. The lots pointed to Jonah, who confessed to being a runaway prophet. Jonah told them to throw him overboard to save the ship. The sailors refused at first, fearing divine wrath, but when the storm increased in intensity, they threw Jonah into the raging sea. The storm stopped immediately.

The prophet didn't drown; instead, he was swallowed by a large sea creature. Inside the fish Jonah prayed:

> I called to you, O Lord
> And you answered me.
> The raging waters engulfed me,
> Yet I said I will look toward your holy temple.
> As I sank beneath the waves,

You snatched me from waters of death.
I will keep my vows,
Because salvation comes from the Lord. (See Jonah 2.)

After Jonah admitted his rebellion and promised to serve God, the fish spit him out.

The Lord spoke to Jonah a second time; this time he obeyed and went to Nineveh. His preaching was surprisingly successful. The people listened to his warning that in forty days the city would be destroyed.

They responded by repenting and fasting. Even the king exchanged his royal robes for garments of mourning. He issued a decree ordering everyone to turn away from wickedness. Because the citizens of Nineveh repented, God did not destroy the city.

Instead of celebrating the success of his mission, Jonah was angry. He wanted God to destroy the city, not spare it. He was so disappointed and angry that he wanted to die. "Just kill me, Lord. I'd rather die than see Nineveh survive," he complained.

The Lord admonished Jonah, who went to a nearby hill and sat down, still anticipating the possibility that God would destroy the city. The hot sun made him uncomfortable, and he was relieved when the Lord caused a plant to grow that gave him shade from the scorching heat.

But God sent a worm to attack the plant, causing it to wither during the night. The next day Jonah had to endure the scorching sun and hot wind, and he was miserable.

The Lord exposed Jonah's hardheartedness with the object lesson of the plant. The prophet was more concerned about a plant he had not created than he was about people, whom God had created. "Shouldn't I be concerned about the people of this great city?" said the Lord.

Meanwhile, back in Israel, the prophets Hosea and Amos tried to warn Jeroboam II that there was a limit to God's mercy. He would judge Israel for their religious hypocrisy, economic greed, and ruthless exploitation of the poor.

After Jeroboam II, the political and military situation deteriorated rapidly due to conspiracy and assassination.

Zechariah, son of Jeroboam II, was evil and ruled Israel for only six months. Shallum assassinated him and declared himself king.

Shallum was king for a month before he was assassinated by Menahem, who launched a scorched-earth campaign to force Israel to recognize him as king. He massacred entire populations and even ripped open pregnant women.

Menahem ruled for ten years and never repented of the sins of idolatry. Like all the other kings before him, he persisted in the sins of Jeroboam I. When the king of Assyria invaded Israel, Menaham was forced to pay tribute to prevent Israel's total destruction.

Pekahiah ruled for two years before he was assassinated by Pekah. Both kings persisted in idolatrous religion. Tiglathpileser, king of Assyria, invaded Israel a second time and captured several towns, deporting the citizens to Assyria. Pekah's twenty-year rule ended when he was assassinated by Hoshea.

Hoshea was evil, though not to the same extent as previous kings. Forced to pay heavy tribute to the king of Assyria, he formed an alliance with King So of Egypt. When Assyria discovered the conspiracy, they captured Hoshea and took him to Assyria.

The Assyrians invaded Israel and devastated the land. After a three-year siege, they captured Samaria and deported the population to other locations in their empire.

The fall of Israel was not because of superior Assyrian military might. God would have protected his people if they would have remained faithful to him. But instead of worshiping the Lord, they rejected him, bowing to worthless idols and detestable pagan gods of the nations. They despised the warning of the prophets and stubbornly refused to obey the Lord until he became so angry he exiled them from the Promised Land.

In addition to deporting Israelites, the Assyrians resettled foreigners in the land of Israel; the Lord killed some of them with lions because they worshiped their gods. When this was reported to the king of Assyria, he ordered one of Israel's exiled priests returned to the land to teach the foreigners how to worship.

He returned to Bethel and taught the people from other nations how to worship the Lord. But instead of worshiping only the Lord, each nation continued to worship its own gods. Though the Lord had made a covenant with his people and commanded them to worship only him, their faith became a confusing mixture of the worship of the Lord and the gods of the nations.

♫ Chapter Summary

Because Solomon was not totally devoted to the Lord, Israel would be divided.

In the north, Jeroboam I compromised devotion to the Lord by encouraging the people to worship idols. His sin led to his downfall; it was repeated by every king in the north and was the eventual reason for Israel's total destruction.

Ahab, the north's most infamous king, married Jezebel and instituted Baal worship, plunging the northern kingdom deeper into religious apostasy. The Lord commissioned Elijah to stem the tide of Baalism; Elijah demonstrated the powerlessness of Baal and the power of the Lord. Elijah repeatedly warned Ahab of God's judgment, but Ahab stubbornly refused to repent, and Jezebel tried to kill the prophet.

When Jezebel had Naboth murdered, Elijah announced judgment on Ahab's family.

Before he was taken to heaven, Elijah transferred his prophetic ministry to Elisha. Like Elijah, Elisha used divine power to show that the Lord was the only true God.

Elisha anointed Hazael to become king of Aram, and Jehu to execute judgment on Ahab and Jezebel. Jehu killed all of Ahab's relatives and slaughtered the priests of Baal.

Though Israel enjoyed times of peace and prosperity, the northern kingdom was in political, military, and spiritual decline until its end.

The ruthless and powerful Assyrians invaded Israel twice. Assyria practiced a policy of resettling conquered nations; they relocated most surviving Israelites to other parts of their empire and resettled foreigners in the land of Israel.

The foreigners worshiped the Lord, but they also worshiped their own gods. Though the Lord had made a covenant with his people, they disobeyed him and worshiped the gods of other nations.

Eleven

A KINGDOM DIVIDED: SOUTHERN KINGDOM

Main Characters
Kings of Judah
Rehoboam (first king of Judah)
Hezekiah
Manasseh
Josiah
Nebuchadnezzar

Setting
Israel (Judah, in the south)
Assyria
Babylon

THE DIVISION OF THE KINGDOM

When Rehoboam attempted to become king of all Israel, he acted arrogantly. The leaders of the northern tribes and Jeroboam met with him and complained about the harsh demands imposed on them by Solomon. They asked for relief, but instead he demanded more work and threatened them with brutal punishment. In response, they shouted, "Down with the dynasty of David! Rule over your own house."

When Rehoboam ordered the supervisor of the workers to force compliance, the people stoned him to death and tried to kill Rehoboam, who barely escaped in his chariot. The northern tribes made Jeroboam their king.

On returning to Jerusalem, Rehoboam mobilized 180,000 troops from Judah and Benjamin to crush the revolt. However, Shemaiah the prophet intervened, informing Rehoboam that the division of the kingdom was God's will.

THE HISTORY OF JUDAH—KINGS AND PROPHETS OF THE SOUTHERN KINGDOM

Rehoboam not only committed political folly; he was a religious apostate. He promoted the practices of the pagan nations the Lord had driven from the land. The people built shrines on all the high hills and practiced cultic prostitution.

In Rehoboam's fifth year, King Shishak of Egypt invaded Judah and stole the temple treasures, including the golden shields made during Solomon's reign. To give the temple the appearance of its former glory, Rehoboam replaced them with bronze shields.

Though he had initially refrained from going to war with the north, Rehoboam and Jeroboam became bitter enemies and fought continually.

Early Kings

Abijam continued the sinful practices of his father Rehoboam, but because of his promises to David, the Lord continued to allow David's descendants to rule over Judah.

The conflict with Israel continued and, during a strategic battle, the Lord helped Abijam, whose army destroyed Jeroboam's though it was outnumbered two to one. Abijam had fourteen wives, twenty-two sons, and sixteen daughters.

Though Abijam was not fully devoted to the Lord, his son Asa was a godly ruler. He prohibited religious prostitution, destroyed pagan idols, and even deposed of his grandmother who was a cultic priestess.

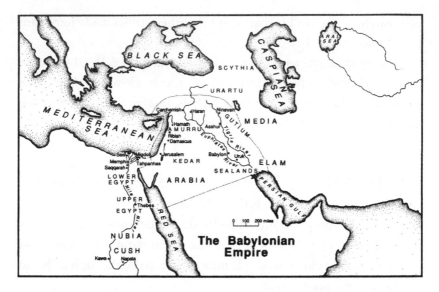

The Babylonian Empire

When a massive Ethiopian army invaded Judah, Asa cried out to the Lord for help. The army of Judah defeated the Ethiopians and captured vast amounts of plunder.

The Spirit of God inspired Azariah the prophet to remind Asa of God's covenant promises: "Listen, the Lord will bless you if you honor him, but if you abandon him, he will abandon you." Asa returned the sacred treasures to the temple and led Judah in a memorable covenant renewal ceremony. They sacrificed thousands of animals, and the people enthusiastically swore to seek the Lord with their whole heart.

Judah enjoyed peace until the thirty-fifth year of Asa's rule, when they were attacked by Israel. Asa paid Ben-Hadad of Aram for help, and for failing to trust the Lord, he was rebuked by Hanani the prophet. But instead of repenting, Asa threw him in prison. For his sin, Asa was inflicted with a disease in his feet from which he never recovered. He ruled forty-one years and was buried with honor in the City of David (Jerusalem).

When Jehoshaphat began his rule, he made Judah's security a priority. He fortified strategic cities and built garrisons on the borders.

Jehoshaphat did not worship Baal as in the northern kingdom of Israel. The Lord blessed Jehoshaphat because he obeyed his commands. He was highly respected by the people, and they brought him so many gifts he became wealthy. He also was highly regarded by other nations— even the Philistines brought him gifts.

In the third year of his rule, he sent officials, Levites, and priests throughout Judah to teach the people the book of the law (the law of Moses).

He made an alliance with King Ahab of Israel, a Baal worshiper. Ahab persuaded him to go to war against Aram. Jehoshaphat insisted on counsel from a true prophet rather than the phony prophets who advised Ahab; Micaiah contradicted Ahab's prophets and warned of defeat. After Ahab was killed in battle, Jehoshaphat returned to Jerusalem and was rebuked by Jehu the prophet for his error in joining with a wicked king.

Jehoshaphat continued to promote worship of the Lord. He demanded his officials govern with integrity and justice. He instructed some of the Levites and priests to judge both religious and civil cases and ordered them to make decisions that would honor God.

When the Moabites, Ammonites, and Meunites (identity uncertain) joined forces to attack Judah, Jehoshaphat declared a national fast. He prayed publicly in front of the temple, confessing Judah's sins and asking for the Lord's help. While he was praying, the Spirit of the Lord inspired one of the men present to encourage Judah. He assured them the Lord would defeat their enemies; they wouldn't even need to fight.

The next day the army marched out of Jerusalem singing and praising the Lord. As they were singing, the three coalition armies destroyed one another. Jehoshaphat's army picked up the plunder and returned to Jerusalem, singing and praising God for victory. From that time until the end of Jehoshaphat's rule, Judah was at peace.

Jehoshaphat made another alliance with a king of Israel. He and Ahaziah built a fleet of ships, but the Lord destroyed them before they sailed.

When Jehoshaphat died, he was buried in Jerusalem, the City of David.

Jehoshaphat's son, Jehoram, was a ruthless king. Jehoshaphat had designated his oldest son to rule Judah, but this didn't matter to Jehoram. When Jehoram became king, he murdered his two brothers and some of the leading officials. Instead of worshiping the Lord, Jehoram married one of Ahab's daughters and plunged Judah into the detestable worship of Baal. It was only because of the covenant the Lord had made with David that he did not destroy Judah.

During Jehoram's rule, Edom rebelled, and when he attempted to put down the revolt, the Edomites surrounded his forces. He escaped under the cover of darkness, but his army deserted him.

Elijah the prophet warned Jehoram of divine judgment. A combined force of Philistines and Arabs attacked Jerusalem, plundered the royal palace, and captured all of Jehoram's wives and sons except Ahaziah. The Lord inflicted Jehoram with a fatal intestinal disease, and he suffered two years before he died. No one mourned Jehoram, and he was the first king in the line of David not buried in the cemetery for kings.

Ahaziah became king when he was twenty-two. His mother, Athaliah, a worshiper of Baal, encouraged him to sin against the Lord. Some of Ahab's descendants became his advisors.

He made an alliance with King Joram of Israel and went to see him after he was wounded in a battle against Aram. Jehu, who had been appointed by the Lord to destroy Ahab's dynasty, found out that officials from Judah and Ahaziah's family members were in Israel, and he killed all of them. Ahaziah tried to hide in Samaria, but Jehu's soldiers found him, and Jehu killed him. Because he was the grandson of Jehoshaphat, a godly king, Ahaziah was honored with a royal burial.

When Athaliah received word that her son was dead, she seized the throne in Judah by attempting to murder the royal family. She killed all of David's descendants except one. Jehosheba, daughter of King

Jehoram, rescued Ahaziah's son Joash and his nurse. Joash was hidden in the temple for six years.

Athaliah's murderous rule ended in the seventh year, when Jehoiada, the high priest, conspired with five military leaders, the Levites, and tribal leaders to overthrow her. He positioned his allies at strategic temple locations to protect Joash, then brought him out from hiding. Jehoiada crowned Joash on the Sabbath, and everyone shouted, "Long live the king!"

When Athaliah heard the shouting, she rushed to the temple to find out what was happening. When she saw the people celebrating the coronation, she cried out, "Treason! Treason!" She was right about treason but wrong about the identity of the traitor. Jehoiada ordered soldiers to seize Athaliah and kill anyone who tried to protect her. They took her outside and publicly executed her.

Jehoiada then made a covenant with the king and the people. After they dedicated themselves to the Lord, they destroyed the altars and idols of Baal and killed Mattan, Baal's high priest. Jehoiada assigned the priests and Levites to supervise worship in the temple according to the instructions of David and the law of Moses. The people rejoiced because there was peace in Jerusalem now that Athaliah was dead.

Joash was only seven when he began his rule that lasted forty years. Joash faithfully served the Lord during Jehoiada's lifetime. The high priest chose two wives for Joash.

Joash ordered the temple repaired; after consulting with Jehoiada, he ordered the Levites to collect a tax for maintaining it. He also had a special chest made and placed at the entrance of the temple so the people could voluntarily give offerings to the Lord.

The people were so grateful for the opportunity that they quickly filled the chest with silver. When it was full, the Levites would bring it to the royal accountant, then return the empty chest to the temple. They did this daily until they had collected large sums. Joash and Jehoiada used the money to pay skilled workers for the temple's restoration. They also had enough money to make some furniture out of gold and silver.

Jehoiada lived until he was 130. He was honored with burial in the cemetery of the kings because he had done so much good for God and his temple.

But after the death of Jehoiada, Judah committed apostasy. The leading officials convinced Joash to abandon the temple and to worship Asherah poles and idols.

The Lord was angry with Judah and Jerusalem; he sent prophets to call them back to himself. However, they ignored the prophets and even killed Jehoiada's son, Zechariah, who courageously said, "Why have you disobeyed the Lord's commands? Because you have abandoned the Lord, he will abandon you!"

Though Zechariah was Jehoiada's son, Joash ordered him stoned to death. As Zechariah was dying, he said to Joash, "May the Lord see what you have done and avenge my death."

The Lord did, using military defeat to punish Joash. Though the Arameans attacked with a small force, the Lord helped them defeat Judah. They wiped out its leaders and plundered the nation.

Joash was badly wounded, and some of his officials plotted to kill him for the murder of Jehoiada's son. Two hit men assassinated him on his bed. He was buried in Jerusalem but not in the royal cemetery.

Amaziah, Joash's son, ruled twenty-five years. He was a godly king but not totally devoted to the Lord. As soon as he had consolidated his power he executed his father's assassins. He didn't kill their children because the law of Moses prohibited punishing children for the sins of their fathers.

He increased the size of the army to 300,000 and recruited 100,000 troops from Israel; however, a prophet warned him that the Lord would not help him in battle if he used troops from the northern kingdom. Though Amaziah had paid them 7,500 pounds of silver, he sent them back to Israel. They were outraged.

Amaziah fought the Edomites in the Valley of Salt and killed ten thousand. He captured another ten thousand and threw them off the top of a cliff. During this battle, though, the soldiers from Israel he had turned away raided towns in the north, killing three thousand and capturing large quantities of plunder.

Amaziah angered the Lord by worshiping idols he had captured. A prophet rebuked him, saying, "Why worship the gods of the Edomites that could not save their own people from you?" Amaziah interrupted and said, "Stop prophesying or else you will be killed!" He stopped but warned Amaziah the Lord would destroy him because of his idolatry and refusal to listen.

After consulting with his advisors, Amaziah decided to attack Israel. He challenged King Jehoash to meet him in battle, but Jehoash ridiculed Amaziah: "You are proud because you have defeated Edom, but I advise you to stay home. You will only bring disaster on yourself and Judah." Amaziah didn't listen. When the two armies fought at Beth Shemesh, a town in Judah, Judah was defeated and Amaziah captured. Jehoash then destroyed part of the wall of Jerusalem, seized treasures from the temple and palace, and took hostages back to Israel.

Amaziah outlived Jehoash yet was killed in a conspiracy; he tried to flee but his assassins tracked him down. He was buried in Jerusalem in the royal cemetery.

Uzziah was only sixteen when he was crowned king, and he ruled fifty-two years. He was taught by Zechariah the prophet to respect the Lord, and because he looked to the Lord for guidance, he was highly successful.

Uzziah was an aggressive military leader and industrious builder. His army consisted of more than 300,000 highly trained and well-equipped soldiers. He expanded his kingdom to the south by defeating the Philistines, the Arabs, and the Ammonites. He fortified the walls of Jerusalem and built forts at strategic locations in the desert. He loved the soil and built cisterns to provide water for his livestock, farms, and vineyards.

He became famous and powerful, but his success was also his downfall. When he became strong, he became proud. He ignored the priestly laws regarding worship in the temple, and offered incense on the sacred altar. The high priest and eighty other priests had the courage to reprimand him: "It is the duty of the priests, who are descendants of Aaron, to offer incense, not the king. Get out of the holy place because you have sinned, and the Lord will not honor you."

Uzziah was furious with the high priest, but while he was ranting and raging, leprosy broke out on his forehead. The priests rushed him out of the temple; Uzziah wanted to leave because he knew the disease was the Lord's judgment. He lived in isolation and was banned from the temple for the rest of his life. Uzziah was buried in the cemetery of the kings but in a separate burial plot because of his leprosy.

His son Jotham was unable to keep the people from sinning. Like his father, he continued the construction of defensive fortifications in Jerusalem and Judah. He forced the Ammonites to pay an annual tribute and became powerful because he obeyed God.

Jotham's son Ahaz was evil. He followed the example of Israel's kings and worshiped Baal. He offered human sacrifices in the valley of Ben-Hinnom (south of Jerusalem), and he even sacrificed his own son, imitating the horrible sins of the pagan nations the Lord had driven from the land.

Because of his apostasy, Ahaz suffered terrible military losses. When threatened by Syria's King Rezin and Israel's King Pekah, Isaiah the prophet urged Ahaz to ask the Lord for help.

He refused: "No, I will not test the Lord by asking for a sign."

Isaiah rebuked Ahaz, saying, "Though you won't trust the Lord, he will not abandon his people. The virgin will conceive and give birth to a son. He will be called Immanuel, which means 'God with us!' "

(The New Testament writers consider this promise a prediction of the virgin birth of Jesus Christ.)

Ahaz was defeated by the Syrians, who took captives to Damascus, and Israel, who killed 120,000 of Judah's soldiers in a single day. In one battle, the king's son, palace commander, and second in command were killed; 200,000 women and children were captured and taken to Samaria.

When Israel's army arrived in Samaria with the prisoners, the prophet Obed met them and said, "The Lord God was angry with Judah and let you defeat them. But you have not shown them mercy, and God is watching you. Don't make them slaves; instead return them to their families."

Some of the leaders confronted the victorious soldiers and declared, "Don't bring the captives here! Don't make our guilt worse. It is already great, and the Lord is very angry with us!" The soldiers released the prisoners and returned the plunder. The leaders took clothes and sandals from the plunder and gave them to the prisoners who were naked. They gave them food and water and dressed their wounds. They placed the ones who couldn't walk on donkeys and brought them to their own people in Jericho.

Because Ahaz was so unfaithful to the Lord, there was no end of trouble for him. When the Edomites and the Philistines invaded Judah, Ahaz asked the king of Assyria for help, but the Assyrians, instead of attacking Ahaz's enemies, attacked Judah. Ahaz was forced to rob the temple and some of his own officials to pay tribute to the Assyrians.

Paying tribute didn't help, so Ahaz decided to worship the gods of Damascus (the Syrian capital city), since the Syrians had defeated him. But instead of strengthening Judah, the worship of foreign gods led to spiritual ruin. Ahaz closed the temple, set up altars to foreign gods on every street corner in Jerusalem, and offered sacrifices to other gods throughout Judah. This infuriated the Lord God, who had made a covenant with his people. When Ahaz died, he was buried in Jerusalem but not in the royal cemetery.

Hezekiah

Hezekiah became king when he was twenty-five and ruled for twenty-nine years. In contrast to his father, Ahaz, Hezekiah was godly and immediately began a process of restoring the worship of the Lord. His program of restoration was in three stages.

First, he reopened the temple and gave an inspiring speech to the priests and Levites on the terrible consequences of abandoning God: "The Lord was angry with Judah and Jerusalem and made them an appalling object of horror at which people hiss out their scorn, as you can see with your own eyes. Our fathers died violently and our families were carried off because of this. Now I intend to make a covenant with the Lord God of Israel, so that he may relent from his raging anger. My sons, do not be negligent now, for the Lord has chosen you to serve in his presence and offer sacrifices."

The Levites consecrated themselves and then began purifying and restoring the temple. All of the priests and Levites dedicated themselves to the work and completed the restoration in sixteen days. When they reported that the temple was ready for worship, the king organized a massive rededication service.

The priests offered sacrifices while the Levites played musical instruments and the people sang and worshiped the Lord. The response far exceeded the expectations of the priests. The people brought so many animals, the priests had to ask the Levites to help prepare them for sacrifice until more priests could be consecrated for service.

Hezekiah and the people were extremely happy about how quickly the temple had been restored and gave thanks to the Lord for what he had done.

In the second stage of his restoration, Hezekiah sent out an announcement to both Israel and Judah inviting them to a Passover celebration in Jerusalem. The response was so overwhelming that there was not enough time for the priests to purify themselves or for people to travel to Jerusalem; they had to delay the celebration for a month.

The runners Hezekiah sent carried a royal letter of invitation: "O

Israelites, return to the Lord God of Abraham, Isaac, and Jacob, and he will return to you. Now, don't be stubborn like your fathers who were unfaithful to the Lord. Submit to the Lord and come worship him at his sanctuary. If you return to him, he will show you mercy."

When the king's messengers went to the tribes of Ephraim and Manasseh in the north, most of the people mocked them; some, however, humbled themselves and went to Jerusalem. In Judah, the Lord moved the people's hearts to accept the king's invitation.

So many people traveled from remote locations that they were not able to ceremonially prepare themselves to celebrate Passover, so Hezekiah asked the Lord to accept their worship without ritual purification. The Lord answered his prayer because he knew the people honored him in their hearts. They celebrated for seven days and were so grateful for the opportunity to worship the Lord that they decided to continue another seven days.

There had not been a Passover celebration like this since the time of Solomon. The priests and Levites blessed the people, and God took note of their prayers.

In Hezekiah's third stage of restoration, when people returned to their homes, they destroyed their pagan idols and altars. Hezekiah made a personal contribution to temple worship and required the people to give a portion of their income to the priests and Levites. The people gave generously and brought so many offerings that the priests didn't have room to store the gifts.

Hezekiah ordered them to build new storerooms and put a Levite named Konaniah in charge of managing the offerings. The supplies were equitably distributed to the priests and Levites in Jerusalem and all the towns in Judah so they could fully devote themselves to serving the Lord. All of Hezekiah's efforts to follow God's commands pleased the Lord, and as a result of his wholehearted devotion, Hezekiah was highly successful.

Hezekiah was more than a religious reformer—he also knew Judah needed protection from foreign invaders. When Sennacherib of Assyria invaded and captured several fortified cities, Hezekiah realized the Assyrians intended to attack Jerusalem. He met with his military advisors and made plans to deny water for the Assyrian army. They reasoned, "Why should the king of Assyria come here and find plenty of water?"

Hezekiah organized workers to keep water from the fields around Jerusalem; he fortified weak sections in the city walls; he manufactured additional weapons to defend the city. To provide water for Jerusalem and deny water to the Assyrians, workers dug a tunnel from the Gihon spring outside the walls to the pool of Siloam inside the walls.

He encouraged the people to be strong and courageous: "Don't be afraid of the king of Assyria and his mighty army, for there is a greater power on our side! He may have a great army, but they are only human. We have the Lord our God to fight our battles!"

The king of Assyria attempted to intimidate Hezekiah into surrendering. He sent messengers who shouted in Hebrew to the defenders on the wall, "This is what Sennacherib says: 'What makes you think you can withstand the siege of Jerusalem? Hezekiah is misleading you. He has told you the Lord will deliver you. He won't. None of the gods of the other nations rescued those people from my power; why do you think your God will rescue you?' "

Instead of becoming paralyzed with fear, Hezekiah turned to the Lord in prayer. Both he and the prophet Isaiah cried out to the Lord for help. God sent an angel who destroyed the Assyrian army. Sennacherib was forced to return to Assyria in disgrace. When he went into the temple of his gods, his own sons killed him.

After the Lord delivered Jerusalem from the powerful Assyrians, other nations respected Hezekiah and honored the Lord by bringing gifts to Jerusalem.

Hezekiah faced a personal crisis when he became ill. Isaiah informed him that the disease was life-threatening: "This is what the Lord says: 'Prepare to die. You will not recover from this illness.' "

Unlike Ahaz, who refused to ask the Lord for help, Hezekiah wept and pleaded for mercy. Isaiah informed Hezekiah that the Lord had heard his prayer and taken note of his tears; he would add fifteen years to the king's life. He ordered Hezekiah's servants to make an ointment and put it on the infected area to promote healing. Hezekiah asked, "What is the confirming sign that I will be healed and able to worship in the temple?"

Isaiah said, "Look, the sun's shadow will move ten steps backward on the sundial of Ahaz." The shadow immediately went back ten steps. Hezekiah recovered from the illness and worshiped the Lord in the temple. (Chronological note: This account of Hezekiah's sickness is recorded after that of the siege of Jerusalem, but it's clear from 2 Kings 20:6 and Isaiah 38:6 that his illness preceded the siege.)

When the king of Babylon heard Hezekiah was ill, he sent envoys to wish Hezekiah well. Unfortunately, Hezekiah succumbed to pride and showed off the treasures in the temple and his palace; he showed everything of value in his whole kingdom.

His attempt to impress was a huge mistake. Isaiah confronted him and announced, "The time is coming when the Babylonians will carry away all of the valuable treasures in your palace and Judah. Even some of your own descendants will be taken into exile to serve the king of Babylon."

Hezekiah realized he had acted in pride and acknowledged that the Lord's judgment was just. He was grateful Judah would continue to enjoy peace during his lifetime.

Hezekiah's son was a wicked king. Manasseh deliberately and aggressively immersed himself in the terrible sins of the Canaanite nations that the Lord had driven out of the land. He rebuilt the pagan shrines Hezekiah had destroyed and set up altars for worship of Baal and Asherah. He worshiped the stars and made altars to them in the temple courtyard. He practiced human sacrifice, including his own son. He consulted with sorcerers and mediums. He led Judah into so much evil that the prophets warned that the Lord would bring judgment fierce enough to make the ears of those who heard tingle.

In addition, Manasseh murdered the prophets who tried to tell him the consequences of his outrageous apostasy. The consequences came quickly.

The Assyrians captured Manasseh. They put a hook in his nose, bound him with bronze chains, and took him to Babylon. In an amazing change of heart, Manasseh repented and humbled himself before the Lord. When he prayed, the Lord answered his plea for mercy. When Manasseh got back to the kingdom of Judah, he honored the Lord as the only true God.

After returning from captivity, Manasseh tried to restore the damage he had done. For protection against another invasion, he fortified the walls of Jerusalem. He initiated religious reforms, removing idols from the temple and throwing pagan altars in the trash dump outside the city. He built an altar and gave peace offerings and offerings of thanksgiving to the Lord. He urged people to worship God. People continued to worship at pagan shrines, but they only sacrificed to the Lord.

Manasseh was buried in the palace garden but not in the royal cemetery.

His son Amon was an evil king. Amon worshiped other gods, but unlike his father, he never repented of his apostasy. Instead of humbling himself, Amon became progressively sinful. After two years, his own officials assassinated him, but the people killed the officials and made Amon's son Josiah king.

Josiah

Josiah began his rule when he was only eight. By age sixteen, Josiah's love for the Lord became obvious to the people. When he was twenty, Josiah initiated a campaign to remove all remaining pagan idols and altars, and he ordered the bones of pagan priests burned on the altars to other gods. His purge was not limited to Judah. He destroyed altars and idols in the northern tribes of Manasseh, Ephraim, Simeon, and Naphtali.

Josiah did not leave Judah in a spiritual void. He commissioned

Shaphan and Joah to restore and refurbish the temple. To pay for the work, they gave money collected from all over Judah and Israel to Hilkiah, the high priest.

While bringing out some of the money, Hilkiah discovered the book of the law. Shaphan took the book (scroll) and read it to the king. When Josiah heard it, he tore his clothes in grief because he realized he and the people had not fulfilled their spiritual responsibilities to the Lord.

Josiah ordered Hilkiah and other officials to find out what they needed to do to obey the Law. They went to the prophetess Huldah, who resided in a suburb of Jerusalem. She had good news and bad news. Because of Judah's apostasy and idolatry, the Lord was going to bring judgment on Judah according to all the curses written in the Law. The good news was the impending judgment would be postponed until after Josiah's death.

When Hilkiah informed Josiah of Huldah's message, the king summoned the leaders and people of Judah to the temple. Josiah set the example for the nation to follow. After reading the book of the covenant, he pledged to obey the Lord's commands with all of his heart, and then he had all the people make the same pledge. For the remainder of Josiah's rule, the people were faithful to the Lord's covenant requirements.

As the final event of his religious reforms, Josiah organized a massive Passover celebration. He assigned the priests and Levites to their designated positions in the temple and instructed them to explain to the people the significance of Passover. He ordered them to leave the ark of the covenant in the temple and not carry it in procession as they had in the wilderness so that more Levites would be available for making sacrifices.

So that as many people as possible could participate in the festival, Josiah personally provided thirty thousand lambs and goats and three thousand cattle. His officials and the leaders of the Levites gave thousands more animals for the offerings. All the preparations and sacrifices were made exactly as prescribed by the law of Moses. The celebration lasted for seven days and was the largest Passover festival since the time of Samuel.

When Pharaoh Neco of Egypt attempted to pass through Judah to attack Babylon, Josiah made a fatal choice: He marched out to intercept them. Neco warned Josiah it was a mistake for him to fight the Egyptians. He said, "I am not attacking you! God told me to attack another kingdom. Do not oppose me, or God, who is with me, will destroy you."

Josiah refused to listen. He was mortally wounded in the battle and brought back to Jerusalem, where he died. The nation mourned his death, and Jeremiah the prophet composed a lament.

Josiah, the last godly king in Judah, had four sons. The people chose Jehoahaz as king, but he ruled for only three months. Pharaoh Neco removed him from power, forced Judah to pay tribute, placed Jehoahaz's brother Eliakim on the throne, and renamed him Jehoiakim. Jehoahaz was taken to Egypt as a prisoner.

Jehoiakim was evil and ruled eight years before being captured by Nebuchadnezzar, king of the Babylonians. At first Jehoiakim was a loyal subject, but then he rebelled. The Babylonians invaded Judah and put Jehoiakim in chains. Nebuchadnezzar took some of the valuable sacred items from the temple and put them in his palace in Babylon; he also took hostages, including Daniel and his friends. Jehoiakim either was released or escaped because he was buried outside of the gates of Jerusalem.

Jehoiachin was eighteen when he succeeded his father Jehoiakim. He was evil and ruled about three months before Nebuchadnezzar invaded a second time. Jehoiachin surrendered and was taken as a captive to Babylon, where he was a prisoner for thirty-seven years and then released.

Nebuchadnezzar plundered the temple and took ten thousand soldiers and skilled workers to Babylon. He placed Mattaniah, Jehoiachin's uncle, on the throne and changed his name to Zedekiah.

Zedekiah was evil and ruled eleven years. He rebelled against Babylon, and Nebuchadnezzar invaded Judah a third time. The Babylonian army surrounded Jerusalem and put the city under siege for eighteen months. When they broke through the walls, Zedekiah attempted to escape under the cover of darkness. He was captured near Jericho and taken to Nebuchadnezzar, whose headquarters was at Riblah (north of Damascus). They made Zedekiah watch the execution of his sons, and then they gouged out his eyes. He was placed in bronze chains and taken to Babylon.

Nebuchadnezzar sent the officer of his security guard to Jerusalem to totally destroy the city. He looted and burned the temple, the palace, and the important buildings. He ordered the army to destroy the city walls and took those who had not been killed in the siege as slaves to Babylon. He left a few of the poorest people to work the fields but took the high priest and other leaders to Riblah. Nebuchadnezzar ordered them all put to death.

Nebuchadnezzar appointed Gedaliah, a Judean, as governor of Judah. He assured the people they had nothing to fear and tried to convince them to serve the king of Babylon.

Ishmael, who was of royal descent, and some army officers conspired to assassinate Gedaliah. They killed him along with the Judeans and Babylonians at Mizpah. Fearing reprisals from the Babylonians, the conspirators fled to Egypt and forced Jeremiah the prophet to go with them.

When Evil-Merodach became king of Babylon, in the thirty-seventh year of the exile, he released Jehoiachin from prison and gave him special privileges, including eating with the king.

🎵 Chapter Summary

Rehoboam's egotistical response to the northern tribes led to the division of the kingdom. Now the king of Judah (the southern kingdom), he incited Judah to worship other gods and reintroduced the detestable practices of the nations the Lord had driven from the land.

Most of the southern kings followed Rehoboam's evil example, abandoning the Lord despite prophetic warnings.

Though his father Jehoshaphat was a godly ruler, Jehoram did not honor the Lord and lost control of vast amounts of territory.

Manasseh was incredibly evil; God's judgment on him was swift and severe. While in captivity, Manasseh repented and the Lord allowed him to return to rule in Judah.

A few southern kings made the mistake of forming military alliances with pagan kings for protection.

Uzziah and Hezekiah were remarkable, successful leaders who were faithful to the Lord. During his fifty-two-year rule, Uzziah expanded the kingdom, fortified Jerusalem, reorganized the army, and developed a water supply for farming in the desert.

With Isaiah's help, Hezekiah undertook some of greatest reforms in Judah's history. He commanded the priests to repair and reopen the temple, organized a massive Passover festival, and challenged people in both Judah and Israel to destroy their idols.

After Josiah's godly rule, Judah went into a freefall that ended with the exile. The Babylonians, under Nebuchadnezzar, invaded Judah three times. The third time they captured Jerusalem, looted and burned the temple, destroyed strategic buildings, and broke down defensive walls. Most of the people were taken to Babylon as captives.

Twelve

GOD'S PEOPLE IN EXILE

Main Characters
Kings of Babylonia and Persia
Daniel
Shadrach, Meshach, and Abednego
Zerubbabel
Ezra
Esther
Mordecai
Haman
Nehemiah

Setting
Babylonia (modern-day Iraq)
Babylon (capital of Babylonia)
Persia (modern-day Iran)
City of Susa (winter palace of the king of Persia)
Jerusalem

DANIEL AND HIS FRIENDS

After a two-year siege, the Babylonians breached the walls of Jerusalem, looted the temple, and destroyed the city. They executed the king's sons and blinded Zedekiah. They took him and many thousands of Jews as captives to Babylon, which became the new home for the Jews of the exile.

The exile had actually begun years earlier when Nebuchadnezzar invaded Judah for the first time. He had forced the king of Judah to pay tribute and taken some of the royal family and nobility as hostages. From among the captives, Daniel and three of his young friends were chosen to train for service in the court of Nebuchadnezzar in Babylon.

While in the royal college, the young men were privileged to eat the lavish food served to the king but refused because it would have defiled them, according to Jewish law. Instead they asked the official in charge of their training for permission to eat the food of their own choosing and then evaluate their health. He agreed to a ten-day test period and was surprised to discover they were in better health than the other trainees.

The official soon discovered that Daniel and his friends were gifted, and they advanced ahead of the other men in training. God endowed them with knowledge and understanding, and to Daniel he gave the ability to interpret dreams and visions.

They graduated with the highest honors. Nebuchadnezzar questioned them and found them far wiser than all the other royal advisors.

In the second year of his rule, Nebuchadnezzar had a perplexing dream and demanded that his advisors interpret it, though he doubted their ability to honestly do so. The king threatened to execute all of them if they didn't interpret it correctly. Daniel informed his friends of the threat and urged them to ask God to reveal the mystery. God answered their prayer in a vision to Daniel.

Daniel reported to Nebuchadnezzar that his God had revealed the dream. Nebuchadnezzar had dreamed of a large statue containing different metals. Nebuchadnezzar was the head of gold. The other metals represented other kingdoms that would rise and fall. In the end the entire statue was crushed by a stone representing the kingdom of God.

Nebuchadnezzar was so impressed that he recognized the God Daniel worshiped as the highest of all the gods. He made Daniel the governor of the province of Babylon and put him in charge of all the other royal advisors.

Nebuchadnezzar praised Daniel's God, but he promoted himself. He ordered the construction of a ninety-foot golden statue and summoned all government officials to the dedication ceremony. When Shadrach, Meshach, and Abednego found out they would be expected to worship the statue as a god, they refused to attend.

It was reported to Nebuchadnezzar that these Jews refused to obey his decree, and he flew into a rage. He warned them and said he would give them another chance. If they still refused to worship the statue, they would immediately be thrown into a blazing furnace, and, he said, "No god would be able to rescue them."

The men replied, "If we are thrown into a blazing furnace, then our God will rescue us; if not, you can be assured we will never worship your gods or the statue."

Their defiance made Nebuchadnezzar so angry his face was distorted with fury. He ordered the furnace heated seven times hotter. It was so hot that the men who threw Shadrach, Meshach, and Abednego into it died from its heat.

When Nebuchadnezzar looked in the furnace, though, he jumped up from his throne in amazement. He saw four men walking in the furnace; the fourth man looked like a god. He shouted to Shadrach, Meshach, and Abednego and told them to come out. They didn't have a single burn mark on them. Not even the hair on their heads was singed.

Nebuchadnezzar praised the God of Shadrach, Meshach, and Abednego and issued a decree that if anyone cursed their God, he would be torn limb from limb. He said, "There is no other god who could have rescued these men from the blazing furnace."

Though he never stopped worshiping the gods of Babylon, Nebuchadnezzar continued to respect Daniel's God. He even issued a decree to his entire empire honoring the Lord as the Most High God.

Nebuchadnezzar had a terrifying dream that no one but Daniel could explain. Daniel said it was a warning from God because of Nebuchadnezzar's arrogance and cruelty: "Stop sinning and be merciful to the poor and the oppressed."

Daniel told the king that if he abandoned his wicked past, perhaps the Lord would have mercy on him. If he didn't, Daniel said Nebuchadnezzar would be inflicted with a disease that would cause him to lose his sanity for a period of time and act like an animal.

Daniel's prediction came true. Nebuchadnezzar was forced to give up his rule, but after his sanity returned he was restored as head of his kingdom. His decree read, "I, Nebuchadnezzar, praise the God of heaven, who is able to humble the proud."

Even after Nebuchadnezzar's death, Daniel continued to advise Babylon's rulers. During the first year of King Belshazzar's rule, Daniel saw in a vision four vicious beasts arise out of the sea. The first was a lion with eagle's wings; the second a lopsided bear with three ribs in its mouth; the third a leopard with wings; the fourth a monster with iron teeth and ten horns. Three horns were uprooted by a larger horn with eyes and a mouth.

In the vision, the Ancient of Days (God) destroyed all the beasts and set up his everlasting reign. The beasts symbolized various kingdoms of this world that oppressed the people of God. God eventually will overthrow the kingdoms of this world, and God's people will rule with him in his kingdom forever.

Daniel had another vision in Belshazzar's third year. He saw a ram with two horns standing on the banks of a river. The ram charged unchallenged in all directions until a male goat came from the west and trampled it to death. The horn of the goat was broken and replaced by four horns. One of the horns grew large and attacked a holy sanctuary.

God sent the angel Gabriel to explain the vision to Daniel. The ram, the goat, and the horn represented earthly kingdoms. The kingdom of the horn would inflict terrible destruction on the people of God, but would suddenly be destroyed by a divine prince.

Daniel warned Belshazzar that his empire was about to come to an end. Thinking that Babylon with its massive defenses was invincible, Belshazzar invited a thousand of his officials and their wives to a drunken orgy.

He planned to use the sacred vessels captured from the temple in Jerusalem for his wild party, but when they began to drink, the fingers of a human hand began to write on the wall: MENE, MENE, TEKEL, PARSIN. The terrified king asked his diviners and magicians to interpret the message and offered them a huge reward. When they couldn't, the queen remembered that Daniel could interpret dreams.

Daniel wasn't interested in the reward but explained the cryptic message. He said Belshazzar was arrogant and had insulted the Most High God by using the sacred vessels to toast the gods of the Babylonians. Daniel said, "Your days are numbered. You have been weighed in the scales of divine justice and found deficient. Your kingdom is doomed."

That night the Medes and the Persians captured the city, and Belshazzar was killed.

Daniel continued to serve as senior administrator. He so effectively and loyally distinguished himself that Darius, king of Persia, planned to put him in charge of his entire empire. This made the other administrators jealous of Daniel, and they tried to find a way to discredit him.

Unable to uncover any fraud in his official duties, they plotted to incriminate Daniel because of his devotion to his God. They persuaded the king to issue a decree prohibiting anyone from worshiping his god for thirty days. Daniel defied the king's command and continued to pray to God three times a day.

Daniel's enemies informed the king. Realizing he had been set up, Darius tried to find a way to save Daniel but had to follow his own edict. Daniel was thrown to the lions, while Darius hoped he would somehow survive. He said, "May your God rescue you!"

Darius worried all night about Daniel and rushed to the lion's den early the next morning. He called to Daniel from outside the den: "Daniel, has the God whom you serve protected you?" Daniel answered, "My God sent an angel to protect me from the lions. I have not been disloyal to you or to my God." The relieved king ordered Daniel released.

Darius had Daniel's enemies arrested and fed to the lions, and he issued a public proclamation acknowledging the God of Daniel: "The God of Daniel is the living God, who rules over an everlasting kingdom. He delivers those who trust him as he has rescued Daniel from the lions."

If Daniel was in his teens when he was deported to Babylon as a hostage, he would have been in his eighties when Cyrus became ruler of Persia. Though Daniel never returned to his own country, he never lost hope that God would restore his people to the Promised Land and that he had a future for the people of Israel.

While reading from Jeremiah, Daniel observed that the prophet had predicted the captivity would last only seventy years. Realizing that the years were almost fulfilled, Daniel prayed and confessed the sins of his people as if they were his own sins. He acknowledged that God is just and righteous. He was confident God would keep his promises to Israel.

Before he finished praying, the Lord sent the angel Gabriel to inform Daniel about the future of Israel. The message focused on the number seventy and the coming of an individual identified as "the anointed one." It gave assurance to Daniel that God had not abandoned his people and that he had a definite plan for Israel.

After Daniel had spent three weeks in prayer and fasting, a divine messenger gave the elder statesman a preview of future events. The messenger described future rulers and the rise and fall of empires. The vision gave assurance that God cares for his people, and ended with a personal promise that Daniel would one day be resurrected from the dead.

REBUILDING THE TEMPLE

Cyrus, king of Persia, had been on the throne less than a year when he proclaimed that the Lord, the God of heaven, had motivated him to rebuild the temple in Jerusalem. He made a decree allowing any willing

Israelites to return to their homeland, encouraging those who didn't want to return to give money and supplies.

Meanwhile, God was stirring up the hearts of the leaders of Benjamin, Judah, and Levi to go back right away and get started. Everyone who decided not to go helped them with provisions and gifts, as Cyrus had instructed. King Cyrus himself even donated the gold and silver trays and bowls that had been taken from the temple by Nebuchadnezzar.

Led by Zerubbabel, 42,360 Israelites made the trip, and thousands of servants and singers came with them. There were even some who went along but couldn't prove they had Jewish blood. There were some who claimed to be priests but couldn't prove their lineage; the leaders decided not to let them serve as priests until their heritage could be proven. Hundreds of horses, mules, and camels came along, as did thousands of donkeys. They brought hundreds of thousands of dollars' worth of gold, silver, and priestly robes.

The priests, Levites, and some of the common people settled in and around Jerusalem, and the rest of the people returned to the places in Judah from which they'd originally come.

In the seventh month of the year, everyone who came back to Judah gathered in Jerusalem. Then Jeshua and his fellow priests and Zerubbabel and his family rebuilt the altar on its old site and burned sacrifices on it, exactly the way the law of Moses told them to. They sacrificed morning and evening and kept all the special celebrations and rituals, though they were afraid of the non-Israelites who still lived in the area.

They hired bricklayers and carpenters from among the locals (non-Israelites) of Tyre and Sidon, paying them with food, oil, and wine. These people helped them ship cedar logs from Lebanon down to Jerusalem, which Cyrus had authorized in his grant.

After gathering supplies, the actual construction of the temple began in the second month of the second year after their arrival. Everyone over twenty years old helped out; Zerubbabel, the governor of Jerusalem, and Jeshua, the high priest, managed the project. Once the foundation was laid, they had a big celebration with singing and shouting and cymbal crashing. But some of the older people, who still remembered Solomon's beautiful temple that had been destroyed, mourned. It was impossible to distinguish the weeping from the shouts of joy.

Now when the enemies of Judah and Bethlehem heard the news about the return of the Jews and the rebuilding of the temple, they came to Zerubbabel and other leaders and offered to help. They claimed they were just as interested in the Jewish God as the Jews, saying they'd sacrificed to him ever since they'd been relocated there by Esarhaddon, former king of Assyria. But Zerubbabel and Jeshua said no. The temple needed to be built by the Israelites, just like Cyrus had said.

So these people tried to frighten and discourage the Israelites by writing letters and sending others to tell lies to Cyrus about them. This went on throughout Cyrus's entire reign and kept going through the reigns of several other Persian rulers.

Their tactics finally worked; the king halted the rebuilding. Leaders from around the empire joined together in saying that once the Jews finished their rebuilding, they would stop paying their taxes. To bolster their argument, they told the king to look back in Jerusalem's historical records to confirm that the city had rebellious, seditious tendencies.

When the king looked, he agreed and told the letter-writers to use force to make the Jews stop building immediately until further notice. Further notice didn't come until the reign of King Darius.

Finally, when Darius was in his second year as king of Persia, the prophets Haggai and Zechariah preached messages to Zerubbabel and Jeshua urging the people to get back to work. Soon after they had started up again, Tattenai, the governor of the province, demanded to know who had authorized them to rebuild the temple. The governor also made them name names, making a list of everyone involved with the project. But the Israelites kept building until King Darius could personally look into the matter.

Tattenai told Darius what was happening, including how the Jews had answered his questions. They had told him God had been working through their history, and that many years ago Cyrus had given an official order to rebuild the temple. Tattenai asked Darius to look into it himself.

Darius did look into it and, after a search of the royal archives, found Cyrus's decree. Darius sent a message to Tattenai, telling him that the Israelites could continue rebuilding. Better still, he also told Tattenai to pay the cost of reconstruction himself out of the taxes he had raised. He also made the governor donate sacrificial animals and told him to have the Israelites pray for Darius and his sons. Anyone who disobeyed Darius's decree would be hanged from beams pulled down from his own house.

The Jews were encouraged and continued to rebuild, finally finishing the temple in Darius's sixth year on the throne. They had a huge celebration and offered many sacrifices. The Passover was celebrated that year, after the Levites had consecrated themselves. Meanwhile, many of the local non-Jewish residents turned from their immoral ways and worshiped the Lord.

ESTHER

In the third year of his rule, King Xerxes of Persia sponsored a 180-day royal celebration to show off the great wealth he'd accumulated in his conquests. At the end he held a seven-day banquet in his garden for every man in his city regardless of rank.

The garden was elegant with white and violet linen curtains on silver rods and marble pillars. There were gold and silver couches on a marble, pearl-like floor. Everyone drank from golden cups and could drink as much as they wanted. Meanwhile, Queen Vashti held a banquet for the women of the palace.

On the seventh day of the king's banquet, when Xerxes was drunk, he ordered seven eunuchs to bring the queen, wearing her royal crown, to his party. He wanted the nobles and officials to see how beautiful she was, but Vashti refused his summons.

Xerxes, outraged, consulted with his closest advisors. An official named Memucan spoke up: "Not only has Queen Vashti wronged the king, but she's wronged all the rest of us as well. When other women hear what she's done, they'll start disobeying their husbands! What you should do is issue a royal decree saying that Vashti can never appear before you again, and then give her position to a more worthy woman."

Xerxes approved of this plan and issued the decree. Soon his advisors told him he should start searching for an attractive young replacement: "Appoint assistants to scour the provinces for beautiful young virgins. Then have your eunuch get them ready for you to judge. Whoever pleases you will become your new queen." The king agreed.

Meanwhile, in the walled city of the king lived a Jew named Mordecai. Mordecai had adopted his cousin Hadassah, also known as Esther, because her parents had died.

Esther was very beautiful and was taken to Hegai, the king's eunuch. She became a favorite of Hegai's, and he gave her special food, servants, beauty treatments, and the best rooms in the women's quarters.

Mordecai had told Esther not to tell anyone she was a Jewish exile. Every day he walked back and forth in front of the women's quarters to check up on her. The beauty treatment for the women lasted twelve months: six months of myrrh and oil, six months of perfume. Once this was completed, the woman would visit the king, with whom she would spend the night. She would only get a second visit if he requested it.

When it was Esther's turn, the king loved her more than all the others and placed the royal crown on her head. He ordered a royal banquet in her honor and invited all his officials, even declaring the day a holiday and handing out gifts.

Mordecai continued to linger at the king's gate. One day he found out that two of Xerxes' eunuchs were plotting to kill the king. Mordecai told Esther, who told the king. Investigators discovered that what Mordecai had said was true, and the eunuchs were impaled on a pole. This event was documented in the official daily records.

Some time later, King Xerxes promoted a man named Haman to a position higher than anyone else but himself. The king commanded all the other advisors to bow to Haman with their faces against the ground. Everyone bowed except Mordecai.

The king's advisors asked Mordecai why he disobeyed the king's command, but he ignored them, so they told Haman. Haman was furious. Rather than kill only Mordecai, he decided to destroy all the Jews in the kingdom to get revenge on him.

Haman said to the king, "There is a certain nationality scattered throughout your kingdom that hasn't mixed with the others. They have their own laws and do not obey your commands. You should write a decree to destroy them. I'll even pay 750,000 pounds of silver to see that it's done."

The king gave his signet ring to Haman and said, "Keep your money; do what you like to these people."

Haman's orders were written down, sealed with the king's ring, and sent to all the rulers and officials of the empire. The people were ordered to kill all the Jews, young and old, men, women, and children, on a certain day in the near future, and were told they could confiscate the property of those they killed.

When Mordecai found out, he tore his clothes, put on sackcloth, and wept in the streets. Jews mourned in all the provinces, fasting and sleeping on sackcloth and ashes. Queen Esther didn't hear the news at first, but when she heard that Mordecai was in sackcloth, she was shocked.

She sent clothes to him, but he refused to wear them. She called for Hathak, a eunuch who served her, telling him to learn from Mordecai what was happening. Mordecai told him and said that Esther should beg the king for mercy for her people.

Esther sent a message back, saying that everyone knows no one is allowed to approach the king without being summoned. She hadn't been summoned in thirty days.

Mordecai answered, "Just because you're in the king's palace doesn't mean you'll be safe either. Even if you remain silent, after you and your family are killed someone else will come along to save the Jews. And who knows, maybe you were placed in your position for a time just like this."

Esther sent a message back: "Gather all the Jews in the city. Fast for three days. My servants and I will fast too. Afterward, I'll go to the king. If I die, I die."

After three days of fasting, Esther put on her robes and went to see the king. As soon as he saw her he held out his scepter in welcome. "What's bothering you?" he asked. "I'll give you anything—up to half the kingdom."

"Please come to a special dinner I'm preparing for you and Haman," she answered.

As they were drinking at dinner, the king asked Esther a second time what she wanted. She asked him to come to another dinner she was preparing for him and Haman the next day. She told him that was when she'd tell him what she wanted.

Haman left feeling good about being invited to these special dinners, but as soon as he saw the fearless Mordecai outside the king's gate, he became furious. He sent for his friends and his wife. He boasted to them about his riches and his power and the special dinner he was to have with Xerxes and Esther, but seeing Mordecai at the king's gate was ruining everything. Haman's wife and friends suggested they put up a seventy-five-foot pole and ask the king in the morning to hang Mordecai on it. Haman loved this plan.

Meanwhile, when King Xerxes was having trouble sleeping, he had a servant read the official daily records to him. He read what Mordecai had done to save him from the assassination plot.

"What did I do to reward him for this?" the king asked.

The servant answered that nothing had been done.

Haman happened to be in the courtyard at that moment, so the king ushered him in. "What should I do for a person I want to reward?" Xerxes asked him.

Haman, in his pride, thought the king was talking about him. He suggested Xerxes give the man royal clothes and the king's horse to parade around the city square as servants shouted that this is what the king does for people he wishes to reward.

"Do this for Mordecai the Jew," Xerxes ordered.

Haman did as he was told but went home in despair. When he told his wife and friends what had happened, they said, "If this man is Jewish, you will never be able to destroy him, and you will suffer great loss if you oppose him."

That evening at dinner the king again asked Esther what she would have him do for her. She answered, "Spare my life and the lives of my people. If they were only going to be enslaved, I'd have kept quiet. But they are to be exterminated."

King Xerxes interrupted her. "Who dares to do such a thing!"

"Our enemy is the wicked Haman!" Esther answered.

The king was furious, and Haman was terrified. As Xerxes left the room, Haman begged Esther to spare him, falling on the couch she lay on. When the king came back and saw Haman on the couch, it looked like he was trying to rape Esther. This made him even angrier.

One of the eunuchs mentioned to the king that Haman had built a tall pole for hanging Mordecai.

"Hang Haman on it!" the king commanded. The servants obeyed by hanging Haman on the pole. The king also gave Haman's property to Esther. She told him that she was related to Mordecai, and so the king met with Mordecai and gave him the signet ring he'd earlier given to Haman. Esther gave Haman's property to Mordecai.

But they still had to deal with the upcoming day of evil against the Jews. When Esther begged Xerxes to cancel the order to destroy them, the king told Esther and Mordecai to write a new decree as they saw fit and use the signet ring to seal it.

In Xerxes' name, Mordecai wrote that on the appointed day the Jews would be allowed to defend themselves. The document was sent by messenger on the king's fastest horses to all the provinces. The Jews celebrated. In fact, many other people pretended to be Jews because they were scared of them.

On the day that Haman had selected for destroying the Jews, the Jews defeated their enemies. No one could stand against them because all the people had become terrified of God's people. All the officials and leaders fought alongside the Jews for fear of Mordecai and the power he now wielded in the palace.

In every province the Jews killed those who attacked them, including Haman's ten sons. Esther asked the king to allow a second day of battle against the Jews' enemies, and the king agreed. He even gave the Jews permission to hang Haman's sons on poles.

The Jews again destroyed their enemies, but they did not take their possessions. Afterward, they rested and celebrated. Mordecai established these two days as a yearly holiday to be filled with feasting and giving gifts, especially to the poor. (This is the Jewish Feast of Purim.)

NEHEMIAH AND THE WALLS OF JERUSALEM

Nehemiah, one of the Jews in exile, served as cupbearer to Artaxerxes, now king of Persia. In the king's twentieth year as ruler, Nehemiah's brother returned from a trip to Jerusalem. Nehemiah asked how the Jews were faring back home, and the answer was discouraging: "The survivors are oppressed and insulted. The walls of Jerusalem are broken down and the gates have been burned to the ground."

When Nehemiah heard this he mourned for days, fasting and praying to God, asking God to keep his promise that if his people repented, he would restore them to their homeland. The king noticed Nehemiah was sad, so he asked what was troubling him.

"May the king live forever," said Nehemiah. "But why shouldn't I be sad when my homeland is in ruins?"

"What would you like?" Artaxerxes asked.

Nehemiah prayed, and then said, "If it pleases you, let me go to Jerusalem so I can rebuild it."

"How long will you be gone, and when will you return?" the king asked.

Nehemiah answered, and the king agreed to let him go. Then Nehemiah asked one more thing: "Could you also give me letters addressed to the rulers of the provinces along the way to guarantee me safe passage? Also, I'd like a letter to the supervisor of your forest to let me have wood for the gates, city wall, and my own house."

Surprisingly, the king agreed. Nehemiah trusted in God, who helped him.

The king also sent army officers and cavalry with Nehemiah for protection on the dangerous journey to Jerusalem. On arrival in Judea, Nehemiah went to the governors of the provinces and gave them the letters. Two men, Sanballat the Horonite and Tobiah the Ammonite, felt threatened by Nehemiah's arrival and were angry that the king had authorized such an important person to help the Jews rebuild the walls of Jerusalem.

Nehemiah went to Jerusalem and stayed three days. Without telling anyone what he was doing or why he'd come, he went out by night with a few men to inspect the walls.

After he had assessed the city's condition, Nehemiah told the Jewish leaders and the priests how God had helped him get permission for rebuilding. Convinced that God was with him, the leaders responded immediately and encouraged each other to get started.

When Sanballat and Tobiah heard about this, they began to mock the Israelites. "Do you think you can rebel against the king?" they asked.

"The God of heaven will help us succeed," Nehemiah answered. "You have no right to this land."

The workers began by rebuilding the Sheep Gate, dedicating it and setting its doors in place. They moved on to other gates and towers, with various workers, priests, and supervisors using their skills to repair and rebuild. Many of the workers repaired sections of the wall that were near their own homes. Unfortunately, the prideful nobles wouldn't work under supervisors.

Sanballat continued to harangue the Jewish builders in front of his allies and a Samaritan army who had come to watch. "What are these ridiculous Jews doing? Are they going to offer sacrifices? Do they think the burned stones that are in the garbage piles are strong enough to use for the walls?"

Tobiah added, "Even a fox could knock that wall down by walking on it!"

Nehemiah prayed to God, asking him to turn the insults around because these men were insulting God himself.

As progress on the wall was made, Israel's enemies—Sanballat, Tobiah, the Arabs, and the Ammonites—became even more furious. They planned to attack Jerusalem to slow the Israelites down. Nehemiah prayed for protection and appointed guards to watch the walls day and night.

After a while the Jews became tired, and at the same time their enemies plotted to attack and kill them. The Jews who lived among their enemies became aware of their plans and let the builders know about them. So Nehemiah organized people by families, arming them and positioning them in places where the wall was weakest. He said, "Don't be afraid of them. Remember the power of the Lord and fight for your families!"

The enemies of the Jews found out that their schemes were known and didn't attack. From that point on, half the Jews continued rebuilding the wall, and half served as armed guards to protect them. Many of the men held swords in one hand while they built with the other. Since the wall was long and the workers were spread out along it, Nehemiah set up men with trumpets to sound the alarm to gather the men together if any portion of the wall was attacked. The men stayed day and night, working by day and guarding the wall by night. Many of Nehemiah's men never even had the chance to change their clothes.

Some of the men and their wives began complaining, saying they didn't have enough to eat. They had to borrow money to pay the king's taxes and even sell their children to the Jewish leaders as slaves.

Nehemiah grew angry with the nobles and leaders when he heard about this. "How can you treat your own people this way? You shouldn't be charging them interest and selling them as slaves! You should live in fear of God rather than giving our enemies an opportunity to mock us." The leaders agreed.

During Nehemiah's twelve years as leader of the returnees, he and his brothers never ate food from the governor's food allowance; the previous leaders and their servants had taken the food for themselves in addition to charging the people taxes. Because Nehemiah feared God, he worked hard and made sure everyone had food and other necessities. He adamantly refused to allow officials to prosper at the people's expense.

When Sanballat, Tobiah, and other enemies heard that the wall was completed and no longer had gaps, except for the doors of the city gates, they asked Nehemiah four times to meet them on the plain of Ono. They were planning an attack.

Nehemiah repeatedly told them he was still busy with the project and didn't have time for them. On the fifth time they sent an additional message: "Word has spread that you and the Jews are rebelling against the Persians. You've set prophets up to announce that there's a king in Judah. This news will get back to the king, so we should get together to talk about it." Nehemiah said their accusations were absurd.

One day Nehemiah went to the house of a man named Shemaiah, who asked Nehemiah to come with him to the temple and close the doors—he said some men were plotting to kill him that night. Nehemiah refused to run away, realizing that Shemaiah was being used by Sanballat and Tobiah to intimidate him and cause him to sin by entering the temple. There were other Jewish traitors also working with Tobiah.

The wall was completed in fifty-two days despite the opposition and intimidation. When it was done, the Jews' enemies became afraid, for God had helped the builders.

Once the wall was built, the gatekeepers, singers, and Levites were given jobs. Nehemiah put his brother Hanani in charge of Jerusalem, alongside Hananiah, the governor of the citadel; they both feared God. Nehemiah also told them to post guards and to close the gates during the heat of the day, when gatekeepers might be resting.

Not many people lived in the city at that time, as homes had not yet been rebuilt. Nehemiah gathered everyone together to read from ancient documents so the people could determine their genealogies. Some of the Jews couldn't prove their heritage, so they had to stop eating the holy food from the temple until a priest could determine whether or not they were true Israelites.

The total number of Jews assembled was 42,360, plus 7,337 servants and 245 singers. They also had 736 horses, 245 mules, 435 camels, and 6,720 donkeys. Many of the heads of families donated money, bowls, and robes for the treasury. Afterward everyone settled back in their own cities.

Several months later all the people gathered in the courtyard by the Water Gate. They brought out the book of Moses' teachings; Ezra the priest read to all the men, women, and children from dawn until noon. When he opened the book, everyone stood up. Ezra thanked the Lord God, and all the people shouted, "Amen!" and raised their hands and bowed their faces to the ground in worship of the Lord. Not only did they read the Word of God, but the Levites also explained it to the gathered crowd.

As the book was read the people began crying. But Nehemiah, Ezra, and the Levites told them not to. "This is a holy day. Go and celebrate with feasting and drinking, also giving food and drink to those who don't have enough. Be strong in the joy of the Lord!" The people obeyed and had a huge celebration because of the words of the Lord.

The next day the leaders gathered with Ezra to study again. They discovered that God had declared a festival in the seventh month, which they were in. They were to live in booths made of branches of olive, myrtle, palm, and other thick-leaved trees. They celebrated for seven days, all the while continuing to read God's teachings.

Later that month the Jews fasted, wearing sackcloth and throwing dust on their heads. The Israelites separated themselves from all foreigners and confessed their sins along with the sins of their ancestors. They worshiped the Lord with Levites leading them to stand up and thank him in prayer.

Their prayers told of how God had taken care of his people through history, how the people had rebelled, and how he'd restored them again. Then everyone who was old enough to understand took an oath before God to live by his commandments regarding marrying foreigners, offering sacrifices, celebrating feasts, and taking care of the temple.

The Jewish leaders settled in Jerusalem, and the rest of the people drew lots so that one out of every ten would move into the city. Many also volunteered to move there. When it was time for the walls to be dedicated, they gathered the Levites to help celebrate with singing and instruments.

The priests and Levites cleansed themselves and the people, along with the gates and the wall. Nehemiah placed leaders on the wall and set up two choirs to give thanks and march through Jerusalem in a parade.

Nehemiah, the leaders, and the choirs all met together in the temple. They offered sacrifices and rejoiced so loudly it could be heard from a great distance. That day they also arranged the storerooms and organized the distribution of food and gifts for the priests and Levites who were doing God's work.

Once again the book of Moses was read in front of the assembled crowd. They heard the stories about how the Moabites and Ammonites had hired Balaam to curse Israel when they were in the wilderness on their way to the Promised Land. When the people heard that, they immediately banned all foreigners from assembling in the temple.

Nehemiah had to return to King Artaxerxes as he'd promised, but then he asked for the king's permission to go back to Jerusalem. When he returned to Jerusalem, he discovered that Tobiah (a foreigner) had been given one of the storage rooms in the temple by one of his relatives, the priest Eliashib.

Nehemiah was furious. He removed Tobiah's belongings and told people to clean the room and return the temple utensils to it. To make matters worse, Nehemiah also learned that the Levites were not being supported according to Moses' law. They were forced by necessity to abandon their temple duties and work their own fields in order to survive. Nehemiah summoned the Levites back and made the people bring grain, wine, and olive oil for their support. He also set up new management to take care of the distribution of goods.

Nehemiah knew that he was making radical reforms, so he asked God for his help. "Remember my work for you and help me according to your compassion and unfailing love, O Lord," he prayed.

The temple and its workers weren't the only things malfunctioning upon Nehemiah's return. When he also observed labor and commerce happening on the Sabbath, he scolded the leaders of Judah, telling them this was one of the reasons God had punished Israel in the first place. He ordered the gates of Jerusalem to be shut for the day of worship so that people wouldn't be carrying loads in and out and selling goods. He also wouldn't let merchants spend the night outside the walls, waiting for the gates to open.

Nehemiah also scolded and beat Jews who had married foreign women, especially since they were not teaching their children their Jewish heritage. Nehemiah warned them that intermarrying like this had led their ancestors into sin. He made them swear they would never allow their children to marry unbelieving foreigners.

Nehemiah made certain the people had removed every pagan object from their homes and the temple. He organized the priests and Levites so they met the requirements of the Law when leading the people in worship. He offered a personal prayer asking the Lord to remember him for his courageous effort to honor him.

◊ Chapter Summary

When the Babylonians invaded Judah, Daniel and other nobility were taken as hostages. Daniel and his friends would serve as special advisors; Daniel distinguished himself with Babylonian and Persian rulers as a man mightily blessed by God. He interpreted cryptic dreams and saw the future for Israel and the world.

King Cyrus of Persia issued a decree allowing captive people to return to their homelands and worship their gods. Thousands of Jews returned to Judea.

The returnees focused on restoring worship of the Lord, and soon they began rebuilding the temple. Through opposition and difficulty, the Lord sent Haggai and Zechariah to encourage them to complete what they had started. When finished, the Jews dedicated the temple to the Lord and celebrated Passover.

Many Jews remained in exile under Persian rule rather than return to their land. Under Xerxes, Esther became queen and, along with her cousin Mordecai, helped to save Jews in the empire from being exterminated.

Nehemiah, cupbearer to Artaxerxes of Persia, asked the king for permission to go back to repair Jerusalem's city walls. Against harassment and stiff opposition, he and his workers finished the walls in fifty-two days with God's help.

Though the city was now protected by walls, the Jewish leaders were concerned about the spiritual life of the returnees. They asked Ezra, an expert in Jewish law, to read from the law of Moses. Afterward the people rededicated themselves to the Lord, and Nehemiah demanded they honor God in worship and marriage.

Thirteen

BIRTH AND CHILDHOOD OF JESUS

Main Characters

Zechariah and Elizabeth
Gabriel
John the Baptist
Mary and Joseph
Jesus (Messiah)
Wise men (Gentiles from the east)
Herod the Great

Setting

Land of Israel
Galilee (province in the north)
Nazareth (town in Galilee)
Judea (province in the south)
Jerusalem (capital of Israel, in Judea; location of the temple)
Bethlehem (seven miles south of Jerusalem)
Egypt

PREPARING FOR JESUS' BIRTH

The birth of Jesus fulfilled the promises God had made to Abraham and David.

God had promised to bless Abraham, make him the father of a great nation, and bring a blessing to all people through him. As a descendant of Abraham, Jesus Christ came to bring salvation to the entire world.

Christ was also in the line of David and fulfilled the promise that one of David's descendants would rule forever.

Four hundred years passed from the time of Malachi, the last Old Testament prophet, to the coming of John the Baptist. John came as a prophet to announce the coming of the Messiah, Jesus Christ.

John was born to Zechariah and Elizabeth when Herod was king of Judea. Zechariah was a priest and served in the temple in Jerusalem. He and Elizabeth were older and had been faithful to the Lord all their lives. They did not have any children.

While Zechariah was on duty, he was startled to see an angel from the Lord standing next to the incense altar. Gabriel said, "Don't be afraid, Zechariah. The Lord has answered your prayer. Elizabeth will give birth to a son, and you are to name him John."

Gabriel told Zechariah that John would bring them joy and that he would have the power of the Holy Spirit from birth. John's mission was to prepare Israel for the coming of the Lord by calling on them to return to their God.

Gabriel's message was astounding. Zechariah asked, "How can I be sure of this? I am old, and so is my wife."

Gabriel said the Lord had sent him to announce this good news to Zechariah, and because Zechariah didn't believe it he would not be able to speak until it came true.

Zechariah stayed so long in the temple that the people began to wonder what had happened to him. When he came out he could only make signs; he couldn't speak.

He returned home after his time of service was completed, and, as Gabriel had promised, Elizabeth conceived.

In the sixth month of Elizabeth's pregnancy, God sent Gabriel to Mary, who was a virgin. She lived in Nazareth, a town in Galilee (northern Israel). "Greetings!" Gabriel said. "You are highly favored, and the Lord is with you."

Mary was frightened, but Gabriel reassured her. "You have found favor with God and will give birth to a son, whom you are to name Jesus. He will be the Son of the Most High God and given the throne of David. His kingdom will last forever."

Mary was bewildered. "How can this be, since I am a virgin?"

The angel said the Holy Spirit would cause her to conceive by the power of God, so her son would actually be God's Son. Elizabeth, six months pregnant, was proof that nothing is impossible with God.

Mary humbled herself before the angelic messenger and answered, "May everything happen as you have promised." Then Gabriel left her.

Mary decided to visit Elizabeth and Zechariah, who lived in the hill country of Judea (south of Nazareth, where Mary and her husband-to-be, Joseph, lived). When Mary arrived and greeted Elizabeth, Elizabeth felt her son jump in her womb. She was filled with the Spirit and cried out, "You are blessed, and the son you are carrying is blessed."

Mary responded by praising the Lord for the son he had given her: "My soul praises the Lord, for he has been gracious to a lowly servant girl. The Mighty One has done a wonderful thing for me and for all of Israel. He has remembered the promises he made to Abraham and his descendants."

Mary stayed with Elizabeth for about three months before returning home.

When Elizabeth gave birth, all her neighbors and relatives rejoiced because the Lord had been so gracious to her.

On the eighth day, when it was customary to circumcise and name a newborn son, Elizabeth gave him the name John. The neighbors were surprised; they thought he would be named after Zechariah, and they wanted to know if Zechariah approved.

He was still unable to speak, so he wrote "John" on a clay tablet. As soon as Zechariah wrote it, his speech was restored, and he began to praise God.

The news of these strange and unusual events became the conversation of every household in the Judean hill country. They wondered what John would become, because he was obviously a special child, blessed by the Lord.

Zechariah, filled with the Holy Spirit, sang a prophetic song about his son:

> *Praise to the Lord, the God of Israel, because he has come to save his people. He has sent a mighty Savior, as he promised David and Abraham. My son will be called a prophet of the Most High God, because he will prepare people for the coming of the Lord. He will tell them how to find salvation and forgiveness of their sins. He will be a light for those in darkness and living in the shadow of death. He will guide us to peace with God.* (See Luke 1:68–75.)

As John grew physically, he also grew spiritually. He became a remarkable man of God. When he was old enough, he chose to live alone in the wilderness.

Mary was engaged to Joseph, and when he discovered she was pregnant, he decided to break the engagement; he thought she had been unfaithful to him. He was godly and considerate, so he planned to do it discreetly rather than disgrace Mary publicly.

The angel of the Lord, however, spoke to Joseph in a dream and explained that Mary had conceived by the Spirit's power—there was no reason he should not marry her. The angel said Mary would give birth to a son, and that they should give him the name Jesus (which means "Savior"), because he would save people from their sins.

When Joseph woke, he did exactly as the angel had commanded. He married Mary but did not have sexual relations with her until she had given birth to their son, Jesus.

JESUS' BIRTH

Jesus was born during the rule of the Roman emperor Caesar Augustus, who issued a decree requiring all Jews to register in the town of their birth. Joseph, from Bethlehem, went there to register and took Mary with him even though she was expecting a child.

In Bethlehem, Mary gave birth. They had to place their newborn baby in a feeding trough for animals because they couldn't find a room in the inn.

The birth of Jesus would have gone unnoticed had not the angel of the Lord appeared to shepherds. It was during the darkness of night while they were watching sheep that he appeared to them and the glory of the Lord surrounded them.

They were terrified, but the angel said, "Do not be afraid. I have good news. The Savior, who is Christ the Lord, has been born in the City of David (Bethlehem). You will know who he is because he is lying in a feeding trough."

Suddenly, a large group of angels appeared and praised God, singing, "Glory to God, and peace to men on earth." They disappeared as suddenly as they had appeared.

The shepherds discussed what had happened and decided to go to Bethlehem. They found Joseph and Mary and the baby exactly as the angel had said. They told everyone what they had seen. Mary, however, kept silent and treasured everything in her heart.

Jesus' parents were devoted Jews. As instructed by the angel, Mary and Joseph named their son Jesus on the eighth day after his birth.

They also fulfilled all the requirements in the law of Moses in raising Jesus. After forty days, they went to Jerusalem to dedicate him to the Lord.

Many in Israel were longing for a messianic Savior. Simeon had lived his entire life assured he would not die until he had seen the Anointed One. On the day of Jesus' dedication, the Spirit led Simeon to the temple; when Mary and Joseph came to dedicate Jesus, Simeon took Jesus in his arms and praised God, saying, "Now I can die in peace, because I have seen the Savior you have sent to save the nations and your people Israel."

Simeon also blessed Mary and Joseph and predicted Mary would experience intense pain because of people's rejection of her son.

A prophetess named Anna was also in the temple at the time of the dedication. Her husband had died after they had been married only seven years. She was now eighty-four and had never left the temple; she had devoted herself to prayer and serving the Lord.

When she heard Simeon speaking to Mary and Joseph, she began praising God and told everyone that God had sent their son to save Israel.

In addition, people from distant lands were looking for the Messiah. In the east, wise men had seen a star and made the journey to Jerusalem to worship the King of the Jews.

JESUS' CHILDHOOD

Not everyone considered the Messiah's birth an amazing work of God. When King Herod heard about the birth of Jesus, he feared Jesus would challenge him as king. He asked the religious teachers for information, and they told him a prophet had predicted that the Messiah would be born in Bethlehem. Herod met with the wise men and asked them to report to him after they had found the child—"so he could worship him also," he said.

After the wise men met with Herod, the star guided them to Bethlehem and stopped over the house where Mary and Joseph were staying. When they saw Mary's son, they bowed and gave him gifts of gold and valuable spices.

After worshiping the child, they returned to their own country by a different route because an angel had warned them that Herod intended to kill the child, not worship him.

The angel also warned Joseph in a dream of Herod's murderous intentions: "Flee to Egypt and stay there until I tell you to return; Herod is plotting to kill your son." Joseph didn't even wait for daylight. He left for Egypt during the night.

Herod was furious when he realized the wise men had departed without informing him of the child's exact location. He went on a rampage and ordered his soldiers to kill all the boys under two years of age in the Bethlehem area.

After the death of Herod, the angel of the Lord told Joseph it was safe for him to return to Israel. Instead of returning to Bethlehem, they went to their hometown of Nazareth, in the northern province of Galilee.

Jesus grew up in the town of Nazareth. God's favor was on him. He was a healthy young man and filled with wisdom.

Jesus' parents continued to honor the Lord by meeting all the requirements of the Law. They made the yearly trip to Jerusalem to celebrate Passover (an annual feast for celebrating Israel's escape from slavery in Egypt). When Jesus was twelve, they took him with them to Jerusalem.

After they started home, though, they couldn't find him. When they rushed back to Jerusalem to look for him, they found Jesus in the temple discussing complicated issues of the Law with the religious teachers. Everyone was greatly impressed with his wisdom and his understanding of the Law.

His parents were perplexed. They didn't know what to think. Mary said, "Son, why have you done this? Your father and I have been frantically searching for you."

Jesus replied, "Why were you searching? Didn't you know I would be in my Father's house?" But they didn't understand.

Jesus returned to Nazareth with his parents and was obedient to them. He continued to develop physically, intellectually, and spiritually. He was highly regarded by both God and people.

𝕎 Chapter Summary

When Israel was occupied by the Romans, and Herod was king of Judea, God sent Gabriel to a priest named Zechariah, informing him that his wife Elizabeth was going to have a son. John would be filled with the Holy Spirit from birth; his purpose in life would be to prepare Israel for the coming of the Lord by calling on people to return to their God.

Six months later God turned the world of a young Jewish girl upside down when he informed her she had been chosen to give birth to the Son of God. Mary was only engaged to Joseph, so having a son seemed impossible. Gabriel told her anything is possible with God, and she would conceive by the Holy Spirit's power.

When Joseph learned Mary was pregnant, he made plans to break the engagement. The angel of the Lord, however, spoke to him in a dream, assuring him that Mary had not been unfaithful.

Jesus was born in the small town of Bethlehem in the province of Judea. The long-awaited Savior's birth was announced by the angel of the Lord to shepherds. A large group of angels appeared and praised God. Then the shepherds went to Bethlehem to see the child; they praised God, telling everyone about the birth.

Having received word of this new Messiah, Herod felt his kingship was being challenged. Thus, he ordered all the male infants in Bethlehem executed.

Joseph, Mary, and Jesus sought refuge in Egypt, and after Herod's death they returned to Nazareth, where Jesus spent the rest of his childhood years.

Fourteen

Jesus' Early Ministry

Main Characters
John the Baptist
Jesus
Satan
The first disciples
Mary, mother of Jesus
Nicodemus
Samaritan woman

Setting
Galilee (northern province in Israel)
Cana (a village in Galilee)
Judea (southern province in Israel)
Samaria (central province in Israel)
Sychar (a village in Samaria)
Jordan River

In the fifteenth year of the rule of Emperor Tiberius Caesar, a strange individual appeared suddenly in the Judean desert. John dressed and acted like an Old Testament prophet. He lived and ministered in the wilderness; he wore a coarse camel-hair robe and a leather belt. He ate locusts and wild honey.

John was abrupt and bold, yet people came from everywhere to hear him. He said to repent because the Lord was coming; when people confessed their sins, he baptized them in the Jordan River.

John's preaching was courageous and confrontational. When a group of religious leaders came to see what he was doing, he told them they needed to repent and called them a nest of snakes: "Flee God's coming wrath. Turn to him. Don't think that because you are descendants of Abraham, you won't be judged."

He warned that the ax of God's judgment was about to fall on people, and "every tree that does not produce good fruit will be chopped down and thrown into the fire."

When the crowds asked, "What should we do?" John told them they must be compassionate, honest, and just. He told the affluent to help the poor, and he told tax collectors to collect only what people owed. He warned soldiers to be content with their pay and not use their power to extort money or make false accusations.

One day Jesus surprised John. He came while John was baptizing people, and he asked John to baptize him also. John protested, "I'm the one who should be baptized by you. You don't need to repent." But Jesus told John that even he needed to obey God.

When John baptized Jesus, the heavens were opened, and John saw the Spirit of God descend on Jesus like a dove. God spoke from heaven, saying, "This is my Son, whom I love. I am pleased with what he has done."

Immediately after this, the Holy Spirit led Jesus into an isolated area of the Judean desert. Jesus hadn't eaten for forty days when Satan came and tempted him three times. The first time he said, "If you are the Son of God, make these stones into bread." Jesus replied, "The Scriptures say, 'Man does not live by bread alone but by the word of God.'"

Satan tempted Jesus a second time, telling him to jump off the temple because God would send angels to catch him. Jesus said, "It is written in the Scriptures, 'You must not test the Lord your God.'"

Then the devil took Jesus to the top of a high mountain and showed him the kingdoms of the world. He said, "If you will worship me, I will give you all of these kingdoms." Jesus commanded Satan to leave: "You must worship the Lord your God and serve only him." After Satan left Jesus, God sent angels to serve him.

Even after Jesus' baptism and temptation, John continued his public ministry. He created quite a stir in Israel. Everyone was expecting the Messiah, and some even thought he might be the Messiah, but he denied it:

> I am only a voice crying out in the wilderness to prepare people for the coming of the Lord. I am only baptizing you with water. Someone greater is coming. I am not even worthy to untie the straps of his sandals. When he comes he will baptize you with the Holy Spirit and with fire.

When John saw Jesus, he shouted, "Look, there is the Lamb of God! He is the one who has come to take away the sin of the world." John testified to people that he knew for certain who Jesus was. He said, "I saw the Spirit of God descend on Jesus when he was baptized, and I know he is God's Son."

Jesus began preparing for ministry by calling men to become his disciples ("disciple" refers to someone who is a learner). The next day, when John was meeting with his followers, he saw Jesus again and shouted, "Look, the Lamb of God!"

Two of his disciples decided to follow Jesus. When they began walking behind him, he turned and asked what they wanted. They said they wanted to become his followers; they spent the rest of the day with him.

One of the men was Andrew, who had a brother named Simon. Andrew told Simon that he had found the Messiah, and he brought him to Jesus. When Simon met Jesus, Jesus changed his name to Peter, which means "rock."

The following day, before Jesus left for Galilee, he called Philip to become a disciple. Philip went to his friend Nathanael and told him they had found the one whom Moses and the other prophets had predicted would come to Israel. He was Jesus, the son of Joseph, from Nazareth.

Nathanael, surprised, asked, "Are you sure Jesus is from Nazareth? Can the Messiah really be from there?" Philip told Nathanael to talk to Jesus and decide for himself.

As the two men approached, Jesus said to Nathanael, "You are a sincere person and a man of integrity."

Nathanael asked, "How do you know about me?"

Jesus said he knew about Nathanael even before Philip spoke with him.

Nathanael exclaimed, "Teacher, you are the Son of God—the King of Israel!"

Jesus replied, "You will see greater things than that simple statement. You will see heaven open, and angels going up and down on the Son of Man; I am the stairway between heaven and earth."

Galilee

Jesus' first miracle was in the village of Cana, in Galilee.

When Jesus and his disciples traveled north, they were invited to a wedding. Jesus' mother, Mary, was in charge of the food and drink, and when the party ran out of wine, she asked Jesus if he could help. He said, "Woman, this is not my problem. Though you mean well, you have no authority to tell me when to use my divine power."

Mary told the servants to do whatever Jesus commanded.

Jesus found the stone waterpots that were used for ritual hand- and foot-washing. Combined, the six pots held between 160 and 180 gallons, but they were empty because the guests had used all the water.

Jesus ordered the servants to fill the pots with water and then take them to the master of ceremonies. The water miraculously changed to wine, but the master didn't know what had happened. When he tasted it, he said to the bridegroom, "A host usually serves the best wine first, but you have saved the best wine until the end of the celebration."

Turning a large quantity of water to wine was convincing evidence to his disciples that Jesus was definitely the promised Messiah and the Son of God.

Jesus and his disciples then spent a few days with his mother and brothers in Capernaum (by the Sea of Galilee) before going to Jerusalem for the Passover Feast.

Jerusalem and Judea

In Jerusalem, Jesus went to the temple. There in one of the courts he discovered merchants selling animals and traders exchanging foreign money.

Jesus was furious. He grabbed some rope, made a whip, and drove out the sheep and cattle. He threw the money on the floor and overturned the trading tables. He yelled at the merchants, saying, "Get these things out of here! You have no right to use my Father's house for a marketplace."

When his disciples saw Jesus' intensity, they remembered that the Old Testament prophets had predicted the Messiah would be a passionate defender of God's house. The Jewish leaders, however, challenged his authority. They demanded Jesus show them a miraculous sign as proof that God had given him divine authority.

Jesus gave a cryptic answer: "Destroy this temple, and I will raise it up in three days."

"What!" the leaders said. "It has taken forty-six years to build this temple, and you claim you can rebuild it in three days?" They didn't know Jesus was referring to his body, not the Jewish temple; after the Resurrection, his disciples remembered what he had said because they knew what Jesus said agreed with the Scriptures.

Not everyone doubted Jesus. Many who were in Jerusalem for Passover believed he was the Messiah because of his miracles. However, even though many believed in him, Jesus knew that some only had superficial faith.

One of those impressed by Jesus was a religious leader named Nicodemus. He came one evening and said, "Teacher, I know God sent you because of your power to work miracles."

Jesus replied, startlingly, "Unless you are born again, you cannot enter the kingdom of God."

Nicodemus, confused, asked, "How can a man be born physically a second time?"

Jesus explained that he meant a spiritual (not a physical) birth. He said, "Humans can reproduce physically, but only the Holy Spirit can give a spiritual birth."

Nicodemus asked, "How is this possible?"

Jesus reprimanded Nicodemus because he was a leader and still didn't understand spiritual realities. "If you can't understand a basic earthly fact, how could you possibly understand heavenly truths?" he said.

Jesus stated that the reason he came from heaven to earth was to give eternal life to people everywhere: "God loves everyone. He didn't send his Son into the world to condemn it but to save it." He explained that the reason not everyone believes in God's Son is that they don't want to abandon their sin: "They would rather live in darkness than come to the light."

When Jesus left Jerusalem, he went into the Judean countryside to spend time with his disciples. John and his disciples were in the same area baptizing people.

One of the Jewish men started an argument with John's disciples over ritual cleansing. When they went to John, instead of asking about ritual cleansing, they complained that Jesus was more popular than John.

That didn't bother John. In fact, he said that was the way it should be. "I am not the Messiah," John reminded them. "I am only here to prepare people for the coming of the Messiah." John said he couldn't be more pleased that Jesus had become so successful.

Jesus decided to return to Galilee for two reasons: (1) he found out that the religious leaders in Jerusalem were concerned about his growing popularity and that his disciples were increasing rapidly, and (2) he was informed that John had been imprisoned.

John had publicly condemned Herod Antipas, governor of the

province of Galilee, for marrying his brother's wife. Herod had arrested John and thrown him into prison.

Samaria

On his way to Samaria, Jesus revealed how radically different he was. Most Jews despised Samaritans and avoided Samaria, but as Jesus walked north from Judea to Galilee, he stopped at the village of Sychar.

It was about noon, and it was hot, so Jesus went to a well on the outskirts of town. Tired from the long walk, he sat on the well's edge. His disciples had gone to buy food, so Jesus was alone.

When a woman came to draw water, Jesus asked her for a drink. She was shocked; she said, "You are a Jew, and I am a Samaritan woman. Why are you asking me for a drink?"

Jesus engaged her in a conversation with a perplexing statement: "If you knew the gift of God and who I am, it is you who would ask me for a drink."

She was puzzled, because Jesus didn't have a rope and a bucket. She asked Jesus how he was going to get water and if he thought he was greater than Jacob, who had dug the well.

Jesus' reply was even more baffling: "Anyone who drinks the water from this well will become thirsty again, but if you drink the water that I give you, you will never be thirsty. The water that I give will become like a spring of fresh water bubbling up with eternal life."

The woman asked Jesus for this water because she misunderstood; she thought she would never be physically thirsty and would never need to come to this well again.

Jesus then redirected the conversation with a command: "Go and call your husband."

The woman replied, "I don't have one."

Jesus said, "That's true. You have had five husbands, and the man you're now living with isn't your husband."

It was the woman who then altered the conversation, seeking to change the subject. She said it was obvious Jesus was a prophet, and she said, "You Jews worship God in Jerusalem; we Samaritans worship here. Where are people supposed to worship?"

Jesus said the place doesn't matter. "God is a Spirit, and those who worship him must worship him in spirit and truth."

She said, "I know the Messiah is coming, and he will be able to explain everything."

Jesus said, "I am the Messiah."

As Jesus' disciples returned from town, they were surprised to see him talking with a woman, but none of them dared ask about it.

The woman left her bucket and ran back into town. She told everyone about her conversation and how Jesus knew all about her past life. The Samaritans rushed out to see him.

Jesus' disciples urged him to eat, but he refused, saying, "I have other food you don't know about."

When they asked one another if someone else had brought him food while they were gone, Jesus explained that he was speaking about the spiritual nourishment he receives from doing God's will. He said, "Look, open your eyes! The fields are ripe for harvest."

Many of the Samaritans believed in Jesus because of the woman's testimony; they begged him to stay in their village. He stayed two more days, and many more became believers because of what he said. They told the woman, "We now believe, because we have heard Jesus for ourselves. We know that he is indeed the Savior of the world!"

♆ Chapter Summary

John the Baptist was a prophet with a single purpose: to prepare Israel for the coming of Jesus Christ (the Messiah). He told people to repent of their sins, and he baptized those who repented. He also baptized Jesus.

Satan tempted Jesus three times, but Jesus did not sin. After forty days, the devil gave up and waited for another opportunity to tempt Jesus.

In preparation for ministry, Jesus began calling men to train as disciples. He performed his first miracle at a wedding in Cana.

After Jesus went to Jerusalem, he angered the religious elite during a confrontation in the temple.

Many people believed in Jesus because of his miracles. A Pharisee named Nicodemus commended him as an inspired teacher of God. Jesus shocked Nicodemus by saying that unless he was "born again" he would never enter God's kingdom. Jesus was referring to a radical and miraculous spiritual transformation.

Jesus assured Nicodemus that God loves the world (all people); the reason some people don't believe in the Son of God is that they don't want to abandon their sinful lifestyle, preferring the darkness of wickedness to the light of moral and ethical integrity.

When Jesus realized the Pharisees were investigating his ministry in Jerusalem, he decided to return to Galilee. He took the most direct route, through Samaria.

There Jesus met a woman at a well. Jesus surprised her by speaking with her; Jews despised Samaritans and did not associate with them. Jesus offered her "the water of life," which is eternal life.

The woman went and told everyone about this amazing man she had met. When the other Samaritans met Jesus, they realized he was "the Savior of the world."

Fifteen

GREAT GALILEAN MINISTRY

Main Characters
Jesus
The twelve disciples/apostles
The Pharisees and other Jewish leaders

Setting
Galilee (province in the north)
Nazareth (town in Galilee)
Capernaum (town in Galilee)
Sea of Galilee

TEACHING AND HEALING

When Jesus arrived in Galilee, he received an enthusiastic welcome. Many Galileans had been in Jerusalem for Passover and had seen his miraculous works.

It was in Galilee that Jesus began his extensive public ministry. He taught in synagogues and preached to large crowds about God's kingdom. He healed people of all kinds of diseases and delivered others from demon-possession.

Jesus was extremely popular with the common people. In addition to his disciples, large crowds followed him wherever he went.

While Jesus was staying in Cana, where he had turned water to wine, a government official heard he had come to Galilee. He went and begged Jesus to come to Capernaum to heal his son, who was terminally ill.

Jesus said, "Will people never believe unless they see miracles?"

The official, desperate and determined, pleaded, "Please come before my son dies!"

The man's persistence convinced Jesus of his faith. Jesus didn't even go to Capernaum. He simply said, "Go home, your son will live."

The man believed Jesus and left for home. While on the road to Capernaum, he received incredibly good news. His servants met him and told him his son was well. The official asked when his son had recovered, and they said that previous afternoon his fever was suddenly gone. The boy's father calculated that his son had recovered at the exact time Jesus had told him, "Your son will live." His entire household believed in Jesus.

On the Sabbath, Jesus went to the synagogue in Nazareth and read from Isaiah the prophet.

> *The Spirit of the Sovereign Lord is on me,*
> *because the Lord has anointed me*
> *to proclaim good news to the poor.*
> *He has sent me to bind up the brokenhearted,*
> *proclaim freedom for the captives*
> *and release from darkness for the prisoners,*
> *to proclaim the year of the Lord's favor.* (Isaiah 61:1–2)

After reading, Jesus rolled up the scroll and said he had come in fulfillment of Isaiah's prophecy. Though the people were impressed with Jesus, they didn't believe he was the Messiah; they thought he was merely Joseph's son.

Jesus was not surprised they didn't believe he was the Messiah, because he knew the proverb "No prophet is accepted in his hometown."

Jesus responded to their unbelief by telling two Old Testament stories about Elijah and Elisha. When the Lord devastated the land of Israel with a severe famine, Elijah didn't help anyone in Israel; instead he provided food for a Gentile widow who lived in another country. Elisha also ministered to a Gentile. Though many in Israel suffered from leprosy, Elisha didn't heal any of them but healed Naaman, a Gentile and general of the Syrian army.

These stories made the people furious. They physically attacked Jesus and tried to throw him over a cliff. Jesus just walked away.

One day when Jesus was teaching, so many people crowded around him to hear that he decided to get into a boat. He asked Peter, who had met him previously, to row him out a short distance from the shore. He sat in the boat and taught the people.

When he had finished speaking, he told Peter to go out farther and cast his net. Peter said they wouldn't catch anything—they had fished all night and caught nothing—but if Jesus insisted, they would try again. This time they caught so many fish the boat almost sank. Fishermen in other boats had to help them get their catch to shore.

When Peter got to shore, he fell on his knees before Jesus and said, "You shouldn't associate with me; I am a sinful man." Jesus said to Peter and to Andrew, who was with Peter, "Come, follow me, and I will show you how to fish for people!"

They responded immediately, leaving their boat and fishing nets to become Jesus' disciples. Jesus saw two more fishermen and called them to follow him. James and John also left their fishing business to be with Jesus.

On the Sabbath, Jesus went to the synagogue in Capernaum and began teaching. People were amazed at how he taught with personal authority. Suddenly a demon-possessed man there started shouting at Jesus. "Stop interfering with us!" the demon cried out. "Have you come to destroy us? I know you are the Holy One of God."

Jesus silenced the demon and ordered him to come out of the man. The evil spirit screamed, shook the man, and threw him down, but he came out and didn't hurt the man.

Everyone in the synagogue was amazed at Jesus' authority and power. Word about what he had done spread throughout Galilee and the surrounding areas.

As soon as they left the synagogue, Jesus and his disciples went to the home of the brothers Andrew and Peter. When they told Jesus that Peter's mother-in-law had a fever, Jesus took her by the hand and helped her get out of bed. She instantly regained her strength and prepared a meal for her guests.

That evening, sick and demon-possessed people came from everywhere to get help. Jesus healed all who were ill and drove out demons. When the demons came out, some shouted, "You are the Son of God!" but Jesus would not allow demons to proclaim that.

Though he had ministered late into the evening, Jesus got up early the next day and went out to an isolated place to pray. When his disciples finally found him, they said, "Everyone is looking for you!"

Jesus replied, "I must go to other towns and preach there."

Jesus and his disciples continued preaching the good news and healing people throughout Galilee. He became immensely popular with people from Galilee, Judea, and even areas east of the Jordan River.

FACING OPPOSITION

One of the most dreaded diseases in the ancient world was leprosy, but Jesus was able to cure it with a mere touch and his word. A leper came to Jesus, knelt before him, and said, "Lord, if you want you can heal me."

Jesus said, "I am willing." He reached out and touched the man, who was instantly cured. Jesus told the man not to tell anyone, but the man ignored his instructions. Because he told everyone what had happened, it was almost impossible for Jesus to enter a town. Jesus spent most of his time in the country, which gave him the opportunity to pray.

A few days later, Jesus returned to Capernaum. So many people came to listen to his teaching that people had to stand outside. While Jesus was teaching God's Word, four men arrived carrying a paralyzed friend on a stretcher. They tried to get to Jesus through the door, but there were too many people. They didn't give up. They climbed up to the roof, dug a hole through it, and lowered their friend down to Jesus on the stretcher.

Seeing the faith of the man and his friends, Jesus said, "Son, your sins are forgiven."

Some of the religious teachers present were upset. They said, "Who does this man think he is? Only God can forgive sins!"

Jesus knew what they were thinking and asked, "Why are you offended? Is it easier to heal a paralyzed man or to forgive his sins?" He then turned to the man and said, "Get up, go home, and take your stretcher with you."

The man jumped up and made his way through the crowd. Everyone praised God. They all agreed they had never seen anyone with this kind of authority and power.

Not all the men Jesus recruited as disciples were fishermen. One was a tax collector. While walking by the Sea of Galilee, Jesus was teaching a large group of people and saw Matthew at his roadside tax booth. Jesus said, "Follow me if you want to become one of my disciples!" Matthew didn't hesitate; he got up and walked away with Jesus.

After he had been with Jesus only a short time, Matthew organized a party for friends. Many of them were tax collectors and other kinds of people that pious Jews despised. It didn't matter to Jesus, the guest of honor. He and his disciples sat down and ate with everyone.

The Pharisees (leaders who strictly followed the law of Moses and didn't associate with anyone they considered unworthy) and religious teachers complained to Jesus' disciples: "Why does your teacher eat with people who are sinful and worthless?"

Jesus answered, "Healthy people don't need a physician; sick people do. I have not come to save those who think they are righteous but those who know that they are sinners and need to repent."

During his ministry, Jesus faced intense opposition from Israel's religious leaders because he repeatedly challenged their traditions about what was honoring to God. This was especially true on issues related to the Sabbath. Because Jesus was more concerned about people than rules, he disregarded their Sabbath restrictions.

Jesus went to Jerusalem for one of the annual Jewish religious festivals. Large numbers of people who were sick would come to a certain pool for healing. A man who had been handicapped for thirty-eight years was lying on his mat next to the pool. When Jesus saw him, he asked a surprising question: "Do you want to get well?"

"Sir," said the man, "I don't have anyone to help me get into the pool when an angel stirs the water. Someone always gets in before me."

Jesus said, "Get up, take your mat, and walk!" The man was immediately healed and walked away carrying his mat.

When the Jewish leaders saw the man, they were shocked. They said to him, "The law prohibits you from carrying your mat on the Sabbath."

The man said, "The man who healed me told me to take my mat and walk." They demanded to know who had dared tell him to do this, but the man didn't know; after he was healed, Jesus had disappeared into the crowd.

Later that day, Jesus met the man in the temple and told him, "Stop sinning or something worse than your handicap might happen to you." The man then went to the Jewish leaders and told them that Jesus had healed him.

They found Jesus and condemned him for breaking the Sabbath

rules. Jesus said to them, "God, my Father, works even on the Sabbath, so I likewise have a right to do works of compassion."

His statement infuriated the Jews. He not only violated the Sabbath rules, he dared to make himself equal to God by calling God his Father. They began plotting to kill him.

After the Jewish holy days, Jesus and his disciples returned to Galilee. When they were walking beside a field of grain on the Sabbath, the disciples were hungry, so they picked grain to eat.

Some Pharisees saw them and complained to Jesus. "Look at that! Your disciples are breaking the Law by harvesting on the Sabbath."

Jesus responded by telling them about the time King David and some of his soldiers were hungry, and they went into the tent of holiness to eat some of the sacred bread that normally only priests were allowed to eat. In addition, the Law permitted the temple priests to perform their sacred duties on the Sabbath. Jesus told the Pharisees they had it all wrong: "The Lord designated the Sabbath for the benefit of man; he did not create man for the Sabbath. I, the Son of Man, am Lord over both man and the Sabbath."

After Jesus claimed this, the religious elite were watching him closely, hoping to find a reason to condemn him. They set a trap one Sabbath when he went to the synagogue. A man with a deformed hand was there, and they planned to accuse Jesus of breaking the Law if he healed him.

They asked Jesus if the Law permitted him to heal on the Sabbath. Jesus didn't answer them directly; he knew what they were plotting. He told the handicapped man to stand up in front of everyone. He then asked the religious leaders two questions: "Is it against the Law to do good on the Sabbath, or is the Sabbath only a day for evil? Is the Sabbath for saving life or destroying it?"

They wouldn't answer because they knew Jesus was talking about them.

Their hardhearted stubbornness made Jesus angry. He said to the man, "Hold out your hand!" When he did, Jesus healed him.

The Pharisees stood up and walked out. They held a secret meeting and further plotted how to kill Jesus.

Knowing the religious leaders were conspiring to kill him, Jesus left for another area of Galilee, but he was so popular that people from everywhere followed him. They came from Judea, Idumea (an area south of Judea), and east of the Jordan River. Others came from as far north as Tyre and Sidon. Jesus healed those who were sick and sternly commanded evil spirits not to tell who he was; they knew he was the Son of God.

One morning, after praying all night, Jesus summoned the people who were following him, and he appointed twelve of them to be apostles. He gave them divine authority to preach and power over evil spirits. He nicknamed James and John "the Sons of Thunder"; another, Simon (not Simon Peter), was a Jewish revolutionary; Judas Iscariot would later betray Jesus.

Later a large crowd began to gather on the mountainside. Many who came had been healed of diseases, and others had been delivered from evil spirits. People were trying to touch Jesus because of his power to heal.

Jesus found a level place, sat down, and began to teach. He began by challenging people to a radically different lifestyle. He said God blesses those who realize they need God; those who are grieved by sin and evil; those who are humble and hunger for righteousness; those who are merciful and are peacemakers; and those who are persecuted because of their devotion to God. Jesus said these are the kind of people that God will honor and reward in the kingdom of heaven.

Jesus challenged his followers to shine as light in a world of moral and spiritual darkness. He emphasized the importance of moral and spiritual integrity. He said that what's in the heart reveals a person's true character.

He taught that his followers should be more concerned about honoring God than about praying, fasting, and impressing others. There's no reason to worry, because God knows what a person needs, and he is just.

Jesus said to pray fervently because God loves to bless those who trust him; he said to leave the judgment of others to God. Jesus said the way to live in relationship with other people can be summed up in the saying, "Treat others like you would want them to treat you."

Jesus concluded his message on the mountain with a call to either accept or reject his challenge to a new and radical way of life. He warned of a day of judgment, and he said those who are wise submit to his teaching.

People were absolutely amazed. They had never heard anything like this teaching from the religious leaders.

Though Jesus was Jewish, he also ministered to non-Jews. As soon as he returned to Capernaum, he was met by several Jewish leaders who had come to ask for his help. They told him about an officer in the Roman army who was a friend to the Jewish people; he had even built a synagogue.

The officer's servant was sick and near death, and they asked Jesus to heal him. But before Jesus arrived at the man's house, the officer himself met Jesus and said he knew Jesus could help his servant—Jesus didn't even need to come all the way to his house. The officer told Jesus he wasn't worthy to have him in his home.

Jesus turned to the crowd following him and said, "I'm amazed at this man's faith. I haven't seen faith like this from anyone in Israel." He told the officer to return home; his servant had been healed. And he had.

Nain was about six miles southeast of Nazareth. As Jesus and his disciples were about to enter the small village, they were stopped by a funeral procession.

A widow's son had died, and Jesus felt compassion for her. He stopped the procession and put his hand on the coffin. "Young man," he said, "Get up!" The boy sat up and immediately began talking.

The crowd was awestruck. They said, "Jesus is a prophet, a man from God." The news of what Jesus had done spread like wildfire throughout Galilee and Judea.

Jesus' ministry was different from what most Jews expected of the Messiah. Even John the Baptist had doubts. After he was arrested and put in prison, John sent two of his disciples to ask Jesus if he was the Messiah or should they look for someone else. Jesus told them to return and tell John that the miraculous healing of the blind and the handicapped and the deaf, and the raising of the dead, were proof that he was the Messiah.

After John's disciples departed, Jesus spoke to the crowds about John. He said John was much more than just another prophet; he had come to announce the Messiah's coming. "Of all who have ever lived, none is greater than John," said Jesus.

The people, even tax collectors, agreed with Jesus, but not the religious elite. They had refused to submit to John's baptism.

Jesus warned about the terrible consequences of rejecting him. His miracles proved who he was, and it was his hope that all people would come to him to fulfill their longing to know God. In contrast to the impossible demands of Israel's religious leaders, Jesus asked only for people to believe in him and follow his teachings. He told them that doing so would bring rest to their souls.

Most of Israel's religious leaders had already decided Jesus was not the Messiah and was instead a threat to them, but some were still undecided. One, named Simon, invited Jesus to his house for dinner. While Jesus was there, a woman who was known to be immoral came to the house, knelt near Jesus, and began to anoint his feet with oil.

Simon, stunned, thought to himself, *If this man were a true prophet, he would know this woman is a sinner, and he would never let her touch him.*

Jesus knew what Simon was thinking and told him a story about two debtors. One had borrowed five hundred silver coins; the other had borrowed fifty. Neither could repay their loan, so the lender graciously cancelled the debt of both men. Jesus asked Simon, "Which of the two debtors would be more grateful?"

The answer was obvious. Jesus turned to the woman but spoke to Simon. "Listen," he said. "When I entered your house, you didn't even offer me water to wash my feet or greet me with a customary kiss. This woman has never stopped kissing my feet and has anointed both my head and feet with expensive oil and perfume. Her sins have been forgiven, and she has shown her appreciation to me."

Jesus then said to the woman, "Your sins are forgiven!" The other startled guests said, "Who does this man think he is, that he can forgive sins?" Jesus told the woman to go in peace; her faith had saved her.

Jesus' followers were not only men; numerous women also traveled with him. Jesus had healed them of all kinds of diseases and delivered them from evil spirits. He had cast seven demons out of Mary Magdalene.

Some women were influential and wealthy. One was the wife of Herod's business manager. Jesus depended on women like them for support for his ministry.

The religious elite concluded that Jesus was a false prophet. He infuriated them because he violated their restrictions, forgave sins, and associated with sinners, tax collectors, non-Jews, and others they despised.

They didn't believe his power to heal was from God, so they tried to discredit him. They brought to him a man with multiple problems, thinking Jesus could not help him. He was not only demon-possessed, he also was blind and couldn't hear or speak.

Jesus cast out the demon and healed the man so he could hear and talk and see. When the people saw the miracle, they thought Jesus must be the Messiah, but the religious leaders charged that Jesus had used the power of Beelzebub (a code name for Satan).

Jesus responded by saying that their charge was absurd. It was ridiculous to think that Satan would work to destroy his own kingdom. Since Jesus had delivered the man from a satanic evil spirit, he was obviously stronger than Satan. Jesus warned the religious leaders that if they persisted in deliberately rejecting him, despite his miracles by the power of the Holy Spirit, they would never find forgiveness.

Their rejection of him was a serious mistake. Though they had seen numerous miracles, they demanded another miraculous sign. Jesus said it wouldn't make any difference, because they had already seen enough miracles to believe.

Because of the leaders' hostility, Jesus began using a new teaching method. Instead of talking directly about his mission as Messiah, he began teaching about God's kingdom in parables (stories from everyday life in first-century Palestine).

He told a story about a farmer who sowed seed in his field. The seed fell on different kinds of soil, but only seed that was planted in fertile soil produced a crop. He applied the parable by explaining that the soil represented different responses to his teaching about the kingdom of God.

Jesus concluded with an illustration from fishing. He said when a fisherman throws his net into the lake he catches all kinds of fish. Some are good to eat, but others are not. He throws the bad ones away. Jesus said that is what will happen at the end of the age: "Angels will separate the wicked from the just, and cast them into a furnace of fire."

That evening Jesus told his disciples he wanted to go to the other side of the Sea of Galilee. He was exhausted from teaching all day, and as soon as they pushed out from shore he fell asleep in the back of the boat on a small cushion.

Without warning, a fierce storm came up, and waves were breaking into the boat. When it began to fill with water, the disciples panicked.

They woke Jesus, shouting, "Teacher, help! We are going to drown. Don't you care?"

Jesus commanded the wind and the waves to be still. There was an immediate calm.

He said to his terrified disciples, "Why are you so afraid? Where is your faith?"

They said to one another, "Who is Jesus? Even the wind and the waves obey him!"

On the other side of the sea, they landed in the region of the Gerasenes. Jesus had taken only a few steps from the boat when he saw a man possessed by an evil spirit.

The man had come out of a cemetery where he lived among the tombs. He was wild and uncontrollable. People put chains on him, but he would break them. At night he roamed the surrounding hills, howling like a wolf and cutting himself with sharp stones.

When the man saw Jesus, he ran to him and fell on his knees, desperate for help. Jesus commanded the demon to come out of the man; it shrieked and screamed, "Have you come to judge me? I know you are the Son of God!"

When Jesus asked the demon his name, it said, "Legion, for we are many." (A legion was an army unit of five thousand men. This describes numerous evil spirits.) A herd of about two thousand pigs was feeding nearby, and the demons begged Jesus to send them into the pigs. Jesus allowed it; the pigs stampeded over a cliff and drowned in the sea.

When the people in the area heard what Jesus had done, they were afraid and asked him to leave. As Jesus and his disciples prepared to leave, the man who had been demon-possessed pleaded to go with them. Jesus told him to go home and tell his family how the Lord had delivered him from demon-possession. The man told everyone in the area east of the Sea of Galilee what Jesus had done for him.

They went back across the sea. On the other side, a large group was waiting. One of them was Jairus, a synagogue ruler, whose twelve-year-old daughter was dying. He fell at Jesus' feet and pleaded with him to come to his house and heal her.

Jesus started for Jairus's house when a woman who had been sick for twelve years came up behind him and touched the edge of his robe. She stopped bleeding immediately and knew she had been miraculously cured.

Jesus realized someone had been healed, so he turned and asked, "Who touched me?"

Because of the size of the crowd, his disciples thought his question was ridiculous. They said, "You are surrounded by people. Why do you ask, 'Who touched me?' "

Jesus kept scanning the crowd, looking for the person who had touched him. Realizing she could not hide from Jesus, the woman fell at his feet and admitted she was the one who had touched him.

Jesus commended her. "Daughter," he said. "Go in peace. Your faith has healed you."

While he was still speaking, some men came from Jairus's house and said, "Your daughter is dead. There is no need to bother Jesus."

Jesus turned to Jairus and said, "Don't be afraid. Trust me. Your daughter will live." When he arrived, he saw people weeping and wailing. He went inside the house and boldly declared, "The child isn't dead; she's only asleep."

Those present laughed at Jesus, so he made them leave. He allowed the girl's father, mother, and his disciples to go into the girl's room with him. He took her by the hand and said in Aramaic, "Little girl, arise."

The twelve-year-old stood and walked. The people were astonished. They didn't know what to think. Jesus told them to give her something to eat and not tell anyone what had happened. But they didn't pay any attention and told everyone about the miracle.

Two blind men were following Jesus when he left Jairus's house, pleading with him, "Son of David, please help us!" They were so desperate they followed him into the house where he planned to spend the night.

Jesus asked them, "Do you believe I can make you see?"

"Yes, Lord, we believe you can," they said.

Jesus said that because of their faith, they would be healed; immediately they were able to see. They told everyone how Jesus had restored their sight, even though he had strictly told them not to tell anyone.

Not everyone believed that Jesus' miracles were proof he was the Son of God. The next morning as Jesus and his disciples were leaving the house, a man who was demon-possessed and unable to speak was brought to Jesus. When Jesus cast the demon out, the man began to speak.

The people said, "Nothing like this has ever happened in Israel!" The Pharisees, however, still charged that Jesus was empowered by Satan, the prince of demons.

Back in his hometown of Nazareth, Jesus went to the synagogue on the Sabbath. People were amazed and perplexed by his ability to teach and his miraculous power to heal. Many believed he was God's Son.

Others, though, stumbled over his human origin. They scoffed and said, "He's just the son of Joseph, the carpenter." Because they knew Jesus' family, they found his claims offensive. Jesus did only a few miracles in Nazareth because of their lack of faith.

EXPANDING THE MINISTRY

Jesus and his disciples left Nazareth to minister throughout the province of Galilee. He taught in synagogues, announcing the good news of God's kingdom, and he healed people of all kinds of diseases. He was moved with compassion because it was obvious people were helpless victims of Israel's religious leaders.

The leaders exploited people for personal gain rather than ministering to their spiritual needs. Jesus told his disciples to pray. He said, "Ask the Lord for more compassionate and devoted workers who genuinely care about people."

After they had prayed, Jesus called the twelve disciples together and gave them power and authority to cast out demons and heal the sick. He instructed them to announce the kingdom's good news and to rely on the hospitality of supporters. He warned that they would encounter opposition yet reminded them that they were of immense value to God and not to fear those who could kill them physically but not spiritually. He promised that anyone who lost his life serving God would not lose his reward in heaven.

The disciples then went from village to village, preaching the good news and healing the sick. As a result of their ministry, Jesus became so well-known that many thought he was John the Baptist raised from the dead. Others thought Jesus was one of the prophets.

Herod Antipas had ordered John the Baptist beheaded. He'd arrested John because John had accused Herod of adultery for marrying his brother's wife.

Herod was reluctant to kill John because the people believed he was a prophet, but at his birthday party, Salome, the daughter of his wife, entertained him and his guests with a sensual dance. Herod then offered to give her anything she wanted, up to half his kingdom. Prompted by her mother, she asked for John's head.

Though surprised, Herod had to keep his word. John's head was brought on a platter to the girl, who then gave it to her mother. When his disciples heard John had been executed, they asked for his body and placed it in a tomb.

When Jesus heard John had been killed, he sailed with his disciples to an isolated place on the other side of the sea. But people found out where he'd gone, and thousands followed. Jesus taught them about the kingdom of God and healed some who were sick.

Late in the afternoon, the disciples told Jesus he should let the people depart so they could get something to eat. Jesus shocked them when he said, "You give them food."

Philip protested, "It would take eight months of wages to buy food for all these people."

Jesus asked the disciples how much food they had with them. They said, "We have five loaves of bread and two small fish."

Jesus directed them to divide the crowd into groups of fifty and have them sit on the grass. Jesus took the five loaves and two fish in his hands and, looking up to heaven, offered thanks. He broke the bread and gave it to his disciples to feed the people. They fed thousands and thousands of people, and they had twelve baskets of food left over.

Jesus sent the disciples back to the other side of the sea. He dismissed the crowd and found a quiet place on the mountainside to pray.

While he was praying, the disciples could only make it about halfway across the sea because of a strong wind. When Jesus saw what was happening, he walked across the water to the boat. The disciples saw him and were terrified; they cried out, thinking he was a ghost.

Jesus assured them he was alive, saying, "It is I; don't be afraid."

Peter said, "Lord, if it is really you, can I come to you on the water?"

Jesus told him to step out of the boat, and he did. But when Peter saw the wind and the waves, he began to sink.

Jesus grabbed his hand and said, "Why did you doubt, Peter? Where is your faith?"

When they climbed into the boat, the wind calmed and they reached the other side of the sea. The disciples didn't know what to think. They worshiped him and said, "You are the Son of God," but they were also confused by his power to control the forces of nature.

As soon as they had landed on the west side of the Sea of Galilee, people recognized Jesus and brought the sick to him. They begged him to allow them merely to touch the edge of his cloak; all who touched him were healed.

The next day when the people realized he was gone, they sailed across the sea to look for him. They found him at Capernaum with his disciples. When Jesus saw the large crowd and realized they were only following him because he had miraculously fed them before, he explained the meaning of the miracle to them. He said, "Don't be consumed by searching for what is temporary and will eventually perish, like food. Seek the life that I can give you. It is eternal and will never perish."

The people still didn't understand and asked Jesus to give them food like Moses had given the children of Israel manna in the wilderness.

Jesus corrected them and said, "It wasn't Moses who gave them food. It was my Father, who now offers you bread from heaven."

When the people said, "Give us this bread," Jesus replied, "I am the bread of life. Whoever comes to me will never be hungry again. I have come down from heaven to do the will of my Father."

His statement that he had come down from heaven confused and angered many because they believed he was merely the son of Joseph. Jesus told them to stop complaining, because those who ate the bread in the wilderness died, but anyone who ate the bread Jesus was offering would never die.

Many in the crowd left and never returned to follow Jesus because they didn't understand that by "bread" Jesus meant to believe in him as the Son of God. Most didn't want to trust Jesus as Savior because it required too much of a commitment.

Aware that many were confused and upset, Jesus asked the twelve disciples if they intended to abandon him.

Peter said, "Where would we go? You are the only one who can give us eternal life; you are the Holy Son of God."

Jesus was grateful for their devotion, but he knew that Judas would betray him.

COMPLAINTS AND MIRACLES

The religious elite continued to look for a way to discredit Jesus. After shadowing Jesus and his disciples while they were ministering in Galilee, a group of Pharisees from Jerusalem accused his disciples of violating the law of Moses. The charge: failing to ritualistically wash their hands before eating.

Jesus said the Pharisees were hypocrites. They observed hundreds of man-made laws but didn't obey God's laws. As just one example, while Moses said to honor one's father and mother, the Pharisees would tell their parents they couldn't help them because they'd promised to give their inheritance to God. This was permitted by their traditions, but it violated God's Word.

Jesus turned to the crowd that was following and said, "It is not what goes into a person that corrupts him; it is what comes out from the heart that makes him evil."

When Jesus and his disciples had gone into a house and were alone, Peter asked Jesus to explain the parable. Jesus said that the food a person eats only goes into the stomach, then passes out of the body into the sewer. But what comes from a person's heart exposes their true character. Immorality, theft, murder, adultery, greed, deceit, lust, envy, slander, pride, and foolishness are the kinds of acts and thoughts that corrupt a person, not eating with unwashed hands.

Jesus left Galilee and went to Tyre and Sidon. Even though he was in a non-Jewish region, he could not keep his identity secret. A Greek woman came and fell at his feet, begging him to deliver her daughter from demon-possession.

His disciples considered her a nuisance and wanted Jesus to get rid of her. Jesus said his first priority was to help his own people, the Jews, and asked her, "Would it be right to help you?"

The woman persisted and humbly said, "I am willing to eat the crumbs that fall from the table of the Jews."

Jesus commended her remarkable faith and told her to go home, saying, "The demon has left your daughter."

The woman found her daughter lying quietly in bed. The demon was gone.

Jesus traveled south to the Decapolis (a region of ten cities southeast of the Sea of Galilee). Large crowds continued to come, and he healed those who were handicapped, blind, and deaf.

A group of people brought a man to Jesus who was deaf and could not speak, but instead of healing him publicly, Jesus took him aside and healed him in a very unusual way. He put his fingers in the man's ears, then spit on his finger and touched the man's tongue. He looked up to heaven and said in Aramaic, *"Ephphatha,"* which means, "Be opened." Instantly, the man was able to both hear and speak clearly. The people were amazed and told everyone about the miracle, though Jesus had said not to tell anyone.

Jesus continued to attract large crowds, and after some had been with him for three days, he told his disciples he didn't want the people to leave hungry. They didn't know what to do because the twelve of them didn't have enough food to feed thousands, plus they were in a remote area and couldn't buy food.

Jesus asked how much bread they had.

"Seven loaves, and a few fish," they said.

Jesus took the bread and fish and, after giving thanks, he gave them to the disciples to feed the people. Everyone had enough to eat, and the disciples still picked up seven baskets of leftover food. Jesus sent the people home after they had eaten; he and his disciples departed for the region of Magadan or Dalmanutha (location unknown).

Israel's religious leaders tried again to discredit Jesus, demanding that he show them a miracle directly from God. Their repeated demands for a miracle troubled Jesus. He sighed and said they knew how to interpret weather signs but did not understand the miraculous signs he'd shown to prove he was the Messiah. He charged they were an evil generation and unfaithful to God; they would only get the sign of Jonah. Like Jonah, who was in the belly of a large fish for three days and nights, Jesus would be in the grave three days before his resurrection.

When Jesus and his disciples had crossed the sea, Jesus told them to watch out for the yeast of the Pharisees and Sadducees. At first they misunderstood and blamed one another for not bringing bread. Jesus stopped the argument and said if they had more spiritual perception they would have known what he was talking about. He repeated the warning, and this time they understood he was referring to the corrupting effect of the teachings of Israel's religious elite.

While Jesus usually healed people instantly, at Bethsaida (a small fishing village northeast of the Sea of Galilee), he restored the sight of a blind man in two stages. After Jesus spit on the man's eyes and put his hands on them, he asked, "Can you see now?"

The man said he could see but not clearly. When Jesus touched his eyes a second time, his sight was perfectly restored. Jesus told the man not to tell anyone about the miracle on his way home.

"WHO AM I?"

As Jesus and his disciples were on their way to Caesarea Philippi (north of the Sea of Galilee near Mount Hermon), he asked, "Who do people say that I am?"

They replied that they were certain Jesus was a prophet. Some thought he was John the Baptist or Elijah; others thought he was Jeremiah or one of the prophets.

Jesus wanted to know what they thought, so he asked, "Who do you think I am?"

Peter spoke for all the disciples when he said, "You are Christ, the Son of the living God!"

Jesus commended Peter for his answer, and for the first time predicted the creation of the church. Jesus promised that all the powers of hell would never be able to stop the advance of the church because he would give his followers God's authority to advance the kingdom on earth.

When Jesus was confident of their faith in him as the Son of God, he made a startling disclosure about his mission. He said he would be arrested by the religious leaders and put to death, but he would rise from the dead on the third day.

This was so shocking that Peter took Jesus aside and tried to refute him. "This will never happen to you, Lord," he said. He did not realize Jesus' mission as Savior included his suffering and death.

Jesus' response to Peter was swift and stern. "Get away from me, Peter," he ordered. "Though you don't realize it, you are setting a satanic trap for me. It is God's will for me to suffer and die."

After predicting his own death, Jesus taught that faith in him requires radical devotion: "True believers must take up their cross and follow me." He warned that the person who is not willing to give up everything and perhaps even die will be condemned in the final judgment.

Several days later Jesus climbed Mount Hermon with Peter, James, and John. As they watched, Jesus' appearance was majestically transformed. His face turned bright as the sun and his clothes turned a brilliant white. Moses and Elijah suddenly appeared and spoke with Jesus about his death, resurrection, and return to heaven.

The disciples didn't know what to do. Peter suggested they build shelters so that everyone could stay on the mountain, but before he finished speaking, they were surrounded by a dense cloud. Frightened, they fell down on their faces and heard a thunderous voice saying, "This is my Son whom I love; believe what he tells you."

Jesus told them to get up and said, "Don't be afraid." When the disciples looked up, Moses and Elijah had disappeared. Only Jesus remained.

As they were descending the mountain, Jesus told them not to tell anyone what they had seen until he had risen from the dead. They didn't tell anyone but discussed among themselves what Jesus meant by "rising from the dead."

The next day Jesus encountered a large group of people arguing with his disciples. When he asked why they were arguing, one of the men spoke up and complained: "A demon repeatedly attacks my son. I brought him to your disciples to cast out the demon, but they couldn't."

Jesus told the man to bring his son. When the evil spirit saw Jesus, he threw the boy into a violent convulsion. The boy rolled on the ground and foamed at the mouth.

The boy's father cried out in desperation, "Help, please help my son if you can!"

"What do you mean, 'If I can'?" said Jesus. "Anything is possible if you believe."

The man said, "I believe; help my unbelief!"

Jesus rebuked the demonic spirit and said, "I command you to come out of the boy and never attack him again." The spirit threw the boy to the ground so hard that the crowd thought the boy was dead. Jesus took him by the hand and pulled him to his feet. The boy stood up and was completely well.

When they were alone with Jesus, his disciples asked why they couldn't cast out the spirit. Jesus said that they still didn't have enough faith to cast out this kind of evil spirit.

JESUS AGAIN PREDICTS HIS DEATH AND RESURRECTION

As Jesus and his disciples continued to minister in Galilee, Jesus tried again to warn them that he would be betrayed and killed yet would rise from the dead after three days. The disciples still didn't understand but were too upset and embarrassed to ask him to explain.

When they arrived in Capernaum, the temple tax collectors from Jerusalem were waiting. They charged that Jesus didn't pay the temple tax. Peter denied this and said Jesus did pay the temple tax. Once inside the house, before Peter could say anything, Jesus told him to go catch a fish. He said Peter would find a silver coin in the mouth of the first fish he caught; he was to use the coin to pay the tax for both of them.

An argument among the disciples about who would be greatest in the kingdom of heaven gave Jesus an opportunity to teach how radically different kingdom values were from those of the world. He said humility is not only a condition for greatness but for entrance into God's kingdom. Jesus took a child in his arms and said, "Whoever is humble enough to honor a little child honors me and my Father who sent me."

The disciples were still concerned about power and positions of honor when they complained about an outsider who used Jesus' name to cast out a demon. They said they had ordered him to stop because he wasn't one of the Twelve. Jesus replied that anyone who was casting out demons in his name was not an enemy but a friend, and he promised that anyone who served others in his name would be rewarded.

Rather than debate about greatness, Jesus told his disciples they should be concerned about sin. He warned that anyone who causes another person to sin puts himself in jeopardy of eternal judgment. Jesus urged believers to deal radically with sin, leaving no place for it in their lives.

He told his disciples that if another believer offends them, they should seek privately to resolve the problem with that person. If they can't settle the issue with the other person, then they should ask the leaders of the church to help.

Peter wanted to know how many times he should forgive someone who offended him. Jesus said that believers should be as merciful as God, whose willingness to forgive is limitless. He said a person who is not willing to forgive is not a true believer.

Jesus then told a story about a man who owed a debt to a king but could not pay it. The king had mercy on the man and forgave his debt, but then the man, instead of showing mercy to one of his own debtors, had that man arrested and thrown into prison. When the king found out, he seized his debtor and put him in prison. Jesus concluded by saying that, like the king, God will punish those who are unwilling to forgive others after God has shown them mercy.

As Jesus and his disciples were walking toward Jerusalem, Jesus again emphasized the high cost of following him. He said that once a person makes the decision to follow him, he cannot return to his former life for any reason.

As the Jewish autumn feast approached, Jesus' unbelieving brothers prodded him to go to Jerusalem. They sarcastically said, "Since you want to become famous, instead of doing miracles in secret, go public. Go to Jerusalem and show yourself to the world."

Jesus refused. He told his brothers to go if they wanted; he wasn't going with them. He stayed in Galilee until he had the opportunity to go secretly to Jerusalem.

When he left, Jesus sent some of his followers ahead to make arrangements to stay in a Samaritan village, but the residents refused to let Jesus stay there. Peter and John wanted to destroy the village with fire, but Jesus reprimanded them and went on to another village before going to Jerusalem.

♆ Chapter Summary

Jesus was received enthusiastically in Galilee. There his ministry began to flourish and his fame spread. He preached about the kingdom of God, healed the sick, and cast out demons. He also healed non-Jews.

Jesus did other amazing things too, like miraculously helping Peter catch huge loads of fish, stopping a storm with the power of his commanding word, and feeding thousands of people with a few fish and bread loaves.

But not everyone welcomed Jesus. The Jewish religious leaders opposed him for "breaking the law" and for taking attention away from themselves. They tried to argue with him, yet Jesus knew too much to become trapped by their games.

The leaders persisted in plotting his demise. Jesus predicted his own death to his disciples, but they did not understand.

Sixteen

LATER JUDEAN MINISTRY, PEREAN MINISTRY, AND JOURNEY TO JERUSALEM

Main Characters
Jesus
The disciples
The Pharisees and religious leaders
Mary, Martha, and Lazarus

Setting
Jerusalem
Mount of Olives (outside Jerusalem)
Judea
Perea (region east of Jordan)
Bethany
Jericho

CONFUSION AND DIVISION

Jesus and his disciples returned to Jerusalem to attend two Jewish religious festivals. He used symbolism from the festivals to teach that he was Christ and the Son of God.

Jesus' teaching created a sharp division between the people and the leaders. Many common people believed in him, but his claims infuriated the Jewish religious leaders and made them even more determined to kill him.

When the leaders heard Jesus was in Jerusalem, they tried to find him but couldn't, even though everyone was talking about him. Some believed he was a good man; others thought he was a fraud. No one had the courage to speak openly about him because they were afraid of the leaders.

Halfway through the seven-day festival, Jesus began teaching in the temple courts. The people were amazed at his knowledge—he didn't have a formal education—and asked, "How do you know so much?"

Jesus said his teaching was not his own and made the startling claim that he had been trained by God, who had sent him. Jesus said if they truly knew God, they would recognize he was from God; but instead they wanted to kill him because he exposed them as religious hypocrites.

This infuriated his audience, who charged that Jesus was deluded and demon-possessed. "Who is trying to kill you?" they asked.

Jesus replied that they wanted to kill him because he healed on the Sabbath (the seventh day) in violation of the law of Moses. However, the Law actually permits acts of mercy on the seventh day. Their problem was they didn't know the Law.

Jesus' response made some people

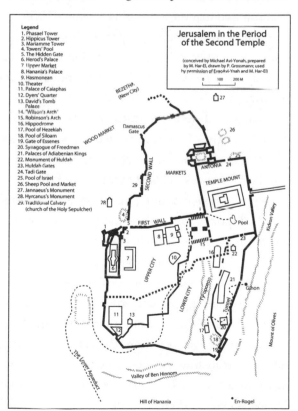

think he truly was the Messiah, but they weren't certain. The leaders, unconvinced, thought about arresting him because he claimed he had been sent by God, yet they still were afraid of the people and confused by his teaching.

As Jesus continued teaching in the temple, more and more people became convinced he was the Messiah. When the Pharisees realized how many were siding with Jesus, they sent the temple guards to arrest him.

Jesus baffled the guards when he said he was returning to the One who had sent him. They thought he was either returning to Nazareth or leaving Jerusalem for another country. They didn't arrest him.

On the last day of the festival, Jesus claimed he was "Living Water." He said, "Anyone who is thirsty and believes in me may come and drink." He promised that the Spirit of God would give that person eternal life.

Jesus' claim divided the people. Some thought he was a prophet, others thought he was the Messiah. Some wanted to arrest him because they thought he was from Nazareth, not Bethlehem, and they knew the Messiah would come from Bethlehem.

The guards returned to the priests and Pharisees, who wanted to know why they had not arrested Jesus. The guards answered, "His teaching is amazing! We have never heard anything like it."

The Pharisees mocked them, saying that anyone who believed in Jesus was stupid and didn't know what they were doing. Nicodemus, who had spoken to Jesus previously, cautioned the leaders: "Is it just to condemn a person without a fair hearing?"

Nicodemus' warning fell on deaf ears. The religious leaders sarcastically asked if he was one of Jesus' naïve followers from Galilee.

That evening Jesus left Jerusalem and spent the night on the Mount of Olives. Early the next morning he returned to the temple.

While he was teaching, the religious leaders and the Pharisees dragged before him a woman who they claimed was caught in the act of adultery. They told Jesus that the Law said to stone her and then asked, "What do you say? How should she be punished?"

Jesus knew they were trying to trap him. He stooped down and wrote something in the sand with his finger. They kept demanding an answer, so Jesus stood and said, "Let the one who has never sinned throw the first stone." Then he wrote again in the sand.

The woman's accusers began walking away, one at a time.

Jesus asked the woman, "Where are your accusers? Didn't even one of them condemn you?"

"No, Lord," she said.

"Neither do I," said Jesus. "You can leave, but don't continue to sin."

As he continued speaking to those who had gathered around, Jesus said, "I am the Light of the World."

The Pharisees attacked immediately. They said Jesus didn't have enough evidence to make that kind of claim—he needed at least one witness.

Jesus said he had two. Because he was the Son of God, he was his own witness; his Father was his second witness.

The Pharisees didn't understand that Jesus meant God was his Father. They wanted to arrest him but didn't know how to charge him.

Jesus had previously angered the Pharisees when he said he had come from heaven. Now he told them he would soon return, and they would not be able to come with him.

Jesus warned that they would die in their sins, but they didn't understand what he meant. He explained, yet they were still confused. Jesus said they would only understand after his death on the cross. Many of the people believed that what he said was true.

Jesus commended those who believed and said they had been set free by believing the truth, while the self-righteous religious people remained slaves to sin.

The Pharisees, not realizing he was referring to spiritual slavery, exploded in anger.

Jesus said that their desire to kill him revealed they were not children of God but, rather, were children of the devil.

The Pharisees responded with a racial slur and called Jesus "a Samaritan devil."

Jesus denied the charge, saying he was not a demon but came to glorify his Father, and that even Abraham had looked forward to his coming with great joy.

They ridiculed him and said, "You aren't yet fifty years old. How can you say you are older than Abraham?"

Jesus made a startling claim: "I am telling you the truth; I am God, and I existed before Abraham was born."

The Pharisees screamed, "Blasphemy!" and picked up stones to throw at Jesus, but he quickly left the temple before they could assault him.

MINISTERING IN JUDEA

Because of the violent opposition in Jerusalem, Jesus left the city to minister in Judea (the southern province that included Jerusalem). Jesus appointed seventy-two disciples, in addition to the twelve apostles, to expand his ministry.

He instructed them to pray and trust God to provide for their needs. He warned of opposition, and he told them to simply leave those towns where they were not welcome. His gave them power to heal those who were sick and who were receptive to the good news about God's kingdom.

The ministry of the seventy-two exceeded their expectations. They were filled with joy when they returned to Jesus, and they told him how they had been victorious over the forces of evil.

Jesus rejoiced with them and thanked his Father for enabling them to serve others in his name.

One day a man who was an expert in religious law came to Jesus and asked, "What should I do to inherit eternal life?"

Jesus responded with a question: "What is written in the Old Testament?"

The man answered, "Love the Lord your God with all your heart, soul, strength, and mind," and, "Love your neighbor as yourself."

Jesus said, "You have answered correctly, and if you demonstrate your faith by loving God and your neighbor, you will have eternal life."

The man wanted to impress Jesus, so he asked, "Who is my neighbor?"

Jesus answered his question with a stunning story about a Jewish man who had been mugged and left for dead, but a Samaritan man stopped to help, while a Jewish priest ignored him.

Back in Jerusalem (there is some uncertainty about the chronology of Jesus' travels through Judea), Jesus and his disciples passed a blind man.

The disciples asked, "Is he blind because he sinned, or because his parents sinned?"

Jesus said, "Neither. This man's blindness happened so that the work of God might be displayed in his life."

Jesus spit on the ground to make mud, and he spread it over the man's eyes. Then he told the man to go and wash in the pool of Siloam (in the southern part of Jerusalem).

When the man washed his face, he was immediately able to see. He tried to find Jesus, but he had gone.

Everyone who knew the blind man was amazed. They asked one another, "Isn't this the blind man who used to beg?" Others weren't sure it was the same man. They thought it was someone who looked like him.

When the man insisted he indeed was the blind beggar, the people wanted to know who had healed him. He said it was the man known as Jesus and told them how Jesus had healed him with mud. The people wanted to know how they could find Jesus, yet the man didn't know where he had gone.

When the Pharisees heard the man's account, they flew into a rage; Jesus had made mud on the Sabbath. They concluded that Jesus could not be from God because he was working on the seventh day.

Others disagreed. They reasoned that Jesus couldn't be a sinner, because a sinful person could not have worked such an amazing miracle.

The Pharisees decided to ask the man what he thought about Jesus. He said, "I believe he is a prophet."

Even with the man's testimony, the Jewish leaders refused to believe Jesus had healed him, so they summoned his parents and questioned them.

The parents were afraid to answer the leaders' questions because they knew the leaders had decided to expel from the synagogue anyone who believed Jesus was the Messiah.

The leaders called in the blind man a second time for questioning. They warned him that they knew Jesus was a sinner, and that he should admit it so God would get the credit for his healing.

The man said, "I don't know whether or not he is a sinner, but I know I was blind and now I can see."

The leaders asked the man again how Jesus had healed him. But he'd had enough of their foolish questions. It was obvious they weren't interested in the facts; they were determined to condemn Jesus. He asked, "Why do you want to hear again how Jesus healed me? Do you want to become his disciples?"

They cursed the man for challenging them. They said, "We are disciples of Moses, but we don't know anything about this man Jesus."

The man said, "What? He healed me, and you don't know anything about him? No one could have healed a blind man if God were not with him."

This made them so angry, they condemned him and threw him out of the synagogue.

When Jesus heard what had happened, he found the man and asked, "Do you believe in the Son of Man?"

The man answered, "Who is he? I want to believe!"

"You have seen him," said Jesus. "I am the one who healed you."

The man believed in Jesus and worshiped him.

Jesus said he had come into the world to give sight to those who are spiritually blind; unfortunately some who think they know God are spiritually blind.

Several Pharisees standing nearby asked, "Are you saying we are blind?"

Jesus said, "Because you claim to know God, yet won't believe in me, you are lost in the blindness of unbelief."

Jesus knew his teaching had opened a chasm between the people and the religious elite. Many were convinced he was the Son of God, but most of Israel's leaders considered him a false Messiah and threat to them.

Jesus made one of his strongest indictments of the leaders using Old Testament imagery. He compared himself to a Good Shepherd and the religious leaders to ruthless shepherds who exploited people for personal gain.

Jesus had come to lead his sheep to green pastures—to a meaningful and fulfilling life now and eternal life in the future. In contrast to leaders who didn't really care about people, Jesus was willing to sacrifice his life to save his sheep. He made a dramatic declaration: "No one can take my life from me. I am a willing sacrifice, and I have both the power to give up my life and the power to restore it." He claimed God was his Father and had given him power over both his death and resurrection.

Jesus' teaching was so bold and amazing that some charged he was demon-possessed. Others remembered how he had healed the beggar and asked, "Can a demon open the eyes of a blind man?"

The heart of the dispute with the religious leaders was Jesus' claim to be Israel's promised Messiah; they didn't have sufficient evidence to condemn him for fraud.

They decided to force Jesus to incriminate himself. They cornered him in Jerusalem during the Feast of Dedication (commemorating the temple's reopening after its destruction by the Greeks) and demanded to know if he was the Messiah.

Jesus did not answer them directly; rather, he offered this evidence: "The miracles I do in my Father's name speak for me. If you were my sheep, you would believe me. I know my sheep and give them eternal life, and no one will ever be able to take them from me because God my Father is more powerful than anyone."

And then, without hesitation, he declared, "I and my Father are one!"

The Jews picked up stones to kill him for blasphemy—claiming he was God.

But Jesus challenged them. He reminded them in the Old Testament Scriptures that some of Israel's leaders were called gods, so why should they object to his calling himself the Son of God? They had seen the proof of his miraculous works, even if they didn't believe in him.

This only made them angrier, and they tried to stone him again. Because of the threat to his life, Jesus decided to leave Jerusalem.

PEREAN MINISTRY

Jesus and his disciples went to the Roman province of Perea, east of the Jordan River. This was the region where John the Baptist first began baptizing people; many of John's followers became followers of Jesus, as they realized that everything John had said about him was true.

While Jesus was there, he continued to teach about the kingdom of God. Some Pharisees warned him that Herod wanted to kill him, but Jesus wasn't concerned. He knew he wouldn't die outside of Jerusalem.

He was invited to a feast at the house of a Pharisee where there was a sick man, swollen with fluid. Jesus asked the Pharisees if it was right to heal the man, since it happened to be the day of worship.

They didn't answer, so he healed the man, saying that if your ox falls into a well on the day of worship, you wouldn't wait until the next day to get him out. He also went on to talk about being humble and being kind to those who can't repay you.

When the crowds excitedly followed him, Jesus warned that they needed to realize that there was a cost to being his disciple. The sinners and tax collectors continued to listen to him, but the religious leaders continued to complain.

Jesus told three parables about the love of God. The first was about a shepherd who cared so much for his sheep that he left ninety-nine to search for one that was lost. The second compared the kingdom to a lost coin of great value; the third, often called the Prodigal Son, was about how God welcomes sinners back when they repent, even after falling into great sin.

Jesus also preached about honesty in business practices and about caring for the poor. He warned against causing others to lose faith, and when his disciples asked for more faith, he said it only takes a very small amount—the size of a mustard seed—to do big things. Finally, Jesus said they needed to humbly do their duties as his followers, not seeking prosperity but wanting to serve only the Lord.

ON THE WAY TO JERUSALEM

While ministering, Jesus received word from Mary and Martha that their brother, Lazarus, was ill. Lazarus lived in Bethany, a small village east of Jerusalem.

When Jesus received the message, he told his disciples that Lazarus's sickness would not end in death; rather, it was an opportunity for Jesus to reveal his power and glory as the Son of God. Instead of leaving immediately, Jesus stayed where he was for two more days, and then surprised his disciples by telling them they were going back to Judea.

They didn't understand what Jesus intended to do, so they questioned his decision: "Teacher, are you certain you want to go back to Judea? It hasn't been that long ago since the Jews there tried to stone you."

Jesus knew they wouldn't understand if he told them he was going to raise Lazarus from the dead, so he said Lazarus was asleep and he was going to wake him up.

They still didn't understand and said, "Lord, if he is asleep he will wake up."

Jesus told them plainly, "Lazarus is dead! We need to go to Bethany now!"

Thomas persuaded the other disciples and said, "Let's go, and we will die with him."

When Jesus arrived in Bethany, Lazarus had been dead four days, and his body had been placed in a tomb. Martha went out to meet Jesus and said, "Lord, if only you had come sooner, you could have kept my brother from dying. But I know that God will do whatever you ask."

Jesus said her brother would rise from the dead.

Not knowing what he intended to do, she said she knew Lazarus would rise from the dead at the end of time.

Jesus said to Martha, "I am the resurrection and the life. Anyone who believes in me will live again after they die. And everyone who believes in me will never die because I will give them eternal life."

Jesus asked Martha if she believed this. She said she believed he was the Messiah and the Son of God.

Martha returned home to get Mary, and Jesus went to the graveyard. When Martha and Mary arrived, Mary fell at his feet and said, "Lord, if you had been here my brother would not have died."

When Jesus saw her weeping and all of the mourners crying and wailing, Jesus wept. He asked, "Where is Lazarus's tomb?"

Jesus went and told some of the mourners to open the tomb.

They refused, saying, "Lord, Lazarus has been dead four days. The smell will be terrible!"

Jesus said, "I told you that you would see God's glorious power if you believed." So they rolled away the stone from the entrance.

Jesus prayed and shouted, "Lazarus, come out!"

Lazarus emerged, still wrapped in graveclothes, his face covered with the burial cloth. Jesus told the people to take off the wraps and free Lazarus.

The raising of Lazarus convinced many mourners that Jesus was God's Son, but others reported what had happened to the chief priests and the Pharisees. The Sanhedrin (a religious council that included the high priest) held a special meeting to discuss the Jesus threat.

Fearing intervention from the Romans because Jesus was stirring up nationalistic hopes, the high priest Caiaphas insisted that Jesus must be put to death. The Sanhedrin unanimously agreed and began to plot how to kill him secretly without causing a riot.

To prevent the Sanhedrin from arresting him before Passover, Jesus stayed in a small village of Ephraim that was within walking distance from Jerusalem. He continued to minister to people in rural areas until Passover.

One day, near Samaria, Jesus was met by ten lepers who begged him to heal them. Jesus did and told them to go show themselves to a priest. All except one left without thanking Jesus. That one, a Samaritan, came back to Jesus, shouting, "Praise God!" Jesus commended him for his faith.

Knowing he soon would be arrested and executed, Jesus continued to teach his disciples about his suffering and death, but they didn't fully understand what he was talking about.

As they were approaching Jericho, a blind beggar heard the noise of a passing crowd. He asked what was happening and heard that Jesus of Nazareth was on his way to Jerusalem. He cried out, "Jesus, have mercy on me!"

The people yelled for the man to shut up, but he shouted louder, "Jesus, help me!"

Jesus stopped and asked, "What do you want me to do?"

The man answered, "Lord, I want to see."

Jesus said, "Your faith has healed you."

When Jesus and the large crowd following him entered Jericho (about twenty miles east of Jerusalem), Zacchaeus, a wealthy tax collector for the Romans, climbed a tree to see Jesus as he passed.

Jesus saw him in the tree, he stopped and said, "Zacchaeus, come down. I would like to have dinner in your house."

When the people saw Jesus talking to a tax collector, they were outraged and grumbled, "Why would Jesus eat with a man who is corrupt and sinful?"

On meeting Jesus, Zacchaeus was convicted of his own dishonesty. He declared, "Lord, I will sell half my possessions to give to the poor and repay with interest those I have cheated."

Jesus said to Zacchaeus, "Salvation has come to your house because you have faith like your ancestor Abraham. For the Son of Man has come to seek and save the lost."

Because Jesus was near Jerusalem, his followers thought he was about to establish the kingdom of God on earth. Instead, to counter their expectation for the immediate coming of the kingdom, he told them a story:

"A nobleman left for a distant country and planned to become king, but while he was gone he found out that some of his subjects hated him. When he returns, he will judge those who rejected him, and he will reward his supporters."

♕ Chapter Summary

In Jerusalem, Jesus and his disciples faced continued opposition from the religious leaders. While the Pharisees focused on the Law and on judgment, Jesus was showing compassion to sinners.

When Jesus traveled throughout Judea, he sent his disciples off two by two so that they could learn how to preach about God's kingdom and minister to people's needs for themselves. They performed miracles in Jesus' name.

Back in Jerusalem, Jesus healed a man who had been blind from birth. There was no denying the miracle, though the Pharisees tried their best to expose the miracle as a trick. Later, when they questioned Jesus about whether or not he was the Messiah, he said he and the Father were one. The Jews tried to stone him for blasphemy, but Jesus escaped.

Jesus used parables to teach about the kingdom of God. His raising of Lazarus from the grave caused many to believe in him; it also fully convinced the religious leaders that he was a serious threat to their power.

Jesus traveled from Bethany through Jericho, on his way to Jerusalem, where he said he would be killed.

Seventeen

THE CRUCIFIXION OF JESUS

Main Characters
Jesus
The disciples
The Jewish religious leaders
Pilate

Setting
Bethany
Jerusalem

SUNDAY: TRIUMPHAL ENTRY

When it was almost time for the Passover Feast, everyone expected Jesus to come to Jerusalem. The chief priests had given orders that if anyone knew where Jesus was, they were to report it. They planned to arrest him.

Meanwhile, Jesus arrived in Bethany, where Lazarus lived. When the residents of Jerusalem heard Jesus was there, they rushed to see him and Lazarus, whom he had raised from the dead. The chief priests heard about all the excitement and made plans to kill Lazarus as well; many Jews had believed in Jesus because of him.

Jesus arranged his entry into Jerusalem, on a donkey, to fulfill prophecy. As he rode into the city, enthusiastic crowds cut palm branches and put them on the road. They sang, "Hosanna, blessed is he who comes in the name of the Lord. Hosanna in the highest."

Some of the Pharisees complained, demanding that Jesus silence his cheering supporters. Jesus refused but was saddened by the opposition. He wept for the city and said, "I wish you would have realized that I have come to bring peace, but the truth is hidden from your eyes. Before long this city will be so violently destroyed that not one stone will be left upon another."

At the end of the day, Jesus returned to Bethany for the night.

MONDAY: CLEANSING THE TEMPLE

The next morning on his way back, Jesus saw a fig tree, but when he searched it for fruit, he found nothing but leaves. His disciples heard him say, "This tree will never bear fruit."

When Jesus arrived in Jerusalem, he went directly to the temple and was outraged at what he found. People were exchanging money to buy animals for sacrifices and selling all kinds of merchandise. Knocking over their tables and benches, he threw the merchants out of the temple, yelling, "It is written in the Scriptures that God's house is a place of prayer for all nations, but you have turned it into a den of thieves!"

The religious leaders heard what Jesus had done and tried their best to come up with a plan to kill him, but they couldn't decide what to do because he was so popular with the people.

That same day, Greeks who had come to observe Passover asked his disciple Philip if they could meet Jesus. When Jesus heard their request, he predicted that the time was near for him to enter into his glory. He prayed, "Father, my heart is deeply troubled. Deliver me from the hour of death, but I know this is the reason that I came into the world. Please glorify your name."

A voice thundered from heaven, "I have glorified my name, and I will glorify it again."

Some who heard the voice thought it was thunder; others thought it was an angel. The crowd was puzzled; they didn't understand what had happened. Jesus left, and no one knew where he had gone.

In the evening, Jesus and his disciples returned to Bethany.

TUESDAY: A DAY OF CONTROVERSY

The next morning when they returned to Jerusalem, they saw that the fig tree had withered, and Peter remembered Jesus' words.

The disciples asked, "How did the tree die so quickly?"

Jesus answered, "If you have faith in God, you can say, 'Let this mountain be thrown into the sea,' and it will happen. Whatever you ask for in faith will be given to you. But when you pray you should always forgive those who have offended you, keeping in mind that God has forgiven your sins."

Jesus went to the temple, where he was teaching daily. A combined group of priests, teachers, and elders came and confronted him. "By what authority are you doing all these things?" they asked.

Jesus responded, "I will answer your question if you answer mine: Was John's baptism from heaven, or from men?"

They discussed the question and realized they were trapped in a dilemma. If they said from heaven, then Jesus would want to know why they didn't believe he was the Messiah. If they said from men, they thought they would be stoned for not believing John was a prophet. So they answered, "We don't know."

Jesus said, "Then I won't tell you by whose authority I am doing all of these things."

Jesus told the leaders three parables that warned of awful judgment for rejecting him. He said the kingdom would be taken away from them and offered to others, and they would be cast into darkness where there is "weeping and gnashing of teeth."

The warnings only made the leaders more determined to get rid of

Jesus. They plotted how to get him to incriminate himself so he would be arrested by the Romans.

The Pharisees then sent some of their supporters, along with supporters of Herod Antipas, to question Jesus about paying taxes. They said, "Tell us, in your opinion, should Jews pay taxes to the Romans?"

Jesus knew what they were trying to do and said, "You hypocrites, why are you trying to trap me? Bring me a coin."

When they gave it to him, Jesus asked, "Whose image is on the coin?"

They replied, "Caesar's."

Jesus said, "Give to Caesar what is his, and give to God what belongs to him."

They were dumbfounded and left.

Later that same day, the Sadducees, who didn't believe in resurrection, came with a confounding question. "Teacher," they said to Jesus, "according to the law of Moses, if a man dies without having any children, his brother is supposed to marry his widow to continue the family line.

"Now, there were seven brothers. The oldest one married and died without children, so his brother married his widow. But the second brother also died, and then the third, until finally all seven had died. After that, the woman died. Tell us, whose wife will she be in the resurrection, since she was legitimately married to all seven?"

Jesus answered, "You are mistaken; you do not know the Scriptures or the power of God. When people are resurrected, they will not marry. They will be like angels in heaven."

Then he said, "Have you not read in the book of Moses the account of God's appearance to Moses in the burning bush? God said, 'I am the God of Abraham, the God of Isaac, and the God of Jacob.' The Lord is the God of the living."

The people and even some of the teachers of the Law were astounded.

When the Pharisees heard Jesus had baffled the Sadducees, they sent an expert in the Law to question him. He challenged Jesus: "Teacher, which is the greatest commandment in the law of Moses?"

Jesus replied, "'You must love the Lord your God with all of your heart, with all of your soul, and with all of your mind.' And there is a second commandment: 'Love your neighbor as yourself.' All of the law of Moses and the prophets are based on these two commands."

The man commended Jesus for his answer and agreed that loving God and loving one's neighbor were more important than offerings and sacrifices.

Jesus said, "You are not far from the kingdom of God."

After that, no one dared ask Jesus any more questions.

Jesus asked a group of Pharisees a question: "Whose son is the Christ?"

"A son of David," they answered.

Jesus asked, "Then why does David call him 'Lord'? David said, 'The Lord said to my Lord: Sit at my right hand, until your enemies humble themselves under your feet.' If David calls his son 'Lord,' how can he be his son?"

The Pharisees didn't know how to answer. They were totally silent.

Having frustrated the leaders' attempts to publicly accuse him, Jesus also made a blistering indictment of the Pharisees and teachers of the Law. He pronounced "seven woes" on them, indicting them as hypocrites and blind guides. He charged them with violating God's Law and rejecting and even murdering God's messengers. He warned of impending judgment for their sins and the sins of their ancestors: "On you will come all the innocent blood that has been spilt on the earth from the righteous man Abel to Zechariah. . . . I tell you the truth, judgment will come on this generation."

Jesus longed for Israel to repent. He wanted to gather them as a hen gathers her chicks, but they rejected him. He predicted, "You will not see me again until you say, 'Blessed is he who comes in the name of the Lord.' "

Jesus went with his disciples and sat down near the place where people brought money to the temple. Jesus watched as the rich put in large sums, and then he saw a poor widow who put in two small copper coins, worth only a fraction of a penny. Jesus said to his disciples, "I tell you the truth, this woman has put in a larger gift than all others. The rich gave out of their wealth; she, out of her poverty, gave everything she had to live on."

As they were leaving the temple, the disciples said, "Teacher, look at these large and magnificent buildings."

Jesus replied, "Yes, they are great buildings, but they will be completely destroyed. Not one stone will be left on another."

They asked, "When will this happen, and what will be the sign of your return?"

In answering their questions, Jesus warned of messianic imposters, continuous wars, catastrophic natural disasters, and the persecution of believers. Jesus said these things were only "the birth pains" of more intense suffering, prior to the end of the present age.

The good news about God's kingdom would be preached to all nations before the end. People would know to flee Jerusalem when they saw "the abomination of desolation," which was predicted by Daniel the prophet.

After these times of terrible trouble, Jesus said he would return as the Son of Man: "They will see the Son of Man coming on the clouds of heaven with power and glory. He will send his angels, and they will gather believers from all over the world."

Jesus ended his message about Jerusalem's destruction and his return with a series of parables. He challenged his followers to wait patiently for his return and serve faithfully.

Jesus described the final judgment in the last story. He said that when the Son of Man comes, he will separate the "sheep" from the "goats."

The former will be worthy to enter God's kingdom because they have been compassionate to other people. The latter will be sent into eternal punishment because they have ignored the poor and helpless.

Knowing that Passover was only two days away, Jesus said to his disciples, "The Son of Man will be turned over to the Romans for crucifixion."

The chief priests and elders of the Jews met in the residence of Caiaphas, the high priest, and made plans to secretly arrest Jesus and kill him. They didn't want the people to know what they were doing because they were afraid of a riot.

Jesus had returned to Bethany for the night and was staying in the home of a man known as Simon the Leper. While he was reclining for dinner, a woman came up behind Jesus and poured expensive fragrant oil on his head.

Judas Iscariot complained, "What a waste! This oil could have been sold to help the poor."

Jesus answered, "Stop criticizing this woman. What she has done is wonderful. You will always have opportunity to help the poor, but I will not be with you much longer. Whenever the good news is proclaimed throughout the world, what she has done will be remembered."

Judas Iscariot, one of the Twelve, then left and went to the chief priests. He asked, "How much will you pay me if I betray Jesus?"

They gave him thirty pieces of silver, and he began scheming how he would betray Jesus.

WEDNESDAY (NO RECORDED ACTIVITY)

THURSDAY: PASSOVER AND TEACHING IN THE UPPER ROOM

On the first day of the Festival of Unleavened Bread, Jesus' disciples asked if he wanted them to make preparations for Passover. He told them to go to Jerusalem and find a man carrying a jar of water. They were to follow him and say to the owner of the house, "The Teacher asks, 'Do you have a guest room where I can eat the Passover meal with my disciples?' He will show you a large upper room. Make the preparations there."

The disciples went into the city and found everything exactly as Jesus had told them.

That evening, Jesus and his disciples went to the upper room and reclined at a table to eat the Passover meal. But before they had eaten anything, the disciples began debating about who was the greatest among them.

Jesus intervened, saying, "The kings of this world rule over their subjects, but I want my followers to be different. Instead, the greatest should take the lowest position. I have set an example for you to follow. One day you will rule in my kingdom, but for now I want you to humbly serve others."

Jesus then assumed the role of a servant; removing his outer robe and wrapping himself in a towel, he began washing their feet.

When he came to Simon Peter, Peter protested, "I will never let you wash my feet."

Jesus said, "Unless I wash your feet, you cannot be my disciple."

Peter replied, "Then wash my entire body!"

Jesus said, "That is not necessary. A person who has bathed is clean all over. Because you are my disciples, you are clean, but not all of you." Jesus said this because he knew Judas was planning to betray him.

While they were eating, Jesus said, "Listen, one of you is going to betray me!"

The disciples were distressed and said, "It can't possibly be me, can it, Lord?"

Jesus replied, "It is the one who has eaten this food with me. As I have predicted, the Son of Man will be betrayed, but it would have been better for my betrayer if he had never been born."

Judas said, "Surely, it isn't me, Teacher?"

Jesus answered, "Yes, it is you."

Judas took some bread, and at that moment Satan entered into him.

Jesus said, "What you plan to do, Judas, do quickly!" (Since Judas was in charge of their money, the disciples thought Jesus was telling him to buy food for the meal or something for the poor.)

Judas immediately went out into the darkness of the night.

Then Jesus spoke to the remaining disciples: "My beloved children, I will only be with you a little longer. You will look for me, but you will not find me, and you cannot come to where I am going.

"I am giving you a new commandment. As I have loved you, so you should love one another. By loving one another, you will prove to the world that you are my disciples."

Peter asked, "Lord, where are you going?"

Jesus answered, "Peter, you can't come with me now, but you will follow me later." He warned Peter and all the disciples that they would abandon him, but he promised that after he had risen from the dead, he would meet them in Galilee.

Peter protested and claimed that even if everyone else abandoned Jesus, he would never leave him.

Jesus said that before the rooster crowed, Peter would deny him three times.

Peter insisted, "Even if it means I have to die, I will never disown you."

All the other disciples said the same thing.

After warning that their loyalty would be severely tested, Jesus resumed the Passover meal. He gave thanks for the bread and broke it, giving a piece to each of them. He said, "This bread is my body. Eat it in remembrance of me."

He then took a cup of wine and, after giving thanks, said, "This is the new covenant in my blood, which is poured out as a sacrifice for many. Drink it in remembrance of me. Whenever you do this, you proclaim the Lord's death until he returns."

It was obvious to Jesus that his disciples were upset because he had said he was going to leave them. He said, "Don't let your hearts be troubled. Trust in God, and trust also in me." He promised he was leaving to prepare a place for them, and that they would one day be with him. When they complained they didn't know the way to where he was going, Jesus said, "I am the way, the truth, and the life. No one can come to the Father except through me."

Jesus promised that, in his absence, they would have a new relationship with him. He would send the Holy Spirit (Advocate/Counselor/Helper/Comforter) to be with them forever. The Spirit would guide them into truth, convict the world of its sin and need for righteousness, and bring glory to Christ.

Using the imagery of a grapevine, Jesus told his disciples that they must remain intimately connected to him to be fruitful (productive). He warned they would experience the same kind of hostility and persecution that he had faced, but the Spirit would help them testify to the world.

After telling his disciples about all these things, Jesus prayed. He asked the Father to glorify his Son, to protect the disciples, and to help all believers to become one even as Jesus and his Father are one.

Jesus and his disciples sang a hymn, then walked across the Kidron Valley to the Mount of Olives.

THE ARREST

Once they were in the olive grove called Gethsemane, Jesus said to his disciples, "Wait here while I pray."

He left all of them except Peter and John, whom he took with him for a short distance, before he was overcome with grief. He said to them, "My spirit is crushed to the point of death. Stay here and keep watch."

Jesus went a little farther and then, falling to the ground, he cried out, "Abba Father, please take this cup of suffering from me! Yet I want your will to be done, not mine." Jesus prayed so intently his sweat was like great drops of blood falling to the ground.

When he returned to the disciples, he found them sound asleep. He said to Peter, "Couldn't you watch with me for just one hour? Keep watch, and pray that you will not be trapped by temptation. Your spirit may be willing, but your flesh is weak."

Jesus left them again to pray. As before, when he came back, they were sleeping. They were so embarrassed they didn't know what to say. The same thing happened when he went to pray a third time and returned. Then he shouted, "Are you still sleeping? Look, the Son of Man is betrayed into the hands of sinners. My betrayer is here."

Before Jesus finished speaking, Judas burst into the olive grove with an armed group of soldiers. Judas had told them he would identify Jesus with a kiss, so he went directly to Jesus and said, "Rabbi" (which means "teacher"), and kissed him.

Jesus said, "Friend, do what you have planned!"

As the soldiers seized Jesus, Peter drew a sword and swung at the servant of the high priest. He partially missed and severed the man's ear.

Jesus intervened. "Put away your sword, Peter. Will I not drink the cup of suffering and death the Father has given to me?" He touched the man's ear and healed him.

The soldiers and the Jewish officials grabbed Jesus and tied him up.

Jesus said, "Am I leading a rebellion, that you have come with weapons? I have taught every day in the temple, and you did not arrest me. But now, Scripture is fulfilled."

Jesus' disciples fled, and one of them who was wearing only his outer robe ran away naked when the soldiers attempted to grab him.

JEWISH INTERROGATION AND TRIAL

It was the middle of the night when Jesus was taken to the house of Annas, the father-in-law of Caiaphas, the high priest. Annas asked Jesus about his disciples and his teaching.

"I have taught publicly," Jesus replied. "I have taught either in the synagogues or the temple, and I have not done anything in secret. Why question me? Ask those who heard my teaching. They know what I said."

One of the officials punched Jesus in the face. "Is this any way to answer Annas?" he demanded.

Jesus replied, "If I said something wrong, then what was it? But if I spoke the truth, why did you hit me?"

After briefly interrogating Jesus, they took him to Caiaphas, who had assembled some members of the Sanhedrin (supreme religious council), though it was night.

They were determined to find evidence to condemn Jesus. They brought in false witnesses, but the charges were so inconsistent, they couldn't find enough evidence to convict Jesus. They finally found two witnesses who said Jesus claimed he was going to destroy the temple and rebuild it in three days.

Caiaphas asked Jesus if he intended to respond to the charges, but Jesus didn't say a word. Frustrated, the high priest said, "You are under oath. Confess to us if you are Christ, the Son of God."

"I am," said Jesus. "In the future, you will see the Son of Man seated at the right hand of the Mighty God and coming on the clouds of heaven."

In anger and shock, the high priest tore his clothes and said, "We don't need any more witnesses. You have heard his blasphemy. What is your verdict?"

All of those present said, "Guilty, and he should be put to death." Some of them spit in Jesus' face. They blindfolded him and hit him with their fists. They mocked him, saying, "Prophesy—tell us who hit you." They turned him over to the guards, who also beat him.

Peter and another disciple who knew the high priest had followed Jesus to the house. When the other disciple was granted permission for them to enter the courtyard, a girl at the entrance asked Peter, "Aren't you one of Jesus' disciples?"

Peter replied, "I am not!"

Because it was cold, the guards had started a small fire in the middle of the courtyard. Peter sat down with them, but a servant girl saw him by the firelight and said, "You are one of Jesus' followers. You were with him in Galilee."

Peter emphatically denied it: "Woman, I don't know him!" he said.

About an hour later another person near Peter said, "By your accent I know you are a Galilean. You must be one of his followers."

Peter said, "I swear I am not. If I am, let me be cursed!" Immediately, a rooster crowed, and he remembered Jesus' warning: "Before the rooster crows, you will deny me three times."

At dawn Jesus was brought before the entire Sanhedrin. "If you are the Christ, then tell us," they demanded.

Jesus answered, "Even if I told you, you wouldn't believe me. From now on, the Son of Man will be seated at the right hand of the Mighty God."

They asked, "Are you claiming, then, that you are the Son of God?"

Jesus replied, "I am!"

They said, "That's enough evidence. He has testified against himself."

When Judas, who had betrayed him, saw that Jesus was condemned, he was so distressed he returned the thirty silver coins to the religious leaders. "I have sinned," he said, "because I have betrayed an innocent man."

"We don't care," they said. "That's your problem, not ours."

Judas threw down the money in the temple and soon after committed suicide.

Because the money was a bribe for murder, the priests decided to use it to buy a field to use as a cemetery for foreigners. This was known as "the Field of Blood," and its purchase fulfilled the prophecy of Jeremiah (and Zechariah) that the money paid to betray the Messiah would be used to purchase a potter's field.

ROMAN INTERROGATION AND TRIAL

The Sanhedrin turned Jesus over to Pilate, the Roman military administrator of the province of Palestine. Ironically, the Jewish religious leaders stood outside Pilate's headquarters because they did not want to ceremonially contaminate themselves. Pilate had to come out to meet them.

Pilate asked, "What are the charges against this man?"

The leaders said Jesus was guilty of subversion against Rome and that he claimed he was a king.

Pilate told them to try Jesus according to Jewish law.

They protested, "We don't have the authority to execute anyone."

Pilate went back inside the palace and had Jesus brought in for questioning. "Are you the king of the Jews?" he asked.

"Did someone else tell you I was a king, or is that what you think?" replied Jesus.

Pilate said, "I'm not Jewish. Look, your own people brought you here. What have you done?"

Jesus said, "My kingdom is not an empire of this world. If it were, my subjects would defend me. My kingdom is different from the empires of the world."

"Then you are a king," said Pilate.

"You are right. I am a king. I was born to witness to the world about truth."

"What is truth?" Pilate mused. Then he went out to the Jews and said, "There is no basis for your charges against this man."

The religious leaders would not be deterred. They insisted Jesus was a threat to all of Judea and Galilee.

Pilate went back to Jesus and told him what the chief priests had said, but to his amazement Jesus refused to defend himself.

Pilate found out Jesus was from Galilee, which was under the jurisdiction of Herod Antipas (a surrogate ruler under the Romans), so he sent Jesus to Herod for questioning.

Herod was delighted to see Jesus; he had heard so much about him. He hoped Jesus would perform some entertaining miracle, and he asked Jesus question after question.

Jesus didn't say a word, even though the religious leaders were there hurling all sorts of accusations. Herod and his soldiers started mocking Jesus. They put a royal robe on him and sent him back to Pilate. Herod and Pilate had been enemies, but that day they became friends.

Pilate told the Jews that both he and Herod had questioned Jesus, and neither of them had found evidence of a threat to Rome. He realized that the chief priests had accused Jesus because of envy and not because he had violated Roman law.

It was customary for the Romans to release a prisoner at the Feast of Passover, so Pilate offered to release one of two men: either Barabbas, a notorious criminal, or Jesus, who claimed he was Israel's Messiah.

While Pilate was waiting for an answer, he received an urgent message from his wife: "I had a frightening dream about Jesus. Don't condemn him—he is innocent!"

But the Jewish leaders incited the crowd and persuaded them to insist that Pilate release Barabbas, even though Barabbas had been arrested for insurrection and murder.

Pilate ordered Jesus flogged. Before whipping him, the soldiers twisted a crown of thorns and shoved it onto his head. They put a purple robe on him. They mocked him, saying "Hail, king of the Jews," and gave him a crude reed scepter and then beat him on the head with it.

Then Pilate went out to the Jews and made it clear he was certain Jesus was an innocent man. He even had Jesus brought out with the crown of thorns and purple robe and said, "Look, here is the man!"

When the priests and temple guards saw Jesus, they began shouting, "Crucify him! Crucify him!"

Pilate said, "You crucify him. He is not guilty!"

The leaders were adamant: "By our law he ought to be executed because he claimed to be the Son of God," they said.

This frightened Pilate, and he had Jesus taken back into his headquarters. "Where are you from?" he asked

Jesus didn't answer.

Pilate said, "Why don't you respond? Don't you realize that I have the authority to set you free or crucify you?"

Jesus replied, "You don't have any power at all in this matter except the power that has been given to you from above. Those who turned me over to you are the guilty ones."

Pilate tried again to release Jesus, but the Jews shouted, "If you let this man go, you are not loyal to Caesar! Anyone who claims he is a king is a rebel."

When Pilate heard this, he brought Jesus outside to the judgment seat and sat down. "Here is your king," Pilate said, but the Jews screamed, "Take him away! Crucify him!"

Pilate asked, "Do you want me to crucify your king?" He symbolically washed his hands, saying, "I am innocent of this man's blood."

The people cried out, "Let his blood be on us and on our children!"

"We have no king but Caesar," the chief priests answered.

To satisfy the leaders and the hostile crowd, Pilate ordered Jesus flogged and taken away for execution.

THE CRUCIFIXION

The First Three Hours

Before crucifying Jesus, the soldiers tortured him. They put a staff in his right hand and, mockingly bowing down to him, they said, "Hail, king of the Jews!" They spit on him and beat him again and again with the staff.

Then they took away the robe and put Jesus' clothes on him. Jesus initially was forced to carry his own cross, but eventually the soldiers saw a man named Simon from Cyrene and forced him to carry it. On the way to the place of execution, a large group of people followed Jesus, including women who grieved.

Jesus called out to them, "Daughters of Jerusalem, do not weep for me; weep instead for yourselves and your children. Blessed are those women who have never given birth to children or nursed infants. People soon will beg for death because of the terrible suffering they will be forced to endure."

Jesus and two other criminals were taken to the Place of the Skull ("Golgotha," in Aramaic). At around nine in the morning, the soldiers crucified him between the two thieves. After nailing him to the cross, the soldiers divided his clothes into four parts. Instead of tearing his outer robe, they gambled for it by throwing dice.

Pilate ordered a sign placed on the cross that read, "Jesus of Nazareth, King of the Jews." The inscription was written in Aramaic, Latin, and Greek.

When the chief priests read it, they objected, saying "Do not write 'King of the Jews.' Write that he claimed he was king of the Jews."

Their protest fell on deaf ears. Pilate said, "What I have written, I have written!"

Some of the people walking by mocked Jesus, saying, "You, who claimed you were going to destroy the temple and rebuild it in three days, save yourself. Come down from the cross if you are the Son of God."

The leaders joined the people in mocking Jesus. They said, "He saved others, but he can't save himself. We will believe that he is the Christ and the Son of God if he can come down from the cross."

One of the crucified thieves shouted, "If you are the Christ, save yourself and save us!"

The other thief, though, scolded him: "Don't you fear God? We deserve to die; we are guilty, but not this man. He isn't a criminal." He said to Jesus, "Don't forget me when you enter into your kingdom."

Jesus answered, "You can be certain that today you will be with me in paradise."

Several women were standing near the cross. When Jesus saw his mother and John, the disciple he loved, standing next to her, he said, "My dear woman, this man is now your son"; to the beloved disciple, Jesus said, "This dear woman is now your mother."

From that time on, John took care of Mary as if she were his own mother.

The Last Three Hours

From noon to three, the entire area was shrouded in darkness. Then Jesus cried out in a loud voice, "My God, my God, why have you forsaken me?"

Some didn't understand and thought he was calling for Elijah.

Jesus said, "I am thirsty."

One of the onlookers tried to give him a drink with a sponge on a pole.

Then Jesus prayed, "Father, into your hands I commit my spirit," and he cried out, "It is finished!"

With those words, Jesus bowed his head and died.

That instant, the curtain in the temple ripped from top to bottom. The earth shook, breaking open tombs, and people were raised to life. After Jesus' resurrection, many of them appeared in Jerusalem.

When the commander of the soldiers who had crucified Jesus saw him die, he said, "He surely was the Son of God, and an innocent man."

Three of the women who had watched the crucifixion were Mary Magdalene, Mary the mother of James and Joseph, and the mother of James and John.

♌ Chapter Summary

Though Jesus knew the religious leaders were plotting his death, he went to Jerusalem for the Passover. After his triumphal entry, Jesus challenged the religious establishment by driving the money changers out of the temple. He sternly denounced them as hypocrites and warned his followers that he would be arrested and executed.

Jesus celebrated a Passover meal with his disciples. He told them he was about to leave them, but he promised to send them the Holy Spirit. He was arrested while praying in the garden of Gethsemane.

Pilate finally was harassed into convicting Jesus. He was nailed to a cross, a Roman form of execution. After about six hours he cried out with a loud voice and died.

Eighteen

BURIAL AND RESURRECTION

Main Characters
Jesus
Joseph of Arimathea
Nicodemus
Women
Disciples

Setting
Jerusalem
Galilee

BURIAL

The Jews wanted the three bodies taken down before the Sabbath, which was the next day, so they asked Pilate to have their legs broken. The soldiers broke the legs of the two thieves, but when they came to Jesus he was already dead.

Instead of breaking his legs, they thrust a spear into his side. Blood mixed with water gushed out, fulfilling Scripture ("not one of his bones will be broken" and "they will look on the one they have pierced").

Joseph of Arimathea, a member of the Sanhedrin and a godly man, showed courage when he asked Pilate for the body of Jesus. Pilate was surprised when the centurion informed him that Jesus was already dead. He gave Joseph permission to bury Jesus.

Joseph and Nicodemus (the one who had previously talked to Jesus) took Jesus' body down from the cross and prepared it for burial according to Jewish tradition, by wrapping it in a linen cloth and anointing it with seventy-five pounds of aromatic spices.

To bury Jesus, Joseph used the tomb he had prepared for his own burial. He and Nicodemus placed the body inside and had a large stone placed in front of the entrance.

After watching where Joseph buried Jesus, the women who had followed them went home to prepare for the Sabbath.

Remembering that Jesus had said he would rise from the dead after three days, the religious leaders asked Pilate to station guards at the tomb. They were concerned Jesus' disciples would try to steal the body and tell everyone he had risen from the dead. "That deception would make us look worse than ever," they complained.

Pilate told them to make the tomb as secure as possible. The leaders put a seal on the entrance to the tomb and posted guards.

THE EMPTY TOMB

Early in the morning after the Sabbath, Mary Magdalene, Mary the mother of James, and Salome decided to go to the tomb and anoint Jesus' body with additional spices.

Then there was a strong earthquake, and an angel removed the large stone from the entrance and sat on it. The angel looked like a bolt of lightning; his clothes were as white as snow. His appearance so terrified the guards that they were frozen with fear.

On their way, the women had worried about how they were going to remove the large stone. When they arrived, they were surprised to find it had already been removed.

On entering the tomb, they saw an angel who looked like a young man. The angel comforted the women, saying, "Don't be alarmed. There is no reason to look for the living among the dead. Jesus is not here. He has risen! Go tell his disciples he will meet them in Galilee as he promised."

Despite the angel's assurance, the women fled from the tomb in fear.

Though the women told the eleven disciples they had gone to Jesus' tomb and found it empty, the disciples didn't believe them. When Mary Magdalene told Peter and John that Jesus' body had been stolen, both ran for the tomb.

John outran Peter but didn't go into the tomb. When Peter arrived he didn't hesitate—he rushed right inside. All the burial cloths were there, and the linen face covering was neatly folded, separately. John finally went inside, and when he saw the cloths, he believed Jesus was alive, even though he didn't fully understand the meaning of the Resurrection. Then they went home.

JESUS' RESURRECTION APPEARANCES

After he had risen from the dead, Jesus appeared to women, the eleven, and many other followers before returning to his Father.

To Mary Magdalene and Other Women

Meanwhile, Mary Magdalene returned to the tomb and, standing outside, wept. Then she saw two angels dressed in white, sitting where Jesus' body had been laid.

They asked her, "Why are you crying?"

"Someone has taken my Lord away, and I don't know where they have taken him."

When she turned around, Jesus was standing outside the tomb, but Mary didn't recognize him. "Woman," he asked, "why are you crying? Who are you looking for?"

Thinking the man was the gardener, she asked, "Sir, did you take the body? If you did, please tell me where you put it."

When Jesus said, "Mary," she spun around and cried out in Aramaic, "Rabboni!" (which means "teacher").

Jesus told her to let go; she was clinging to him. "I still must return to my Father," he said. "Go tell my disciples I am returning to my Father, my God and their God."

Mary rushed to tell them she had seen Jesus. They were grieving and didn't believe that Jesus was alive.

Jesus appeared to some of the other women who had discovered the empty tomb. They grasped his feet in worship. He told them to tell his brothers to meet him in Galilee.

The Cover-up

When the guards from the tomb regained their composure, they reported to the chief priests what had happened. The chief priests met with the elders to plan a cover-up.

They bribed the guards and told them to say, "The disciples stole the body while we were asleep." They assured the guards they would intervene if the Roman governor tried to punish them, so the guards took the money and lied about what had happened.

To the Two Men on the Road to Emmaus

On the same day, two of Jesus' followers were on their way to the small village of Emmaus, about seven miles from Jerusalem. They were talking about what had recently happened when Jesus himself joined them. They didn't recognize him.

Jesus asked them what they were discussing. One of them, named Cleopas, was surprised that this stranger didn't know what had happened in Jerusalem.

Jesus asked what had taken place.

They said Jesus of Nazareth, a powerful prophet and an amazing teacher, had been executed by the religious leaders. "We had hoped he would save our nation," they said.

But, they went on, some women claimed they had gone to the tomb and couldn't find a body. While the tomb didn't seem to have been robbed, they didn't see Jesus.

Jesus said, "How foolish of you, that you didn't believe what the prophets predicted. They said that Christ had to suffer and die before entering into his glory." Then, beginning with Moses, Jesus explained what was written in the Scriptures about himself. They still didn't know who he was.

As they were nearing Emmaus, the two men invited Jesus to stay with them. When they sat down for the evening meal, Jesus took a loaf of bread and gave thanks for it. When he broke it and gave it to them, they recognized him, but he suddenly disappeared. They said, "Didn't our hearts burn within us when he explained the Scriptures to us?"

They immediately returned to Jerusalem and found the eleven disciples. They were saying, "It is true. The Lord has risen and has appeared to Peter."

The men told the disciples they had seen Jesus and had eaten a meal with him.

While they were trying to explain what had happened, Jesus was suddenly standing in the room with them. He said, "Peace be with you."

They thought he was a ghost.

Jesus said, "Don't be alarmed, and don't doubt. Look at my hands and feet. Touch me! A ghost does not have flesh and bones as you see I have!"

They were so bewildered they still couldn't believe it was Jesus.

He asked, "Do you have anything to eat?"

They gave him a piece of fish and watched him eat it.

To Thomas

Thomas wasn't with the disciples when they saw Jesus, and when they told him they had seen the Lord, he didn't believe them. "I won't believe," he said, "unless I see the nail marks and put my finger in them, and put my hand in the wound in his side."

A week later the disciples met in the same house, and though the doors were locked, Jesus instantly was standing in the room. He said to Thomas, "Put your finger in the nail wounds, and put your hand in my side. Stop doubting and believe!"

Thomas said, "My Lord and my God!"

Jesus said, "You believe because you have seen me; blessed are those who believe though they have not seen me."

To His Disciples in Galilee

One evening, after Peter and six other disciples had returned to Galilee, Peter said, "I'm going fishing." The others went with him. They fished all night and caught nothing.

Early the next morning, Jesus was standing on the shore, but the disciples didn't recognize him. He called out to them, "Friends, did you catch any fish?"

"None," they answered.

Jesus said, "Throw your net on the other side of the boat."

They did and caught so many fish they could hardly haul in the net.

John, the disciple Jesus loved, said to Peter, "It's the Lord!"

Peter didn't wait for the boat to arrive; he jumped in the water and swam to shore.

When the other disciples landed, they saw a fire with fish on it, and bread.

"Bring some of the fish you caught and have breakfast," Jesus said.

None of them dared ask if he was the Lord, but they knew it was him because this was the third time they had seen him.

When they finished eating, Jesus asked, "Simon, do you love me more than these?"

Peter said, "Yes, you know that I love you, Lord."

Jesus said, "Then feed my lambs," and asked a second time, "Simon, do you truly love me?"

"Yes, Lord, you know that I love you," Peter answered.

"Then take care of my sheep," Jesus said. And for the third time, he asked, "Simon, do you really love me?"

Peter said, "Lord, you know all things, and you know how much I love you."

Jesus said, "Then feed my sheep."

Jesus also told Peter that he would die by martyrdom.

Peter looked over at John and asked how he would die.

Jesus said, "If I want him to live until I return, that is my business. You, follow me."

To the Eleven in Galilee

As Jesus had commanded, all eleven disciples went to a mountain in Galilee. When he appeared, they worshiped him but some still had lingering doubts.

Jesus commissioned them to witness to the world, saying:

> All authority in heaven and on earth has been given to me, go and make disciples of all nations. Baptize in the name of the Father, the Son, and the Holy Spirit. Teach them everything I have taught you, and I will be with you until the end of the age.

To the Disciples in Jerusalem

When Jesus met with the eleven in Jerusalem, he said his death and resurrection was according to Scripture: "It is written in the law of Moses and the prophets that the Messiah would suffer and die but rise from the dead on the third day." He told them they were now witnesses of his resurrection and commissioned to preach repentance and forgiveness of sins to all nations.

To remove any doubts that he had risen from the dead, Jesus spent forty days with his followers before returning to heaven. During this time he showed them evidence again and again that he was alive, and he promised to send the Holy Spirit to give them power as his witnesses.

After forty days, as they watched, Jesus was caught up in a cloud and disappeared.

♔ Chapter Summary

After Jesus' death, Joseph of Arimathea, a follower who was also a member of the Sanhedrin, asked to bury Jesus in his own grave. Pilate sealed the tomb and stationed guards in case anyone would try to steal the body.

Early Sunday morning, some women came to the tomb and discovered Jesus was not there; an angel had removed the stone. They told the disciples that Jesus was alive, but initially they didn't believe.

Over several weeks, Jesus appeared to the women, the disciples, and other followers. At some point during this time, Peter and the disciples went back to fishing. Jesus appeared and filled their nets with fish one last time. He challenged Peter to serve others and predicted how he would die.

Jesus was seen by hundreds over forty days. Then he returned to his Father in a cloud.

Nineteen

THE STORY OF THE CHURCH (ACTS)

Main Characters

Jesus

Peter

The apostles

Stephen

Philip

Cornelius (Roman centurion)

Paul

Barnabas

Lydia (a businesswoman), a slave girl, and a jailer (converts at Philippi)

Luke (not identified in the text)

Felix (Roman governor)

Festus (Roman governor)

Setting

Jerusalem

Judea

Samaria

Road to Gaza

Road to Damascus

Caesarea (Roman provincial capital)

Antioch (location of first Gentile church and sending church for missionary journeys)

Cities and places on the first missionary journey

Cities and places on the second missionary journey

Cities and places on the third missionary journey

Cities and places on the journey to Rome

THE GIFT OF THE SPIRIT

Over a period of forty days after his resurrection, Jesus appeared many times to his followers, teaching them about the kingdom of God. He also commanded them to stay in Jerusalem to wait for the Spirit, whom God had promised.

The apostles asked, "Lord, will you now establish the kingdom of Israel?"

Jesus told them not to worry about when the Father would restore Israel. "In the meantime, go to the nations and tell people about me. Start in Jerusalem, then go to Judea and Samaria, and ultimately testify of me to the ends of the earth."

After commissioning them, Jesus ascended to heaven enveloped in a cloud. The bewildered apostles stared up at the sky until two angels appeared. The angels promised that Jesus would return in the same way he had departed—both bodily and visibly.

The apostles courageously returned to Jerusalem. Both men and women prayed with one mind and purpose. Peter quickly became the leader of the early believers, who numbered 120. He gave a short speech recognizing that even the tragic events surrounding Christ's betrayal and arrest were a fulfillment of Scripture.

Peter then recommended that they choose a replacement for Judas. Two candidates were selected: Joseph and Matthias. The apostles prayed, acknowledging that God knew their hearts and asking him to reveal his will. Then they cast lots, a traditional Old Testament way of making a choice. The lot landed on Matthias.

Approximately six weeks after Jesus' resurrection and only days after his ascension, the apostles were celebrating the Jewish feast of Pentecost. Suddenly a powerful wind blew into their meeting place, along with flashes of fire that appeared over each of the believers' heads, and they were all filled with the Holy Spirit. All of them began to speak in tongues, which meant they were speaking foreign languages they'd not been taught.

The phenomenon attracted people from all over Jerusalem. Though these onlookers were from all over the world, they each heard Christ's followers speaking in their own language. Others, unable to grasp what had happened, thought the disciples were drunk.

Peter took the opportunity to explain to the gathered crowd how the gift of the Spirit fulfilled prophecy, and claimed that the crucifixion, resurrection, and Jesus' return to heaven were proof that he was both Lord and Christ. In conclusion, he told them what to do to be saved.

Peter's audience was shocked. They were not merely convinced that what he said was true, but they were also convicted of their sins. Three thousand believed and were baptized. They became a community bonded together by common faith in Jesus Christ, unselfish love for one another, and determination to proclaim the gospel.

While Peter and John were on their way to the temple, they met a man who was handicapped from birth. Because of his disability, he wasn't allowed to enter the temple area; he had to sit at the entrance, begging for a handout.

The man wanted money from Peter. Instead Peter said, "I don't have silver or gold, but what I do have I'll give you. In the name of Jesus of Nazareth, walk!"

Immediately the man got up and started walking, then began leaping and praising God. A huge crowd of Jews gathered, so Peter once again seized the moment, telling them about Christ. He took no credit for the healing, giving all credit to Jesus.

While Peter and John were speaking, the religious leaders arrived and arrested them because of their teaching about the resurrection. Although they threw Peter and John in jail, their witness had had an effect. Now there were at least five thousand believers.

The next day Peter and John were interrogated by the Sanhedrin, Israel's "Supreme Court." They did not deny the healing, but they asked on whose authority it took place.

Peter said the man was healed in the name of Jesus Christ, who is alive, not dead. Though Peter and John were only fishermen, they were filled with the Holy Spirit and would not be intimidated by the nation's most powerful religious leaders. Peter answered the charges of the Sanhedrin with a message claiming that Jesus is the ultimate person in God's plan of redemption.

The Sanhedrin was astonished by the courageous defiance of these two unschooled and ordinary men. It was obvious they were followers of Jesus.

The Sanhedrin was forced to release Peter and John because they could not deny that the lame man had been healed in Jesus' name. However, they told them not to preach the resurrection any more. Meanwhile, the people praised God for the miraculous healing.

When Peter and John were released, they gathered with the other believers and prayed. God answered their prayer and gave them a fresh filling of the Holy Spirit. They continued to proclaim the Word of God with uncommon courage.

TROUBLE ON THE INSIDE AND THREATS FROM THE OUTSIDE

Believers in the early church were not only courageous, they were compassionate. They shared with one another what they had. One believer, Barnabas, sold his land and turned the money over to the apostles to distribute to those who needed it.

Perhaps motivated by this example, Ananias and Sapphira sold property, but instead of giving it all to the church, as promised, Ananias kept back some of the money with his wife's full knowledge. Peter was made aware of their dishonesty and charged Ananias with lying to God and the Holy Spirit. When his sin was exposed, Ananias collapsed and died.

A short time later Peter confronted Sapphira, who was unaware of her husband's death. Peter asked her if what they had given was the amount they had pledged. Like her husband, she lied and collapsed at Peter's feet. Great awe came upon the whole church.

More and more miracles were performed, and the church continued to grow. Soon the chief priest and the Sadducees, one of the Jewish religious sects, became jealous and ordered all the apostles arrested. But that night they were released by an angel of the Lord. After releasing them, the angel told them to continue to preach about the life that can be found in Christ. In obedience, the apostles returned to the temple and continued teaching as the people arrived for morning prayers.

When the Sanhedrin reassembled the next day for the trial of the apostles, they were shocked by the report from the guards that the apostles had broken out of the city jail. They told the guards to arrest them again.

At the trial, the high priest reminded the apostles that they'd been told to stop preaching about Christ. The apostles, though, were determined to obey God rather than man. This put the Sanhedrin in a predicament.

Gamaliel, one of the most respected Pharisaic leaders of his time, stood up. He cautioned the Sanhedrin against trying to impose their will, when it might possibly oppose God's will. He mentioned two previous revolts against the Romans that ultimately had failed on their own. If Christianity is not of God, he told them, it would fail on its own as well. The Sanhedrin ordered the disciples beaten with rods (the Jewish method of flogging) and commanded them once again not to speak in Jesus' name; then they were set free.

The church had to respond to a serious racial issue when a group of Hellenistic (Greek) Jewish widows complained that they were neglected in the daily distribution of food. But Hebraic (Hebrew) Jews ignored their requests for help.

The twelve apostles reasoned that if they focused their attention on this problem, it could distract them from their primary ministry of prayer and teaching the Word. They recommended the church select seven reputable men to oversee the care of widows. These men were Hellenistic Jews and included Stephen and Philip.

STEPHEN

Because the believers were determined to obey God rather than men, it was inevitable that one of Christ's followers would pay the ultimate price. Stephen was a believer full of grace and power who performed many miracles. The Synagogue of the Freedmen, which consisted of Jews who were formerly slaves from foreign countries, were for some reason offended by Stephen's ministry. They convinced some of their sympathizers to slander Stephen, charging him with blasphemy against Moses and God, and he was soon brought before the Sanhedrin.

As the council stared at Stephen, his face looked like that of an angel. Stephen told the council about the history of the Jews from Abraham to Christ. He exposed Israel's history of rebellion, and then accused them of betraying and murdering Jesus, the Promised One.

The Sanhedrin became furious. Like an angry mob, they rushed him out of the city and began to stone him. They left their coats with a young man named Saul.

Before he died, Stephen cried out, "Look, I see the Son of Man (Jesus) standing at the right hand of God!" When the Jews began stoning Stephen, he knelt down and prayed, "Lord, do not hold this sin against them."

Stephen was the church's first martyr. Devout men honored him by burying his battered body.

PHILIP

The outburst of hostility against believers forced Christians to scatter and seek safety in remote areas. All left Jerusalem except the apostles. Philip went to Samaria and told about the Messiah. He performed miracles, and the city welcomed his message.

A magician named Simon, who lived in the city, practiced sorcery and had impressed people with magical powers. His magic was effective, and the Samaritans regarded him as a channel of divine power.

In response to Philip's preaching, many Samaritans believed, and even Simon believed and was baptized. He followed Philip everywhere.

When the church in Jerusalem heard of the Samaritans' response to God's word, they sent Peter and John. They discovered that, though many Samaritans had believed, they had not received the Spirit. They prayed, and these new converts received the Spirit through the laying on of hands. Simon, intrigued by this, tried to buy the Spirit. Peter sternly rebuked him, saying the Spirit was not for sale. He warned Simon of the consequences of his greed and appealed to him to repent.

Though Samaria was north of Jerusalem, an angel of the Lord directed Philip to go to Gaza, south of Jerusalem. Philip obeyed and met an Ethiopian eunuch, who was an official of the Ethiopian queen, Candace. The Spirit ordered Philip to join the eunuch in his chariot, where he discovered the eunuch was reading from the prophet Isaiah but didn't understand the passage. Philip became the eunuch's guide for interpreting the Scripture, which was a prophecy about Jesus' suffering on the cross.

When they came to water, the eunuch asked if he could be baptized. He stopped his chariot, both men entered the water, and Philip baptized him in the name of Jesus. Immediately the Spirit of the Lord snatched Philip away, somehow bringing him to Azotus. Meanwhile, the eunuch continued his journey with rejoicing because of his new relationship with God through Christ.

Philip continued preaching the good news from Azotus (thirty-five miles west of Jerusalem) to Caesarea.

SAUL/PAUL

Saul, the man who held the Sanhedrin members' coats as they stoned Stephen, hated Christians. With the zeal of a fanatic, he devoted himself to Christianity's destruction, requesting authority from the Sanhedrin to extradite and punish believers who lived in Damascus.

But God had other plans. While traveling to Damascus, Saul was halted by a light more brilliant than the sun, and he fell to the ground. Blinded, Saul heard a voice asking, "Why are you persecuting me?"

Saul answered, "Who are you, Lord?"

"I am Jesus, who you are persecuting. Go into Damascus where you will receive further instructions."

Saul's companions also heard the voice but couldn't understand it. Nevertheless, they escorted him to Damascus. He remained blind for three days while he fasted.

There was a disciple of Jesus in Damascus named Ananias. The Lord spoke to him in a vision, telling him to go to a house on Straight Street where he would find Saul, who was praying and had also seen a vision about the restoration of his sight.

The vision was upsetting. Ananias had heard of Saul. "But Lord, he persecutes your people!"

The Lord assured Ananias that Saul was now a different man, and Ananias obeyed. He restored Saul's sight and gave him the gift of the Spirit through the laying on of hands. Saul was immediately baptized and soon regained his strength.

Saul started spreading the word that Jesus is the Son of God; those who knew how viciously Saul had persecuted Christians were amazed that he now argued that Jesus was Israel's Messiah.

Unable to refute his arguments, the Jews plotted to kill him. Saul was forced to sneak out of the city like a fugitive, being lowered in a large basket through an opening in the city wall.

Saul returned to Jerusalem, but the church was understandably afraid and refused to accept him until Barnabas assured them of his conversion experience. As in Damascus, Saul boldly proclaimed the name of Jesus, and again he faced opposition. When the Jerusalem believers found out about a threat on Saul's life, they sent him to Tarsus, where he remained until Barnabas recruited him for ministering at Antioch in Syria.

All along, the church continued to grow. It experienced peace and strength, living in the fear of the Lord, not the fear of persecution.

PETER AND THE GENTILES

While Peter was visiting believers in the city of Lydda, he healed a paralyzed man named Aeneas, which led many in the area to trust in Jesus. Then Peter went to the neighboring town of Joppa.

Dorcas, a disciple of Jesus, who was known for helping the poor and needy, became sick and died. When the disciples heard Peter was nearby, they begged him to come and help. Through Christ he raised her from the dead. Again, news of the miracle spread, and many believed on the Lord.

While in Joppa, Peter stayed at the house of Simon, a man who tanned leather for a living. Meanwhile Cornelius, a Roman centurion, was stationed at nearby Caesarea. Though a Gentile, Cornelius was a man of God and gave generously to the Jewish people.

During the time of the afternoon prayers, the Lord spoke to Cornelius through an angel and instructed him to send for Peter. He did not question the heavenly messenger, obeying the angel's instructions and sending two of his servants to Joppa.

The next day Peter also had a vision while praying at noon. In a trance he saw a sheet-like object descend from heaven. It was filled with animals that looked good to eat, and he heard a voice saying, "Arise, Peter, kill and eat."

Some of the animals were clean but others were unclean according to regulations in the law of Moses. Peter protested, and God told him that he (God) alone could decide what was clean and what was unclean. The command was repeated three times to confirm that Peter had not misunderstood. Peter realized that the vision signaled the end to legalistic barriers separating Jews and Gentiles.

Cornelius's messengers arrived at the house where Peter was staying, and they stood outside the outer courtyard until Peter invited them in. God told him not to worry that the messengers were Gentiles—Peter was to go with them. He invited them in, and the next morning they all went to Cornelius's house.

Cornelius, knowing that Peter was a Jew, fell down in deference to him.

Peter declared that while Jews did not normally associate with Gentiles, God had shown him that he should not consider any person unclean. Peter explained his vision, and Cornelius was certain their meeting was by divine design. He gathered his family to listen to what Peter had to say.

Peter shared the gospel with them; before he finished, the Holy Spirit came on these Gentiles, and they began speaking in tongues and praising God. Immediately Peter had them baptized in the name of Jesus Christ.

The conversion of Cornelius and his household did not go unnoticed by the Jewish church in Jerusalem. Those who believed in the necessity of circumcision criticized Peter for associating with Gentiles. Peter told them his vision and what had happened to the Gentiles who'd believed in Jesus. They accepted his explanation and confirmed the admission of Gentiles to the church without requiring them to convert to Judaism.

Once the Jerusalem church officially recognized the conversion of Cornelius apart from Judaism, the church was prepared for a universal mission to the Gentiles. Many of the believers who were scattered by persecution after the death of Stephen preached to Jews; others stepped across racial boundaries. They preached to Greeks and established a church in Antioch.

The Jerusalem church sent Barnabas to Antioch to investigate the new church. Barnabas encouraged the new converts to remain whole-heartedly devoted to the Lord.

Because of the explosive growth, Barnabas needed help; instead of returning to Jerusalem, Barnabas went to Tarsus to bring back Paul. The two taught for a year in Antioch, where the church grew and where believers were first called Christians.

Christian prophets came from Jerusalem to Antioch, proclaiming and interpreting God's Word. One, named Agabus, predicted a severe famine. The church collected funds and appointed Barnabas and Paul to take the gifts to Jerusalem to help in their time of need.

In Jerusalem, the church faced a dangerous threat. Herod Agrippa (a local ruler under the Romans) ordered James, the brother of John, arrested and executed. When Herod saw how much the killing of James pleased the Jews, he had Peter arrested, intending to hold a public trial and execution after Passover.

The church prayed fervently, and while Peter was sleeping in his cell, an angel appeared. Peter's chains fell off, and the angel escorted him past the guards, through locked gates, and out of the prison. At first Peter thought his experience was a vision, but once he was on the street, he realized he had actually been rescued.

The angel departed, and Peter went to the house where the believers were praying. He knocked on the door, and a woman named Rhoda answered. She recognized Peter, but the others thought she was out of her mind. Peter kept knocking until they all came and were amazed. After explaining how the Lord delivered him, Peter told them to inform James (the brother of Jesus) about his release. Peter left Jerusalem.

Peter's escape was a mystery to the guards. Herod questioned them and ordered them led away for execution.

Some time later, when Herod visited Tyre and Sidon, the people praised him as a god. Herod did not refuse their praise, so the Lord ordered an angel to judge him, and he died from a painful disease.

FIRST MISSIONARY JOURNEY

The elimination of Herod's threat freed the church for its first missionary endeavor. The Gentile church at Antioch, not the Jewish church in Jerusalem, sent out the first missionaries. Under the direction of the

Holy Spirit, the church commissioned Saul and Barnabas, and they set sail for Cyprus, the homeland of Barnabas.

After they arrived, they walked overland to Paphos. The governor of the island, Sergius Paulus, sent for Paul and Barnabas to hear the Word of God, but a sorcerer named Elymas opposed them, trying to distort the message so the governor wouldn't believe. Paul announced blindness on Elymas, and Sergius Paulus came to faith.

When they sailed from Paphos to the port town of Perga, John Mark returned to Jerusalem. Paul and Barnabas traveled north to Antioch of Pisidia. They went to the synagogue and, after reading from the Law and the Prophets, the elders asked them to speak, as it was customary to read from two sections of the Old Testament—the Law and the Prophets—and then give an interpretation. Paul seized the opportunity to explain how the promises of God to Israel were fulfilled in Christ, who was put to death but raised from the dead.

Some of the listeners begged Paul to speak again the following Sabbath, and many Jews and converts to Judaism even became followers of Paul and Barnabas. They were urged to continue to rely on God's grace and not revert to living by the law of Moses.

When Paul spoke the next Sabbath, the events of Paphos were repeated. When Jews saw the favorable response of many in the audience, they were filled with jealousy and began to slander Paul. In contrast, Gentiles rejoiced and many were saved.

This response led to even greater opposition; the Jews incited upper-class women and the Gentile leaders of the city to persecute Paul and Barnabas, who were forced to leave the district. With a symbolic act of judgment, Paul and Barnabas shook the dust off of their feet and traveled to Iconium, ninety miles southeast.

At Iconium the divided response and hostility of the Jews were repeated again. When the missionaries spoke in the synagogue, a large number of both Jews and Greeks believed. But unbelieving Jews stirred up the minds of the Gentiles, turning them against Paul and Barnabas. Though they authenticated their message with signs and wonders, the people were still divided. Some believed the slander; others sided with the apostles.

They fled to Lystra, where there was a man who was born lame, unable to walk. He listened to Paul's words, and Paul observed him closely. Then Paul said with a loud voice, "Stand up!"

Immediately the man jumped up and began to walk. The superstitious Gentiles mistakenly assumed Barnabas and Paul were the gods Zeus and Hermes, and they wanted to offer sacrifices to them.

Barnabas and Paul vehemently protested. Rather than being worshiped, Paul told the people about God. He said the living God, the Creator of heaven and earth, had revealed himself in his providential care of all people. He urged them to repent and turn to Christ.

Unfortunately, Paul's message did not dissuade the Lycaonians from worshiping the missionaries as gods. Then some Jews convinced the people that Paul deserved death.

They stoned him and dragged him from the city, thinking he was dead. But when the disciples gathered around him, he got up and went back into the city.

The next day Paul and Barnabas left for the city of Derbe, spreading the good news of Christ. They also went back to the other places they'd visited, strengthening and encouraging the disciples there. They preached in Perga and took a boat from Attalia back to Antioch. When they arrived home, they reported to the church, describing how God had opened the door of faith to the Gentiles.

THE JERUSALEM COUNCIL

As a result of the first missionary journey, the conversion of Gentiles alarmed a group of Jewish traditionalists who insisted on circumcision as part of the salvation experience. The issue was not about Gentile participation in the church, but rather the requirements for inclusion in the church.

When a group of these traditionalists came from Judea to Antioch, teaching that circumcision was essential for salvation, Paul and Barnabas correctly viewed this as a threat to God's grace. After a heated debate with them, Paul and Barnabas traveled to Jerusalem and requested that the church resolve the issue.

Peter gave a report on his ministry to Cornelius, identifying the heart of the issue; both Jews and Gentiles are saved by grace, not the works of the Law. Also, Barnabas and Paul reported on their ministry to Gentiles, showing that God confirmed this ministry with miraculous signs and wonders.

James, as the apparent leader of the Jerusalem church, recommended that the council reject the view of the Judaizers and not impose the Jewish law on Gentiles. But he also recommended the council send a letter to the Gentiles asking them to refrain from practices especially offensive to Jews, such as eating things contaminated by idols, fornication, and eating meat that had been strangled or had large amounts of blood in it.

When Paul and Barnabas and Judas and Silas (two respected men from the Jerusalem church) read the letter to the church at Antioch, they rejoiced. The potentially divisive issue of the Law had been officially resolved; unity had been preserved.

Judas and Silas ministered to the Gentile church with a message that strengthened them in their faith, and then they returned to Jerusalem. Paul and Barnabas remained in Antioch, teaching the word of the Lord.

SECOND MISSIONARY JOURNEY—TO EUROPE

Before long, Paul and Barnabas decided to revisit the churches that were started on their first journey, but they disagreed about whether or not to bring John Mark with them. Barnabas wanted to take him, but Paul objected. Both men vigorously defended their position, and this led to a separation between Paul and Barnabas.

Paul took Silas and went to Derbe and then to Lystra, where a disciple named Timothy lived. Because Timothy's mother was Jewish, Jews considered him Jewish and expected him to submit to the requirements of the Law. Paul asked Timothy to submit to circumcision, not as a compromise of the decision of the Jerusalem Council but as an attempt to avoid offending Jews for the purpose of ministry.

Troas

Paul continued strengthening the churches by informing believers in Derbe and Lystra of the Jerusalem Council's decision. It was his intention to minister in Asia, probably Ephesus, after revisiting the churches planted on the first journey in Phrygia and Galatia. However, the Holy Spirit prevented Paul and his companions from entering Asia.

Instead of turning back, Paul turned north, and this time the Spirit of Jesus prevented him from entering Bithynia. He turned west and traveled through Mysia to Troas. (Troas was a coastal city on the northwestern coast of Asia Minor—what's now part of Turkey.) During the night, Paul had a vision of a man from Macedonia, urging Paul to come to his region to help them.

Philippi

The missionaries sailed from Troas to the island of Samothrace, then to Neapolis (a seaport ten miles from Philippi). Philippi was a major city in the province of Macedonia.

On the Sabbath, the missionaries went to a place of prayer. While Paul spoke to the women gathered, the Lord opened the heart of Lydia to respond to the gospel. Lydia was a businesswoman from Thyatira who sold purple fabrics, an indication that she was highly successful. Her household followed her lead in responding to the gospel. She offered to let Paul and his companions stay in her home, and they accepted.

Paul consistently was harassed by a slave girl who was possessed by a demon, which used her to predict the future. Following Paul and his companions, she repeatedly identified them as bondservants of the Most High God. Her constant tirade annoyed Paul, so he delivered the girl from demon-possession in the name of Jesus.

The girl's owners were not happy about her conversion because it meant a loss of income for them. They seized Paul and Silas and accused them of disturbing the peace.

The magistrates punished Paul and Silas without a fair trial, having them flogged with rods and then imprisoned.

In the middle of the night, while Paul and Silas were praying and singing, they were miraculously set free. Instead of sending an angel, God used an earthquake.

The earthquake awoke the jailer; when he saw the cells were open, he assumed the prisoners had escaped. Since he was responsible, he prepared to take his own life rather than risk execution.

He could not have been more surprised, though, by what he discovered. Instead of escaping, all the prisoners had stayed put. Seeing the jailer about to kill himself, Paul cried out with a loud voice, "Do not harm yourself—we are all here!"

The jailer fell on his knees before Paul and Silas and asked, "Sirs, what must I do to be saved?"

"Believe in the Lord Jesus," answered Paul, "and you will be saved, you and your family." His household believed; they were immediately baptized. They opened their home to Paul and Silas and rejoiced greatly.

The officials wanted to quickly and quietly get Paul and Silas out of town; they realized they had violated Roman law by arresting and punishing them without a trial.

Paul, however, was not willing to allow the officials to simply dismiss the issue. Since they had been publicly punished, Paul used the leverage of his Roman citizenship to force the officials to publicly admit misusing their authority.

They apologized and escorted him out of the city. Paul and Silas then returned to Lydia's house to encourage them before leaving.

Thessalonica and Berea

Paul and Silas went to Thessalonica and attempted to minister in the synagogue. Some were persuaded to believe in the Lord, especially Greeks who had converted to Judaism and some wives of prominent men.

But other Jews became jealous. They managed to form a mob and start a riot. Searching for Paul and Silas, they grabbed Jason, the man they'd been staying with, questioning him about their whereabouts. That night the believers helped Paul and Silas escape, sending them to Berea.

There Paul and Silas went immediately to the synagogue. The Bereans were reasonable people, listening to what Paul had to say. They judged his message by the standard of Scripture rather than by their preconceived prejudices.

As in Thessalonica, many, including people of high social and political standing, believed. But again, not everyone was happy about Paul's preaching the gospel. When Jews from Thessalonica discovered that Paul preached the Word of God in Berea, they took action to stop him.

Athens

While Silas and Timothy stayed behind in Berea, Paul went to Athens, where he faced the blind wisdom of pagan philosophers. He was greatly disturbed by the pervasiveness of idolatry. He preached in the synagogue and the marketplace, confronting their philosophies and idol worship.

After conversing with Paul, the philosophers decided Paul was a babbler and proclaimer of strange gods.

They took Paul to the Aeropagus, where the Athenians discussed ideas. Paul was not arrested but was given the opportunity to give them more information about what he believed. He told them he was proclaiming their "unknown god" and said they needed to repent and turn to Jesus, who was resurrected from the dead.

The response was divided. Most ridiculed the idea of resurrection, but a few became believers, including Dionysius (a member of the philosophical society) and a woman named Damaris.

Corinth

Paul went to Corinth, forty miles west. He sometimes worked as a tentmaker to support himself, and in Corinth he met Aquila and Priscilla, also Jewish tentmakers.

Paul began his ministry in the synagogue, proclaiming the gospel first to his own people. When Silas and Timothy arrived with financial support from the Macedonian churches, Paul was able to devote himself full time to ministry.

Intense opposition forced Paul to abandon ministry in the synagogue. In a symbolic gesture, Paul shook the dust off his clothes and said the Jews were responsible for their own fate. Instead of leaving Corinth, Paul relocated his ministry to the house of Titus Justus, a God-fearer who had converted to Judaism. Crispus, the synagogue ruler, and his household were among many of the Corinthians who believed and were baptized.

One night the Lord spoke to Paul in a vision and made two promises. He pledged divine protection, saying "I am with you," and telling Paul he would not be beaten as he was at Philippi. Also, God said many people in Corinth would be saved. Paul preached there for eighteen months, longer than in any other city on his second journey.

Again the Jews attempted to disrupt Paul's ministry by saying he was violating the law. Paul was arraigned before the proconsul, Gallio, and brought before the judgment seat for a hearing. Gallio concluded that the complaint was religious, not political, and ruled that the charges were unwarranted.

Frustrated by Gallio's decision, the Jews assaulted Sosthenes, the new synagogue leader. Gallio ignored the violence.

Back to Jerusalem and Antioch

After staying in Corinth awhile longer, Paul went to the port city of Cenchrea, where he had his hair cut (previously he'd taken a vow not to cut his hair and to abstain from certain food and drink for thirty days). He left with Priscilla and Aquila for Ephesus, and he went into the synagogue to talk to the Jews. They asked him to stay longer, but he refused, saying he'd come back if God wanted him to. Paul sailed from there to Caesarea, then traveled overland to Jerusalem and back to Antioch.

THIRD MISSIONARY JOURNEY—FROM ANTIOCH TO EPHESUS

Paul stayed in Antioch for an extended time and then revisited the churches in Galatia and Phrygia, strengthening the disciples there.

Back in Ephesus, a Jew named Apollos arrived, preaching of Jesus but not knowing anything beyond the baptism of John. Priscilla and Aquila took him home with them and explained the good news more completely.

When Apollos wanted to go to Greece, the believers in Ephesus encouraged him and wrote to the disciples in Greece to welcome him. He was able to refute Jews there by clearly showing from the Scriptures that Jesus was the Messiah.

When Paul arrived in Ephesus, he met a dozen disciples of John the Baptist. He asked if they had received the Holy Spirit when they believed, but they had never heard of such a thing. So Paul baptized them in the name of Jesus and gave them the gift of the Spirit through the laying on of hands. The men prophesied and spoke in tongues as evidence they had received the Spirit.

In the synagogue at Ephesus, Paul argued and attempted for three months to persuade the Jews about the kingdom of God. Ministry in the synagogue, however, became impossible because some of the Jews openly opposed Paul and tried to discredit him.

Instead of giving up, Paul made arrangements to hold daily discussion in the lecture hall of a teacher named Tyrannus. He continued doing this for two years, and all who lived in Asia heard the word of the Lord, both Jews and Greeks.

God did unusual miracles through Paul. Sometimes people would take handkerchiefs and aprons Paul had used and touch the skin of the sick with them. They would be healed and evil spirits would leave them.

Some Jewish exorcists saw Paul cast out demons in the name of Jesus, but when they attempted to cast out a demon in Jesus' name, the demon rebuked them and the man assaulted them. Badly beaten and humiliated, they fled the house naked and wounded.

When the news of what had happened became known to both Jews and Greeks, the superstitious pagans of Ephesus were overcome with fear and magnified the name of Jesus. Some became believers and burned their books on magic, which were worth fifty thousand pieces of silver. The word of the Lord continued to spread and gain strength.

Before leaving Ephesus, Paul made the strategic decision to revisit Macedonia and Greece on his way to Jerusalem and eventually go to Rome. But before he went on this journey, he sent two helpers, Timothy and Erastus, on to Macedonia while he stayed in Asia.

But while Paul was still in Ephesus, a man named Demetrius organized a protest. He and the other silversmiths made their living by selling small silver idols to pagan pilgrims. Because of Paul's ministry, Christianity had become a threat to their livelihood.

Demetrius told the other silversmiths that Paul was preaching against idols, winning over large crowds with his message that man-made gods are not gods at all. They erupted with rage and shouted out praise for Artemis (Diana), the goddess of prosperity. The small crowd grew into a large unruly mob that rushed into the amphitheater, forcibly taking two of Paul's traveling companions with them.

Unconcerned about his safety, Paul wanted to address the mob, but he was constrained by his disciples and some local officials. The mob became so fanatical and chaotic that many of them didn't even know why they were rioting.

A disciple named Alexander was pushed forward to talk, but when the crowds realized he was a Jew they prevented him from speaking by shouting, "Great is Artemis of the Ephesians."

After about two hours of total confusion, the town clerk pleaded for law and order. He reminded the Ephesians of the legend that they were guardians of the temple where Artemis's image fell from heaven, trying to pacify them. Then he emphasized that Paul and his companions had not committed a chargeable crime. They had not actually robbed the temple or directly blasphemed the goddess.

Then he said the action of Demetrius and the other silversmiths was illegal—that they should take the Christians to court if they wanted to deal with it legally. After this, he sent everyone on their way.

THIRD MISSIONARY JOURNEY—FROM EPHESUS TO JERUSALEM

Paul traveled through Macedonia and Greece, strengthening the Gentile churches, but he was forced to alter his plans because of a threat to his life. Instead of sailing from Cenchrea for Syria, Paul went back through Macedonia and sailed from Philippi to Troas.

In addition to danger from the Jews, Paul was carrying an offering for the churches in Judea, and the seaport at Cenchrea would be an easy place for Jews or thieves to attack him. At Troas, Paul celebrated the Jewish Feast of Unleavened Bread.

In Troas, the church met on Sundays to honor the day that Jesus rose from the dead. They shared a meal together, which included the celebration of the Lord's Table, also known as Communion.

Paul preached until midnight because he planned to leave the next day. The church met in the upper room of a private home, and a young man named Eutychus was sitting in the window, listening to Paul, when he dozed off and fell to the ground. He died, but Paul took him in his arms and God performed a miracle, bringing the boy back to life.

Paul continued to talk until after sunrise, then left the city. He went to the cities of Assos, Mitylene, Chios, Samos, and Miletus. He was trying to get back to Jerusalem for Pentecost.

In Miletus he gathered the Christians and told them in an impassioned speech that he would never see them again. The Holy Spirit had warned him of imprisonment and suffering. He charged the church leaders to teach the Word of God and defend their flocks from false teachers. The Christians wept and hugged and kissed Paul, then sent him on his way.

Paul and his companions sailed along the coast, stopping at Cos, Rhodes, and Patara. At Patara, they transferred to a larger ship that was sailing for Phoenicia. The ship made port at Tyre to unload cargo; they went ashore and spent seven days there. Through the Spirit, the disciples warned Paul not to go to Jerusalem, but after prayer with the disciples and their families, Paul continued his journey to Jerusalem.

On the trip to Caesarea, Paul stopped for a day at Ptolemais and greeted the believers. When he arrived at Caesarea, Paul stayed with Philip the evangelist, one of the seven chosen to supervise the distribution of food to the Hellenistic widows.

Also, a prophet named Agabus took Paul's belt and tied his own feet and hands with it, prophesying that Paul would be arrested and handed over to Gentiles in Jerusalem.

Paul's companions again begged him not to go. Paul told them their pleading was breaking his heart, but he wouldn't be deterred. Some of the believers from Caesarea joined Paul and his companions for the overland trip. They stayed at the house of Mnason, a Gentile convert from Cyprus.

RIOT AND ARREST IN JERUSALEM

When Paul arrived in Jerusalem, he was warmly greeted by the church. The next day he told James and the elders how God had blessed his ministry to the Gentiles. They praised God for this and told him that thousands of Jews had also come to faith and were passionately devoted to the law of Moses.

Though thankful for what God had done through him, they informed him that his ministry among the Gentiles had raised suspicions about his loyalty to the Law. "What should we do?" they asked. "The Jewish believers will certainly find out you have come to Jerusalem."

They suggested that Paul, to show his respect for the Law, join four other Jewish men in the completion of a Jewish ritual and pay for their sacrifices.

Somewhat surprisingly, he agreed. The next day he went to the temple and set a date for offering the prescribed sacrifices.

Before Paul and the other men were able to complete the ritual, Jews from Asia spotted him in the temple and stirred up a mob. They claimed his teaching threatened traditional Judaism; they said he encouraged Jewish people everywhere to ignore the Law and abandon worship in the temple. They also accused him of desecrating the temple by taking Trophimus, a Gentile, into the holy place.

The accusations spread through Jerusalem like wildfire, and Jews from every part of the city rushed to the temple. They dragged him out so they could kill him.

But when the Roman commander heard the Jews were rioting, he acted quickly to restore order. He ran to the temple area with officers and soldiers, and when the Jews saw them, they stopped beating Paul.

Thinking Paul had started the riot, the commander ordered him arrested and bound with chains. When he asked the crowd what Paul had done, they were so angry their answers were confusing. He ordered Paul taken to the Roman barracks for protection.

The soldiers had to lift Paul on their shoulders to make their way through the angry mob. The crowd followed, shouting, "Kill him! Kill him!"

Once inside the barracks, Paul asked the commander for permission to speak. The commander was surprised when Paul spoke in Greek; he'd thought Paul was the leader of a band of Egyptian terrorists. Paul told the commander he was a Jew from Tarsus and asked to speak to the crowd that had followed them.

Paul's request was granted, and he spoke in Hebrew (or possibly Aramaic). When the fuming mob heard Paul speaking in their own native language, they quieted down.

Paul appealed to his Jewish brothers to listen to his defense and, as he continued, they became even quieter.

He said he was born and raised in Tarsus and was taught Jewish law and traditions by Gamaliel. He had hated Christians and persecuted them, arresting men and women and putting them in prison. He had been authorized by the high priest and the Sanhedrin to arrest Christians in Damascus and return them to Jerusalem for trial.

On the way to Damascus, a brilliant light surrounded Paul. He fell to the ground and heard a voice saying, "Saul, Saul, why are you persecuting me?"

When he asked who was speaking, he heard a voice saying, "I am Jesus."

Those with Paul saw the light but couldn't understand what was said.

When Paul asked what he should do, the Lord said to go into Damascus and there he would be told what to do.

Blinded by the light, Paul's companions led him into Damascus. Ananias met Paul and said, "Brother Saul, your sight is restored," and that moment he could see again.

Ananias informed Paul that God had chosen him to witness to everyone about what he had experienced; Ananias said, "Why wait? Be baptized, washing away your sins."

Paul then said that he returned to Jerusalem and went to the temple to pray. While praying, he fell into a trance and was told to leave Jerusalem because his own people would reject his testimony about Jesus.

He objected, "Lord, they know how I imprisoned and punished those who believe in you. They know I was a witness when Stephen was stoned."

The Lord answered, "Go, I am sending you to witness to the Gentiles."

When he said that, the Jews exploded in rage, shouting, "Away with him, he doesn't deserve to live!" They screamed at Paul, ripped off their coats, and threw dust in the air.

Not knowing what Paul had said, and assuming that he had intentionally inflamed the crowd, the commander ordered him flogged to force him to confess and find out what he had done to anger them.

Rather than endure unnecessary punishment, Paul claimed his right as a Roman citizen. He asked, "Is it legal for you to flog a Roman citizen who hasn't had a trial?"

This shocked the commander, who ordered the soldiers to stop. He asked Paul how he became a citizen and said, "I had to pay a lot of money to get my citizenship."

Paul replied, "I was born a Roman citizen."

The soldiers who had intended to interrogate Paul backed off. The commander was concerned because he had ordered Paul bound and flogged.

He ordered a meeting of the Jewish religious council to find out why the Jews had rioted, and he freed Paul so he could speak to the council.

Paul looked straight at the council and said, "Brothers, I have a clear conscience before God."

The high priest considered Paul's statement blasphemous, and he ordered him slapped on the mouth. Paul responded by calling the high priest a hypocrite and a corrupt judge for ordering the guard to hit him.

Those nearby scolded Paul. "How dare you insult the high priest?" they said.

Paul apologized and said, "I didn't realize he was the high priest. The Scriptures do tell us we shouldn't speak evil of our rulers."

Paul realized that some council members were Sadducees and some were Pharisees, so he shouted, "I am a Pharisee, and I am on trial because I believe in the resurrection!"

This started an emotional debate, because the Sadducees didn't believe in angels or the resurrection, while the Pharisees did. Some Pharisees jumped to Paul's defense and said he hadn't done anything wrong: "It is possible a spirit or an angel has spoken to him," they said.

This added fuel to the argument, and the commander could see the council was becoming more and more violent, so he ordered the guards to rescue Paul and take him back to the Roman fortress.

That night the Lord appeared to Paul and said, "Be strong, Paul. As you have witnessed for me in Jerusalem, I promise—you will witness for me in Rome."

The Jews were determined to kill Paul. A group of forty conspired to assassinate him and made a suicidal pact, vowing, "May God curse me if I fail to do this." They informed the priests and elders that they had taken an oath not to eat anything until they had killed Paul. They told the high priest to ask the commander to return Paul to the council; they planned to ambush him in the narrow streets of Jerusalem.

Paul's nephew discovered the plot and warned him. Paul asked one of the Roman officers to take his nephew to the commander. Informed of the situation, the commander cautioned him to keep their meeting a secret.

A ROMAN PRISONER

The commander summoned two officers and ordered them to prepare for a secret transfer to Caesarea (the headquarters for the Roman government of Judea). Because of the threat of an ambush, he ordered them to take two hundred soldiers, two hundred spearmen, and seventy cavalry, and to leave at nine at night under the cover of darkness.

Claudius, the commander, wrote a letter to Felix (the military governor of Judea).

> The prisoner [Paul] was seized by the Jews, who were attempting to kill him, when I intervened. When I found out he is a Roman citizen, I placed him under protective custody and made an investigation to find out what had happened. I learned from the Jewish high council that the accusations are related to their religious law but not a crime warranting imprisonment or execution. When I discovered a plot to murder him, I immediately transferred him to you, and I told his accusers to state their charges to you.

The soldiers left that night. The entire contingent accompanied Paul to Antipatris (twenty-five miles from Caesarea). The foot soldiers returned to Jerusalem the next morning, and the mounted troops took Paul on to Caesarea.

They turned Paul over to Felix and gave him the letter Claudias had written. After reading it, Felix asked Paul what province he was from. Paul answered, "Cilicia."

Paul and Felix

Felix told Paul he would hear the charges against him when his accusers arrived. He ordered Paul placed under guard at Herod's headquarters.

Five days later the high priest and a group of Jewish elders arrived with Tertullus, an attorney. Before charging Paul, Tertullus complimented Felix for providing peace and enacting reforms. He then accused Paul of being a troublemaker, a leader of the sect of the Nazarenes, and of defiling the temple. Tertullus told the governor if he questioned Paul he would discover for himself the charges were true. The Jews who had come with Tertullus testified that he was telling the truth—that Paul was guilty of all the charges.

Felix gave Paul the opportunity to answer.

Paul denied the charges. He said that twelve days ago he had gone to Jerusalem to worship at the temple, that he was not involved in civil disobedience, and that the Jews could not prove the charges against him.

He admitted he worshiped the same God as his accusers and that he was a follower of the Way, which they considered a heretical party. He said he believed in everything written in the Law and Prophets, including the resurrection of both the righteous and the wicked. He had done his best to keep a clear conscience before God and men.

He told Felix he had come to Jerusalem with an offering for the poor and to worship God. He had ceremonially purified himself before entering the temple, and no one was with him. He hadn't started a riot. He pointed out to Felix that his accusers, Jews from Asia, were not even present and that they had not presented evidence to support their charges. Paul said he had not committed any crime unless it was

what he shouted out to the Sanhedrin: "I believe in the resurrection from the dead!"

Though Felix knew about the Way, he postponed his decision until Lysias, the commander who had arrested Paul, came from Jerusalem. He ordered Paul placed under guard but with the privilege of having his friends visit and provide for his needs.

Because she was Jewish, Felix invited Drusilla, his wife, to come with him to listen to Paul. With them Paul discussed righteousness, self-control, and future judgment.

All three topics were somewhat disturbing to Felix. He dismissed Paul and said they soon would meet again, when it was more convenient. He hoped that Paul would offer him a bribe, so he sent for him on more than one occasion.

Felix continued to hold Paul as a prisoner in order to win the support of the Jews, but he was replaced by Festus as military governor after two years.

Three days after he arrived in Caesarea, Festus left for Jerusalem, where he met with the Jewish religious leaders. They informed him of the charges against Paul and asked him to transfer Paul to Jerusalem. (They planned to ambush and kill Paul on the way.)

Festus refused. He said they could return with him to Caesarea to make their case.

Paul, Festus, and Herod

As soon as Festus got back to Caesarea, he summoned Paul.

Paul's accusers surrounded him, making serious charges they could not prove.

Paul denied committing a crime against the Law, the temple, or Caesar.

After listening to his defense, Festus attempted to patronize the Jews by asking Paul if he was willing to return to Jerusalem for trial.

Paul replied, "No! I am a Roman citizen, and I have a right to trial in a Roman court. If I have committed a capital offense, I am willing to accept the death penalty, but if I am innocent, no one has the right to turn me over to these men. I appeal to Caesar!"

When Herod Agrippa II (a local and surrogate ruler under the Romans) arrived with his sister Bernice to pay their respects to the new governor, Festus explained that he had inherited Paul's case from Felix, and that when he went to Jerusalem, the Jewish leaders asked him to condemn and execute Paul. But he told them that under Roman law, an accused person has a right to defend himself face-to-face with his accusers.

Festus informed Agrippa that when Paul's accusers had presented their case against him, he was surprised by their charges. He discovered that the dispute was about Judaism and a dead man named Jesus, whom Paul insisted was alive. Festus said he didn't know how to judge their complaint, so he wanted Paul to respond to the charges in Jerusalem, but he refused, instead making an appeal to present his case to the emperor.

Festus said he planned to hold Paul prisoner until he could be sent to the emperor.

Agrippa replied, "If it's possible, I'd like to talk to Paul."

"You can tomorrow," said Festus.

The next day Agrippa and Bernice entered the auditorium dressed in purple robes of royalty and gold, accompanied by several military officers and some city officials.

When all were present, Festus ordered Paul brought in and explained to those present why he needed their opinion and help. He had not found sufficient evidence to support the charge that Paul should be executed. Plus, Paul had made an appeal to Caesar, and Festus didn't know what accusations he should send with the prisoner. "It would be absurd for me to send him to Caesar without credible charges," he said.

Since Festus had asked for his opinion, Agrippa granted Paul permission to speak.

Extending his hand, Paul began his defense by stating that he considered it a unique privilege to make his defense before Agrippa, an expert in Jewish legal matters.

Paul told Agrippa that the Jewish leaders knew he had been trained as a Pharisee to live according to strict demands of the Law. His countrymen had condemned him as a criminal because of his belief in the same hope for Israel that they held. He asked those assembled, "Why do any of you consider it incredible that God raises the dead?"

As a faithful Jew, Paul testified, he originally had felt obligated to oppose those who believed in Jesus of Nazareth. He had received authorization from the chief priests in Jerusalem to imprison believers, and he had personally voted for the death penalty. In synagogues Paul had tried to force believers to curse the name of Jesus. He was so enraged against Christians that he even pursued them to cities outside of Israel.

After describing his life as a Jew who was zealous for the religious heritage of his people, Paul recounted his conversion experience on the road to Damascus. He told of being surrounded by a light brighter than the sun. All had fallen to the ground as Paul heard a voice saying, "Saul, Saul, why are you persecuting me? It is useless for you to resist the power of God!"

When he'd asked who was speaking, the Lord identified himself as Jesus, whom Saul was persecuting. Jesus ordered Paul to stand up and said, "I'm appointing you as my witness to all the earth. I will rescue you from your own people and Gentiles. You are my witness to Gentiles, so they may turn to God and receive forgiveness of sins through faith in me."

Paul said he believed he had been divinely protected so that he could continue to testify what the Prophets and Moses had said about the Messiah, the Anointed One. They had written that Christ must suffer and die, and as the first to rise from the dead proclaim the same message of "good news" to Jews and Gentiles.

Festus exploded and shouted, "Paul, your advanced education has made you crazy."

Paul denied the charge and appealed to Agrippa for support. He was sure Agrippa had heard about Christ's death and resurrection, since what had happened was not done in secret. He asked, "King Agrippa, do you believe in the Prophets? I know you do!"

Agrippa replied, "You think you can persuade me to become a Christian so easily?"

"I pray to God," responded Paul, "whether easily or with difficulty, that everyone here might become as I am—except for these chains, of course!"

They had heard enough. Agrippa, Festus, Bernice, and the others left the room to discuss the case. All agreed that Paul had not committed a capital offense.

Agrippa said to Festus, "You could have released this man, if only he had not appealed to Caesar."

The Storm and the Shipwreck

Paul and several other prisoners were placed in the custody of Julius, an officer in the Imperial Regiment, for transfer by ship to Rome. Aristarchus, a believer from Thessalonica, and Luke, the doctor, booked passage on the same ship, which was from Adramyttium, a seaport on the northeast shore of the Aegean Sea, near Troas. Instead of sailing directly across the Mediterranean Sea, they sailed north to Sidon. There Julius allowed Paul to visit his friends so they could provide him with supplies for the voyage.

As soon as they left Sidon, they encountered strong winter winds from the north, making it difficult for them to keep on course. They sailed north of Cyprus for protection from the wind, and after they passed Cilicia and Pamphylia, they set their course for Myra. At Myra, the centurion transferred the prisoners to a ship from Alexandria that was sailing to Rome.

The voyage became increasingly difficult as they continued west, but they finally reached a port at Fair Havens on the island of Crete.

Because so much time had been lost on the voyage, the weather had gotten worse and sailing had become dangerous. Paul decided to speak to the ship's captain and crew. He said, "Men, it is clear to me that if we continue this voyage, we risk shipwreck and the loss of cargo and lives."

Julius didn't listen to Paul and instead asked the ship's captain what he thought they should do. The captain disagreed with Paul and most of the crew; he wanted to sail to the port at Phoenix for the winter. Phoenix was farther up the coast on the island of Crete and had a harbor that provided better protection from winter storms.

Thinking they could make it to Phoenix, the sailors weighed anchor when a light wind began blowing from the south. They kept as close to the shoreline of Crete as possible, but a "northeaster" came up suddenly. The ship was broadsided by a wind of typhoon strength and blown out to sea. It was so powerful, the sailors lost control of the ship and were driven along by the storm.

The wind drove them twenty-five miles south to the island of Cauda. On the southern side they were able to secure the lifeboat that was towed behind the ship and used rope cables to secure the ship's hull.

The crew feared they would run aground on the shallows of Syrtis (a series of deadly sandbars off the North African coast, infamous as a graveyard for vessels), so they lowered the anchor to create additional drag.

On the second day of the storm, they began jettisoning cargo. On the third day, the crew became so desperate they threw some of the ship's equipment overboard.

The storm continued its relentless assault. After several days without seeing the sun or stars, they lost all hope and resigned themselves to death at sea.

No one had eaten for several days when Paul said to the crew, "Men, you ought to have followed my advice; you would have avoided this life-threatening situation. But don't be afraid, because an angel of my God has assured me that though the ship will be lost, there will be no loss of life. He promised I will stand trial before Caesar and that because God is good, he will protect all who are on the ship." He encouraged the crew to trust him because he trusted in God, but he said they would shipwreck on some island.

On the fourteenth day, about midnight, the sailors sensed they were near land and began taking soundings. Since it was the middle of the night, pitch black, they wished for daylight so they could see to prevent the ship from hitting rocks.

The sailors had had enough; they decided to abandon ship in the lifeboat but under the pretense of putting out anchors from the back of the ship. Paul realized what they were doing and warned the centurion: "Unless these men remain in the ship, you will not be safe." The sailors cut the ropes to the lifeboat, allowing it to drift away from the ship.

When it was almost light, Paul encouraged everyone to eat, reminding them that no one had eaten for several days. After reassuring them that no one would be injured, Paul took some bread, gave thanks to God, and ate it in front of the crew and passengers. After eating, the crew threw the remaining grain overboard to lighten the ship.

At first light they saw land and decided to beach the ship if possible. They cut the lines to the anchors, freed the rudders, and hoisted the small foresail to guide the ship to land. But they hit a reef. The ship became stuck and was pounded by the surf. Realizing that if the ship broke apart the prisoners might escape, the soldiers planned to kill them.

The centurion intervened to save Paul. He ordered those who could to swim for shore and the rest to float on planks and other debris. All made it safely to land.

Malta

Once everyone reached shore, they discovered they were on the island of Malta. The inhabitants were friendly and helped the waterlogged survivors build a fire. Paul pitched in, but as he was adding wood, the heat drove out a snake that struck him.

When the islanders saw the viper clinging to Paul's hand, they said to one another, "This man must be a murderer, and though he has escaped the sea, the god Justice does not allow him to live."

But Paul shook off the snake into the fire and did not drop dead. After a reasonable amount of time, the islanders changed their minds and decided he must be a god.

While staying at the home of Publius, the island's governor, Paul saw that his father was ill with fever and dysentery. Paul healed the man and several others who were sick. They expressed their gratitude with gifts and supplies for the rest of the journey to Rome.

After three months on Malta, Paul and his companions were put on an Alexandrian ship with a figurehead of the "Twin Gods." They sailed from Malta to Syracuse on the island of Sicily and stayed three days. From Syracuse they sailed to Rhegium and then to Puteoli, both on the mainland of Greece. Before going on to Rome, Paul was invited by believers in Puteoli to stay with them for seven days.

After Paul left Puteoli, believers from Rome met him at the Forum of Appius. Other believers met him and his companions at the Three Taverns. This greatly encouraged Paul, and he thanked God.

Rome

When Paul arrived in Rome, he was permitted to stay in a private home guarded by a Roman soldier.

Paul did not waste any time before seeing his Jewish countrymen. After three days he requested a meeting with the leadership. Paul assured them he was not a criminal. Though he had been arrested and turned over to the Romans, he had not committed any crimes against the Jews or Jewish traditions. He explained that his purpose for requesting the meeting was to get acquainted with the leaders and explain why he was a prisoner. "I am bound with this chain because I believe the Messiah has already come."

The leaders informed Paul that they had not received any reports from Judea criticizing him, but they had heard about a new movement everyone was denouncing. They requested a second meeting to find out Paul's opinion on this new movement.

On that day an even greater number of Jews came to Paul's rented house. Paul explained how Jesus had fulfilled Israel's hopes for the kingdom of God, and he appealed to them from both the law of Moses and from the Prophets from morning to evening.

Some were convinced, but most refused to believe. The Jews not only disagreed with Paul, they also disagreed with one another, and they began leaving after Paul warned them of making the same mistake as their hardhearted ancestors. He quoted from Isaiah the prophet, who was inspired by the Holy Spirit to warn his generation of divine judgment for rejecting his message: "Go to this people and tell them they can't hear with their ears or see with their eyes. Their hearts have become hard. They are deaf and blind to God. If they would believe in me, I would save them, but they won't." Paul concluded by saying the Jews' refusal to believe his message justified his preaching to the Gentiles.

For two years, Paul lived in his own rented house and was able to receive visitors. He welcomed everyone who came to visit and, boldly and unopposed, continued preaching about God's kingdom and teaching about the Lord Jesus Christ.

♆ Chapter Summary

After Jesus rose from the dead, he continued teaching his followers about the kingdom and commissioned them to take "the good news" to all the earth. He promised to send the Holy Spirit and then returned to heaven in a cloud, promising to return.

On Pentecost, the Spirit filled all of Jesus' followers, who began to speak in tongues (foreign languages). This attracted a large crowd; Peter preached a sermon claiming that Jesus was Lord and Messiah. Three thousand people believed and were baptized.

The apostles' message and miraculous works in Jerusalem caused a stir that made two things clear. First, Jesus' return to God would not halt the spread of the gospel message, and second, the leaders would continue to oppose and harass those who followed Jesus.

The church continued to grow. But tension between the Jewish religious leaders and the Christians resulted in the first martyr, Stephen.

Paul, who was part of Stephen's execution, was a zealous antagonist of the church. On the road to Damascus, where he wanted to stamp out other Christ followers, Jesus appeared to him, and immediately Paul became a changed man.

Peter's vision, Philip's witness, and Paul's missionary journeys all plainly showed that the message of redemption and salvation was for all people, not just for the Jews. Paul and others effectively spread the good news from Jerusalem to Rome.

In spite of opposition, the church grew as Jesus had promised. The early Christians were threatened, arrested, and flogged. Peter was jailed twice. James was executed. Paul was harassed, jailed, and beaten. But the message of salvation through Jesus Christ continued its powerful march across the Roman Empire and to the world.

Epilogue

The ending to the book of Acts is somewhat abrupt. Paul is in Rome, but he's there as a prisoner. Though he is in chains, the good news is not chained. Paul has the freedom to preach and teach about the kingdom of God and Christ "without hindrance."

From Paul's epistles (the letters he wrote to churches), we know that after two years he was released and continued his ministry for several years before being rearrested and executed. The story of Christianity, however, did not end with the death of Paul.

Though the non-Pauline epistles do not give explicit information about events in the first century, we know the church faced the external threat of persecution and the internal problem of false teaching. The other New Testament epistles were written to inspire and instruct believers to remain faithful to Christ and to the historic truths of Christianity.

Near the end of the first century, the Roman emperor Domitian demanded absolute loyalty and worship from all subjects. Because Christians refused to worship him as a god, they were ruthlessly persecuted. The apostle John was arrested and banished to the small island of Patmos (off the coast of Asia Minor).

While a prisoner there, John wrote the book of Revelation to remind Christians that God is in the process of restoring creation, which had been corrupted by the rebellion of Satan and humankind. Though believers were hated by the world, they were loved by God; they ultimately will rule victoriously with Christ forever.

THE STORY ENDS . . . OR IS THIS JUST THE BEGINNING?

God sent an angel to his servant John to show him what would happen in the future, and John carefully recorded everything revealed to him. The revelation was about Jesus Christ, and it came with a promise of blessing: "Those who read these words are blessed, and those who obey what is written here are blessed."

John greeted seven churches in the province of Asia (currently western Turkey), writing, "Grace and peace to you from the One who is, who was, and who is coming—Jesus Christ, the first to rise from the dead." John reminded the churches that Jesus is the only one who deserves our worship because he loved us and forgave our sins by shedding his blood. John said that when Jesus returns, everyone will see him, and the nations will mourn: "Jesus is the Alpha and Omega—the first and the last, the Almighty God."

John assured the churches that he understood their suffering because he too was suffering. He had been exiled to Patmos for preaching God's Word and testifying about Jesus Christ.

It was the Lord's Day when John heard a voice so loud it sounded like a trumpet. It said, "Write on a scroll what you see and send it to the seven churches—Ephesus, Smyrna, Pergamum, Thyatira, Sardis, Philadelphia, and Laodicea."

When John turned around to see who was speaking to him, he saw seven golden lampstands. Someone like the Son of Man was standing in the middle of them, wearing a long robe with a gold sash across his chest. His hair was like wool and white as snow. His eyes were like two fiery furnaces, and his feet were as brilliant as polished bronze. His voice thundered like a powerful waterfall. He had seven stars in his right hand, and a sharp double-edged sword came out of his mouth. His face was as bright as the midday sun.

John fell to the ground like a dead man. But the man in the vision, who was Jesus Christ, said, "Don't be afraid! I am the First and the Last. I am the Living One. I was dead, but now I am alive forever and ever!

I hold the keys to death and Hades (the place of the dead). Write what you have seen—what is happening now and what will happen in the future. This is the message to the seven churches."

He who testifies to these things says, "Yes, I am coming soon."
Amen. Come, Lord Jesus.
The grace of the Lord Jesus be with God's people. Amen. (Revelation 22:20–21)

About the Author

Dr. William Marty is Professor of Bible at The Moody Bible Institute. He has written two other books: *Surveying the New Testament* and *Survey of the Old Testament: Student Notes*, both by educational publisher Kendall and Hunt. He is rare in the Bible college world in that he teaches and writes on both the New and Old Testaments. He received his MDiv from Denver Seminary and his ThD from Dallas Theological Seminary. Dr. Marty lives in Chicago with his wife, and in his spare time enjoys competing in triathlons.